Heaven Is Beyond Imagination

Heaven Is Beyond Imagination

The music, beauty, waters, flowers, joy, peace, love, relationships, and more, as described by fifty published eyewitnesses

Jacques LaFrance, Ph.D.

Illustrations by **Laurie Brumbaugh**

Published independently with Kindle Direct Publishing
Copyright © 2021 Jacques LaFrance
All rights reserved.
ISBN: 9798709912724

DEDICATION

This book is dedicated to Carolyn Tillman BSN, RN. When I was finishing this, I had a routine outpatient surgery that went well. There were no complications, and I was scheduled to be discharged after I left recovery. But in recovery my heart rate dropped and then quit. Carolyn was alert and promptly started chest compressions to get my heart restarted. Had it not been for her alertness and prompt professional attention, this book may have never been published. So the fact that you have this book in your hands is a testimony to Carolyn. It is very fitting that I dedicate it to her. May she be blessed and continue saving lives as your servant.

It is also dedicated to the Father and to the Son, who endured horrible torture, rejection, and cruel and unusual death to pay for our rebellion and sin. Such is the extent of His love for us. Everything described in this book is a product of that love and is tribute to it.

CONTENTS

PREFACE

"The grass was the most vivid shade of green I had ever seen and the hillside meadow looked like a perfectly manicured golf course dotted with perfect beautiful flowers that were unfamiliar to me. As I stepped on the grass, the three inch blades came up through my foot undamaged and transmitted energy throughout my body."

"I was overwhelmed by the love, peace, and acceptance I experienced there."

"I experienced peace and tranquility there greater than any human has ever known on Earth."

"One thing that is constant in heaven but rarely found on Earth is a constant peaceful happy feeling. It caused my spirit to rejoice and know I was home there."

"In Heaven there is total love, confidence, and peace, and everything is perfect, blissful; there is no fear, just total joy and peace. God's love is so far beyond our experience here that our minds cannot fathom it. We are infused with that love the moment we enter heaven. He is in us and we are in him in wonderful ways beyond anything we can know here."

"Heaven feels like being inside pure joy. We have no words to describe it."

"Music, light, love, and vibrant life permeated everything. It was not just around me, it was in me. It was the most wonderful thing I have ever experienced. It felt like I belonged here; it was what I had been searching for all my life. I didn't want to leave."

"Heaven is not about what we get; it is all about God."

These reactions are common in eyewitness testimonies of heaven from the fifty-eight books in my bibliography. Their visits to heaven resulted from either a temporary clinical death or an out-of-body journey of the spirit. I have ignored the so-called near death out-of-body experiences (NDE) that fall short of seeing heaven or hell and generally considered only those testimonies of actual visits to heaven or hell. Many of these authors believe Jesus gave them this experience beyond death to tell us what He has prepared for us. While each author's own testimony is impressive, very few people will be able to read more than just a few of these books. This book is not just a repetition of others' stories of heaven. I have considered different features of heaven and extracted from the various books what those authors have said about those features. As a result, you get a description of heaven more complete and focused than any other book gives, and it is based only on eyewitness testimony. You can see the consistency between different accounts of heaven and also the variability of different perceptions. Also you see more features of heaven because different people have been shown different things. No one person has seen all there is. Nor has this book captured all of heaven. There is much more that awaits us, but I hope the insight in this book gives you enough of the whole picture to excite you, help you change your life to have eternal priorities, appreciate and praise your Father and our Lord more than before, be excited to tell others either what they can anticipate or what they are going to miss, or encourage those who have lost a loved one. My prayer is that you will be blessed, more than you were before, and that your life on Earth will be filled with more joy, hope, and praise.

I chose the title, *Heaven Is Beyond Imagination: The music, beauty, flowers, landscapes, joy, peace, love, relationships, and more, described by fifty published eyewitnesses*, because, first of all, many of the those giving their testimonies state there aren't words to describe what they saw, heard, smelled, tasted, or experienced. Their experience in heaven surpasses anything they have known here and leaves very little to which they can compare it. Don Piper said he cannot find enough words even to come close to being able to describe the actual experience. (Piper 1018, 132) And he said it is hard to imagine the bliss there is in heaven. (Piper 2018, 135) Mary K. Baxter also said, "[Heaven's] glories, its beauties, its wonders are beyond human powers of description." (Baxter, 27) Furthermore, in many cases their minds cannot recall many of the things since they returned, because those things are incomprehensible without our heavenly minds.

Second, we can only imagine things that are related to our own experience in some way. But some features of heaven are far different from anything in this world. People blind from birth have seen colors, but have not been able to relate them to the colors we see here because having never seen colors they have no point of reference. This is similar to many of the things these authors have seen or experienced. So since much of heaven is far beyond our experience here, we have no point of reference for imagining heaven.

I have provided an annotated bibliography that describes each book. Then throughout the manuscript I have made reference to the book from which I obtained the testimony along with page references. This is provided so if you want to explore further what that author said, you have a link to the place to look. This is recognition that I cannot do complete justice to these other authors' experiences. So I encourage you to take what I have done as a stepping-stone into your own study. You can choose from my descriptions which authors you wish to study further and read their experiences in their own words.

For those who doubt the veracity of any particular account they have read or heard about, this book, by bringing together multiple accounts of the same features, demonstrates that these experiences cannot be attributed to hallucinations or drugs, but must be considered authentic. Hallucinations occur in the brain so it is not possible for two people to hallucinate the same thing. One of the authors included, Eben Alexander, began as a skeptical neurosurgeon assuming all near death experiences[1] were just functions of brain wave activity until he had his own experience out of his body. But it is clear from this book that many people have seen essentially the same things in heaven. Furthermore, these testimonies are from different genders, different ages, different locations (from Australia to the Middle East), and different years, making it impossible for them to be contrived deceptions or fictional stories. You can be assured these authors are faithfully reporting what they saw, heard, and felt. W. Mark Lanier, a trial lawyer, in his book Christianity on Trial, made the statement, "In my courtroom experience, anytime two stories are identical, there is strong likelihood of collusion. The truth is that eyewitnesses notice different things. One may see two cars racing through an intersection while another notices a green one. That does not mean one is right and another is wrong. It means that the stories need to be combined to see if they make sense."[2] In this book none of the eyewitnesses saw exactly the same thing,

---

[1] I call most NDE's Temporary Death Experiences because the individuals were clinically dead but later resuscitated.

[2] W. Mark Lanier. 2014. *Christianity on Trial: A Lawyer Examines the*

but together they give a more complete picture of what heaven is like. So look forward to being treated to the most complete eyewitness testimony to our futures beyond this life.

Christian Faith. Downers Grove, IL: IVP Books, pg. 204.

ACKNOWLEDGMENTS

I acknowledge my gratitude to Alan Bailey for reviewing the whole manuscript and indicating numerous corrections and errors. Marlene McClelland and Janet Gilson also contributed numerous suggestions. Christine Detrick has been an avid supporter from the first edition. Many at First Presbyterian Church of Tulsa (FirstChurchTulsa.org) have also been very supportive from the beginning. I also appreciate the opportunities FirstChurch gave me to teach classes that led to the inspiration for this book. The staff at Christian Faith Publishing was very helpful in getting the first edition published, and the staff at Trilogy Christian Publishers was very helpful in getting the second edition published. And I appreciate all those who bought the earlier editions and gave me encouraging feedback, including testimonials of how they were blessed by the book.

I also acknowledge the artistic contributions of Laurie Brumbaugh that are scattered throughout the manuscript and to Marlene McClelland for putting together the ideas for the cover. I am grateful to the many friends who encouraged me and reviewed some of what I wrote. In addition to the above these include Beth Pielsticker, and John McCormack.

CHAPTER 1
Approaching Heaven

There are different stories of people's first encounter with heaven. Some people describe traveling fast through space, as in a tunnel or on a beam of light. Others' first experience is of being in the arms of Jesus. Some are met by friends who guide them. Others are guided by angels or even Jesus himself. Some pass through a fog or veil into the presence of heaven. And some are just suddenly there. In the next paragraphs, I will share some testimonies of each of these types of travels to heaven.

Friends and Guides

Marvin Besteman was taken by two angels to heaven. Two men showed up in his hospital room. They looked like regular guys except they wore white robes. They did not have wings. He said they unhooked all his tubes, about five in all. That didn't make sense to Marvin either, and he just assumed because of his nature they needed to cross all the t's and dot all the i's. They put their arms around him and took off. The trip was smooth, unlike some airplane trips, and he had no fear just perfect serenity. As they flew for a few seconds or minutes through a clear blue sky he had peace and profound sense of lightness and calm. They climbed for a few seconds and then changed directions, ultimately coming in for a landing like Canada Geese landing. He noticed he was no longer wearing his blue hospital gown but now wore a light brown golf shirt, tan pants, and shoes. As soon as his feet touched down, his two angels disappeared. (Besteman, 31-33,51-52)

Another of those who encountered friends who guided her to heaven was Mary Neal. She is an orthopedic surgeon living with her husband and children in Jackson Hole, Wyoming. They became friends with a family running a canoe and kayak service in Idaho and were excellent kayakers themselves. The families went to Chile one winter for a white-water kayak trip. The trip did not turn out well. A lesser-experienced kayaker preceded Mary over a falls and got stuck between two rocks. Mary couldn't stop or get around and went under the other kayak and got pinned under water. The force of the current prevented her from getting out of her kayak until she lost consciousness. She wrote of her experience dying while submerged in the river. When her spirit was released from her body and began to tumble from her submerged kayak, she felt a pop. She felt released from a shell, freeing her soul. When her soul rose from the water, she encountered a group of fifteen to twenty human spirits sent by God, who greeted her with the most overwhelming joy she had ever experienced and could ever imagine. She says it was an incredible joy. They were like a large welcoming committee. She likened it to the great cloud of witnesses mentioned in Hebrews 12:1. This welcoming committee was wildly cheering for her as she arrived.

She felt a kindred spirit with them and knew they were sent to guide her across the divide of time and dimension that separates our world from God's. She also knew they were to protect her during her journey. (Neal 2012, 68-69)

This was also the experience of Rebecca Springer, who suffered an extended painful illness. One night she had intense suffering and, in the morning, seemed to be standing on the floor by the bed in front of a stained-glass window in her house. She was aware of someone standing beside her. She saw it was her husband's favorite brother, Frank, who had died many years ago. She cried out joyously to her brother-in-law and expressed how glad she was to see him. As he drew her toward the window, she looked back at the room she was about to leave forever she thought. She went with him through the window, out onto the veranda, and from there, in some mysterious way, down to the street. (Springer, 8-9)

Tunnel or Beam

Betty Eadie died from complications after a hysterectomy. At the moment of death, she felt a surge of energy. It was like the pop Mary Neal experienced as her spirit came free from her body. She stayed in her room, studied her body, realized her body was dead, wanted to tell someone, and experienced weightlessness and a freedom from pain. Then three guys in brown robes showed up who seemed to her to exhibit spirituality, knowledge, and wisdom. She left her room in a great whirling black mass. It was as if she was moving faster than the speed of light through a tunnel toward a pinpoint of light. The pinpoint light turned out to be the radiant brilliance of Jesus, as she landed in his presence. (Eadie, 29)

Jim Woodford had trouble moving back toward his truck after he passed out from an overdose of opiods[3]. But when he saw someone slumped over the steering wheel, he recognized that person was him and he had died. He then involuntarily began moving upwards. It appears our movements toward heaven are determined for us; it is not a choice we make. In seconds he was looking at the bed of his truck and then was thousands of feet up and moving faster and faster. When he looked up he saw a tunnel of light, and then a golden circle about sixty feet in diameter appeared. The circle revealed an entrance to an immense distance. It opened up and he entered the tunnel at a very fast speed. As a former pilot he recognized his speed to be at least one thousand miles an hour, yet there was no sound or wind. He was traveling feet first tilted back at about a forty-five degree angle. Inside the tunnel was a swirling cloud, but a cloud more solid that those in the sky on Earth. He focused on a light at the end of the tunnel. For someone who has always arrogantly valued being in control, being out of control was a new and humbling experience for him. When he reached the end of the tunnel the opening widened, he decelerated to a soft landing on his feet in a mist that was the portal to what lay beyond. As he tentatively stepped forward, he looked down and saw he was standing on "the most incredibly beautiful, perfectly manicured green grass anyone could ever imagine." He was also amazed that light rippled out from the grass when he stepped on it. Light was everywhere. (Jim Woodford, 53-54)

Dale Black stayed with his body at the hospital for a while and then he moved out of the room, down the hallway where the walls disappeared into a long corridor of light. It wasn't a tunnel of light but a path in the darkness delineated by light. He was out of his body, but he felt fully complete. He traveled at an incredible speed. Even with the incredible speed of travel, he felt no sense of movement, no g-forces, no wind in his face, no ear popping. Millions of tiny spheres of light were moving past. Two angels were accompanying him. He wondered what

---

[3] See the description in the annotated bibliography.

was happening to him but began to anticipate something wondrous was coming. The light of the corridor was coming from a central source to which he was headed. It was the whitest light he had ever seen, but as he approached the central source, it became yellow-white and then golden. Unlike the sun's light, this light was a living substance. (Black 2010, 98; Black 2018, 156-159, 164)

One of Dr. Maurice Rawlings' patients, Mr. Ledford, died of heart failure. He remembers everything being black, and then seeing the hospital staff working on him. It seemed strange to him because he felt perfectly fine. He couldn't see himself clearly and wasn't sure that the body they were working on was his, so he moved to one side so he could see and verified that the body was indeed his.

He saw three or four people come in, including a boy in charge of oxygen. He thought the others must be nurses from another unit since he had not seen them before. Then everything seemed to be dimming out and going black again. He sensed he was moving through a long corridor. After a while, he became aware of a small pinpoint of light that looked like a bird. The pinpoint of light slowly became larger and larger until it looked like a flying white dove. It eventually became so big and bright that the whole area was lit with the brilliant, beautiful light. It surpassed anything he had ever seen before. (Rawlings, 76)

The moment Crystal McVea closed her eyes in the surgery room, she was suddenly in the presence of God. It happened in the same instant. (McVea, 11) But after being with Him for a bit (described in the chapter on meeting Jesus), she, her two angels (described in the chapter on angels) and God traveled through something like a tunnel of brightness, brightness above and below, toward an even brighter light, more intense, vivid, golden, and beautiful than all other brightness. She knew it was heaven, the gates of heaven, the entrance to heaven. God made it clear that once she reached the gate she could not come back. She had excitement and expectation about getting there, but she also had a vision of her four children. She knew they would be okay without her and she would see them again when they came to heaven. She knew she wanted to stay with God. But as they neared the gates, she knew it wasn't her time to be there. There was someone she was supposed to meet. She eventually met that person at a testimony service she did not want to do.

4

This is described in the chapter on Life after Heaven. (McVea, 149-152)

When Ian McCormack died it was dark and he couldn't see what was around him. He moved around but didn't bump into anything like his hospital bed. He could not even see his hand in front of his face and it was bitterly cold. He tried to touch his face and his hand went right through; he apparently did not have his physical body. Then he sensed evil around him, but he couldn't see the evil beings. He said he felt a terrible encroaching evil all around him. The evil beings began to communicate with him, told him to "shut up!" and that he was in hell. He became aware of other people there in the same predicament as him. He said he used to think hell was a party place where you get to do all the things you couldn't do on Earth. But it is not like that at all. He said it was the most frightening place he had ever been in and people were not able to do anything their evil hearts desired.

But then a brilliant light shown upon him and drew him out of the darkness. It surrounded him and he ascended up into the beam of light. He was drawn to a large circular opening above him, like a tunnel. The source of the light emanated from the end of the tunnel. It was unspeakably bright and it seemed all light came from it. He could see a whole world through the opening. Waves of greater density broke off from the light and came toward him. The first gave him warmth and comfort. The second wave gave off total and complete peace, unlike anything he had tried in his search for peace on Earth including studies, alcohol, sport, drugs, women, and more. But now he had total peace. He also saw that his body was full of the same light he saw coming from the end of the tunnel. The third wave brought him total joy. A voice spoke from the light and asked him by name if he wished to return. He couldn't figure out where he was but the voice spoke again. Then it said if you return you must see in a new light. At that point he realized he was seeing Jesus. (Sharkey, 24-28)

Immediate Arrival

Others just appear in the brilliance of heaven. Richard Eby died from a fall from a second story balcony railing that broke. He hit his head on pavement and it split open. He died instantly, but on the way to the hospital apparently his life functions resumed and the leisurely ambulance ride turned into a lights-flashing, siren-blaring, emergency run. He says one moment he was in Chicago and the next moment in heaven, one moment in miserable humidity and then next in the most beautiful wondrous world he had ever known. He was met with an overwhelming sense of peace and the sharpest mind he had ever had. (Eby, 202-203)

When Betty Malz (Betty Upchurch at the time) died from a ruptured appendix in the hospital, the transition was serene and peaceful, she said. She found herself walking up a green grassy hill. The grass was beautiful, the most vivid shade of green she had ever seen. (Malz, 84)

Don Piper specifically says that he never experienced any of these other arrival patterns. He was crossing a bridge going about 45 mph when he met a semitrailer truck head-on going about 60 mph. One moment he was looking at an eighteen-wheeler coming right at him and the next moment he was standing in heaven. (Piper 2018, 7) He was just suddenly enveloped by a brilliant light when he found himself in heaven. He was filled with joy and saw a crowd of people, including some that he knew, but Jesus was not there. They rushed toward him smiling and praising God. (Piper 2004, 21-22)

An angel and Jesus came to Mary K. Baxter and told her God wanted her to see heaven. He said, "come and see the glory of God," and at that moment she was suddenly standing outside one of the gates of heaven. (Baxter, 22)

Jeanne Enstad was in the hospital for a heart value repair when the repair failed and she was rushed to the operating room. There she heard someone call "code blue", but a warm, comforting voice told her, "Jeanne, you are fine." She tried to tell those working on her that she was fine, and they needn't be worried, but they acted like they could not hear her. She felt tranquility with an incredible kind of unconditional love she had not experienced before. She was surrounded by a beautiful white light and a gentle, loving touch. Looking down she saw her white gown like a princess and looking up, she saw amazing beautiful, sparkling, golden streets. She was suddenly in heaven. (Enstad, 29-30)

Jeff Olsen left his body at the scene of the accident and immediately was in heaven with his wife Tamara. (Olsen, 31)

Immediate Arrival with Jesus

This is the case of Samaa Habib. She is a former Muslim in an unidentified Middle Eastern country suffering through an extended civil war. She was next to a fire extinguisher cabinet when a Jihadist's bomb exploded in the cabinet and knocked her ten feet against a wall. She died immediately. When she opened her eyes, she saw a brilliant white light illuminating Jesus, the Son of Man, the Son of God. She said His face was brighter than the sun, and He was so glorious and transcendent that she was blinded with the brilliant light. His golden light was everywhere around her. She was in awe at His mighty presence and had a great fear of the Lord that made her speechless seeing His majesty and His indescribable beauty. She was totally consumed with praise, saying, "Holy, holy, holy is the Lord God Almighty."

She fell facedown with the weight of His glory. She was prostrate at His feet. She said she was terrified and aware of her uncleanness. She was unable to stand in His presence.

Then Jesus touched her and told her not be afraid. He reminded her that His precious blood was shed for her and that He had washed her clean as white snow, making her holy and pure. It was all because of His love for her. (Habib, 177)

This is like John's experience recorded in Revelation 1:17, *"When I saw him, I fell at his feet as though dead. Then he placed his right hand on me and said: 'Do not be afraid'"* [NIV]

Jesus came to Rhoda "Jubilee" Mitchell as she was lying facedown on her bed, completely overwhelmed by her troubles and feeling defeated. She had cried out to God, "I can't take it any more." Jesus came in response to her call. She said as Jesus took her out of her body, she was acutely aware of her surroundings. They ascended into the night sky, and she saw the celestial vista and Jesus' and the Father's communication. It revealed to her the majesty of God as Creator. (Roth, 44)

Later she says that, all of a sudden, we were in heaven, which she sensed was her home, as it loomed large in front of them. Jesus let her know immediately that she was there only for a visit and would not be allowed to stay. Then He set her down inside the walls. (Roth, 48)

Colton Burpo's experience is hard to decipher because as a four-year-old, he didn't tell a continuous story but added bits and pieces over time. However, one of the first things he reports is being in Jesus' lap, presumably in the hospital. It would appear that Jesus is the one that took Colton Burpo to heaven. (Burpo, xix)

Transporters

Some people report riding in some conveyance like a cable car without the cable. This is what Jesse Duplantis said on the tape recording of his experience. Kat Kerr reported this possibility also. (Kerr 2007, 33-34)

Dawn Cypret was on what she calls a large escalator. There was a long line of people also riding on the escalator. (May, 21)

As reported later in the chapter on the rivers, lakes, and seas in this book, Rebecca Springer saw sea-going conveyances bringing people from the other side. (Springer, 108)

Arrival in Clouds

Dale Reppert saw hazy white light around the blurred individuals in his hospital room when a brilliant soft beam of white light arose from the horizon and formed a dome over him that extended infinitely in all directions. It took away his pain and gave him the feeling of the purest deepest love he had ever experienced. Then he began to see the faces of loved ones who had passed on in heaven. (Reppert, 53)

Dr. Gary Wood, after a fatal car wreck, was caught up into a funnel-shaped cloud that kept getting wider and wider. He describes walking in the cloud on a moving pathway like an airport moving walkway. He kept going up, and as he continued, he was engulfed in a brilliant light with serenity and peace washing over him. Ultimately, he landed in heaven outside the wall and an angel with a sword granted him access to heaven. (Roth, 100-102; Wood, 24)

Richard Sigmund had been driving down the road in his van when, all of a sudden, he was in a fatal single-car accident. He describes being in a thick cloud-like veil, coming through the veil like a fog, and stepping into heaven. There were gold, purple, and amber colors and a bright light. The cloud pulsated as sound was going through it. He was moving through the cloud for a few minutes but felt the cloud moving through him also.

He could hear people at the accident talking only a few inches away. There were sirens and lots of noise. Then he heard someone say he was dead.

He felt a force drawing him through the glory cloud, and he could hear people singing on the other side of the cloud. There was joyous laughter, and he felt total peace. He smelled an aroma, and experienced a taste like strawberries and cream. (Sigmund, 16-17)

When Tony Davis' spirit left his body he floated up toward the clouds. The closer he got to them the more peace, love, and joy he felt. Then the clouds opened and he saw a huge beautiful city and felt more love than he ever had before. He felt joy and peace.

After his glimpse of the beautiful city and feeling the tremendous love and compassion of heaven, he tried to move forward but was held back and a voice said, "It's not your time, go back." But he did not want to go back from what he had seen and experienced already. He said, "No, no, I am not going back. No!" He tried again to pull his way through, but the voice said, "It's not your time." After some more protests, he heard, "Tony, your work is not done yet, I need you to go back." Then with a breath and a whoosh, he went back through the clouds into his body. All of this took place in a four-hour Earth-time period. (Doucette 2013-2)

Summary

Mary Neal and Rebecca Springer both met a family member or friends who welcomed them and escorted them to heaven. Dr. Wood met a friend after he entered heaven that guided him. Mr. Ledford moved through a long corridor, as did Betty Eadie. Dale Black followed a beam of light. Richard Sigmund and Dr. Gary Wood arrived in a cloud. Richard Eby, Betty Malz, Samaa Habib, Mary K. Baxter, and Don Piper just appeared suddenly in heaven. Jesus met Rhoda Mitchell and Colton Burpo and took them to heaven. Jesse Duplantis and Kat Kerr talk about going there in a cable car-like conveyance, although Kat in most of her visions of heaven just appeared in heaven, sometimes only for an instant to be shown one thing for the benefit of someone she was with. This is a sampling of most of the ways people report going to heaven.

CHAPTER 2

First Glimpses Of Heaven

Oden Hetrick said that when we first get there, we go to what might be called the suburbs, being outside the city. It is a lot like earth with trees, flowers, and birds. That is where the pets go. We go there to learn that the Spirit of God controls everything, and it is His spirit that puts it in our minds to go to the river, to the fruit on the trees, to someone with whom to fellowship, to the library, or whatever. There is no disobedience in heaven, but everything we do arises out of our love relationship with God. (Doucette 2013-1)

Emotion

By far the most universal experience of heaven is a love that exceeds any love that author has known on Earth. This is accompanied by a total acceptance and a peace we long for on Earth but don't experience to the degree it is found in heaven. As you read through this book you will see testimony after testimony of this deep emotional experience of each person's experience in heaven. This emotion is so powerful no one wants to come back to Earth, but they all (except those who did stay and didn't come back to tell us) either recognize family members here that need them back, or Jesus sends them back on a mission to tell others, or it is not their time to enter heaven.

Tony Davis felt rays of love pouring out of the window in the clouds where he saw the huge beautiful city. He said it was like the arms of God reached out to him and held him. He felt so much love and compassion that he began forgiving and letting everything go more than he could imagine. (Doucette 2013-2)

Crystal McVea spends most of her book telling all the terrible things that happened in her life and how she broke all ten commandments and was lost to God, including how she knew He could never forgive her. But her experience in the magnificent presence of God's love and healing healed her from all the stuff that hung over her, a gift so great she has tears of joy and gratitude remembering from what she has been healed. (McVea, 14)

Mary Neal said heaven glimmered with Exhilaration. (Neal 2017, 42)

Mary K. Baxter was overwhelmed with the breathtaking beauty she saw all around her. The indescribable beauty of God all around her amazed her. The angel with her appeared to be clothed in a garment of light. Its wings were triangular and glistened with the colors of the rainbow. (Baxter, 22) She saw that the citizens of heaven were exuberant in their happiness and joy. It beamed from their faces beyond anything with which Mary could identify. (Baxter, 25)

Dr. Kolbaba tells the story from Dr. Robin Mraz of Cleveland Manning who experienced rapid bleeding from a failed suture from a minor surgery. He was rushed to the hospital emergency department where Dr. Mraz was on duty. When he arrived his face looked like a ghost and he had no pulse, no blood pressure, and was completely unresponsive. Furthermore, he had been gone for twenty minutes. After CPR, several pints of blood, and surgery, he suddenly had a faint pulse. His eye flickered and at first he couldn't talk. But soon he said, "You guys have beautiful music here. I want to hear it again. Can you get me back to that room where they play the music? It was so peaceful." He described a beautiful white room where there was quiet music from unfamiliar instruments. He clearly had been to some part of heaven but thought it had been in the hospital. (Kolbaba, 14-17)

Jeanne Enstad felt no pain and no fear, nothing negative. But she did experience everyone there as being happy and full of joy. They were laughing and there was no fear of harm or danger. Everything was perfect there with total peace, happiness, and joy. The love was like no other that she knew, a perfect love unlike anything on Earth. (Enstad, 31)

She loved the divine life of being near the Savior all the time. It is one great brotherhood with Jesus as the head, built on love. "Everyone loved one another." (Enstad, 32)

She said, "Heaven is beyond anything we will ever experience on Earth." She anticipates being with the Lord forever. Here God is bigger than any crisis she or we will have and is here for every single one of us with an incredible love. (Enstad, 91)

When Mickey Robinson passed through the portal of pure white dazzling light, he came immediately into the presence of Almighty God. He had a spiritual awareness that he would live here in God's presence forever. He was bathed in the "pure, undiluted, perfect love of God." His glory engulfed all of everything. He did not see an image, form, or shape, just the powerful Presence of God going beyond mere emotion. He experienced the reality of King David's words, "In your presence there is fullness of joy; at your right hand are pleasures forevermore." [Psalm 16:11] He said what he was experiencing was more magnificent than any words can describe. He was more alive than any sense of being alive on Earth and was infused with perfect love and peace. He had an overwhelming knowledge that all human beings were made to be connected and attuned to God's presence. God's radiant energy and majesty were emanating everywhere in all directions. The greatest awe for him in all this experience "was knowing, feeling, and hearing from God Himself the unrelenting, personal, everlasting love He has" for him. (Robinson, 105-107)

Sights

On her first visit to heaven in 1994, Jeanne Enstad, looking down, saw her white gown like a princess, and looking up, she saw amazing beautiful, sparkling, golden streets. She tiptoed gracefully and approached the gates of heaven. She was transformed when she walked through the gates, and the warm comforting voice spoke again, "Come my child. You are home." She saw that heaven is a beautiful place and everything appeared to be pure gold, radiant and sparkling. There were many beautiful sparkling stones everywhere. She said the city is made of gold, as pure as glass. There was no sun or moon; the glory of God illuminated all of heaven. She experienced the most brilliant brightest white light she had ever seen. The colors were radiant and bright, unlike any she had seen before. She marveled at the glory all around her and was amazed at the panoramic view. She was weightless and mobile. There was nothing negative; she felt no pain or fear. There was a perfect kind of love, which cannot be found on Earth. (Enstad, 31)

In her second visit to heaven in 2001, as she stood there, she was surrounded by a beautiful bright light and was surrounded by the warmth, peace, and joy of Jesus' love. She was amazed at the sparkling golden radiance lining the street. The perfect beauty and holiness there is beyond Earthly description. She was held in the comforting warmth and love of Jesus' arms. She had yearned to feel Jesus' love in the seven years since her first visit. (Enstad, 85)

Dale Black came to a radiant city bathed in a golden to white light. It gleamed with a myriad of resplendent colors, every imaginable color. The light was the purest he had ever seen. He said, "The music was the most majestic, enchanting and glorious [he] had ever heard." The city was huge and grand. It exceeded any of the world's cities he had seen in his flying career as an airline pilot, both in size and in radiance. He didn't know how, but he knew that this place was utterly holy. The city was overwhelmingly beautiful and breathtaking. He also knew he was made for this place and it was made for him. As he approached the city, he flew over a glorious colorful countryside with meadows and trees and became aware of indescribable music. (Black 2010, 99; Black 2018, 164-165)

He arrived in a meadow outside the city in view of a massive wall with a huge ornate gateway that was so beautiful it took away his breath. These will be described later. (Black 2018, 16)

Ian McCormack looked through a circular shaped opening behind Jesus and saw a whole new world of meadows, fields, grass, a crystal stream, mountains, clear blue sky, rolling green hills, and flowers. He wanted to say goodbye to the old world he had left, but then he saw his mother's face looking at him. She had prayed for him every day of his life and had tried to show him the way of God. If he never returned she would never know of his radical change. He knew he had to go back. Also God showed him his family and thousands of people, whom God said would not come to Him if he didn't go back. Jesus told him he would have to see things in a new light, by which he understood he would have to see people as Jesus saw them with love and forgiveness. So he came back after being dead for fifteen minutes and shocked the medical staff, who knew he was dead. He did serve God the rest of his life, speaking all over the world, causing many to accept Jesus and become part of God's family. (Roth, 70-73, Sharkey, 32-34)

Jim Woodford said everything in heaven is filled with light: people, flowers, grass, angels. In answer to the question, "Who am I?" he saw

14

that he was just one for whom God banished the darkness when he spoke out a need for God's help. The longer he was there, the more wondrous the things he saw and witnessed. (Woodford, 71) He was amazed that the colors had sounds and the sounds had colors. The sensory spectrum overwhelmed him. He said heaven resembles Earth but the best vistas on Earth are a thousand times less beautiful, serene, and amazing than those in heaven. (Woodford, 79-80)

Steven Musick was hurled out of the tunnel into a rolling green meadow with waist high grass and what he calls a massive shady oak tree, a lush valley on his left and a forest of rolling hills beyond the meadow. He mentions billowy clouds and bright sunshine everywhere. He hadn't yet noticed there is no sun but the light that permeates heaven was like bright sunlight to him, and it permeated everything. He was surrounded by a sense of abundance, completeness, and perfection. He said it is like high definition TV on steroids. The colors are indescribably rich and everything is crystal clear. He found the visual experience overwhelming. (Musick, 37-38)

Tony Davis heard people talking and saw kids playing. He heard a waterfall and saw beautiful radiant colors he had never seen before. He saw speckles of light going through the city and was told those are archangels. (Doucette 2013-2)

Richard Eby arrived in the most beautiful wondrous world he had ever known. He was met with an overwhelming sense of peace and the sharpest mind he had ever had. (Eby, 202-203)

Crystal McVea said everything was much more beautiful, brilliant, and amazing than anything on Earth. It was all so real and clear that by comparison the things of Earth seem hazy and out-of-focus. To her heaven seemed so real that Earth seemed just a dream. However she describes things, her words are inadequate; everything is so much more breathtaking and big that she doesn't have adequate words to express it. She also had a sensation of cleanness, a feeling of absolute purity and perfection, a sense of being unblemished and unbroken. She was immersed in it and had a kind of peace and assurance she had never known on Earth. She was bathed in love. She had the sense that this was finally home, the home for which she was made. No matter how mind-bending something was, she had no problem processing it and was never confused. Thinking in heaven is more certain, natural, powerful, and complete. (McVea, 12-13)

Dr. Gary Wood landed in heaven outside the wall and an angel with a sword granted him access to heaven. His friend John was the first person he saw upon entering the city. Seeing John brought him overwhelming joy. John ran and embraced him in a glorious reunion. When they hugged their arms went all the way through each other. Then John took him on a tour of heaven. (Roth, 100-102)

Richard Sigmund could hear people singing and joyous laughter, and he felt total peace. He smelled an aroma, and it had a taste like strawberries and cream.

He saw other people coming through the veil too. To his right, there appeared to be a receiving area. Just a few feet from him, he could see two women who were of great age, but they appeared to be in their mid-twenties, and they were beautiful. They were hugging each other and seemed very joyful. They were looking through the veil.

Suddenly, the man they were expecting as they looked through the veil came through. He seemed very confused for a moment and didn't seem to know where he was. But he recognized the women, and they began to hug him and praise and worship God in a joyous reunion.

To his right he saw a group of about fifty people with their arms up praising God, when they started saying, "He is coming. I see him coming!" Then their very old pastor came through the veil. Suddenly his age lines disappeared and his gnarled old body straightened up and he looked like he was in his twenties or thirties. (Sigmund, 16-18)

He saw others coming through the veil and being welcomed by those who knew they were coming. When each person stepped into heaven, he/she was immediately transformed into a whole and healthy person in his/her prime of life.

This reminds me of the vision I had of my first wife. She had been tragically murdered the week before the vision. I was looking at her portrait photograph when it suddenly took on a living three-dimensional appearance. At that moment, I saw her more whole and complete and full of joy than I had ever seen her in life. She had struggled with emotional problems all her life, but they were completely gone. She was radiant, confident, whole, joyful, and beautiful. The vision only lasted a second or two, but it spoke a lifetime of what happens to us when we get into the Lord's presence in His kingdom.

Khalida Wukawitz was working in the back room of the shop run by the Christian woman who had given her a job. She was unhappy and wondering where is truth. She cried out, "Jesus, if You are the Son of God, come down and show me." Suddenly the room changed and Jesus was standing before her. He said, "Leave the darkness for the light." As He continued to talk with her, she became aware that she was no longer in the room but had become a part of heaven. Angels were saying, "Holy, holy, holy." She saw many people of every color and race and children under the age of six all worshiping Jesus, calling Him, "Holy, holy Lamb of God." There were the sounds of many languages and tongues all speaking praises. As she looked at things she understood them supernaturally through the Holy Spirit. There was a place by His feet where she could see angels, babies, and birds of the air. (Malick, 81-83)

Jaafar Attaran saw a beautiful city made of clear crystal glass and gold, which Jesus said is the New Jerusalem. It was such that no human effort could have built it. It was beyond anything that he could possibly describe. There he experienced a peace and safety he had never known in his life. Malick, 124)

Heavenly grass

In several cases, the author's first introduction to heaven was landing on a meadow or a hill of a heavenly grass. Here is how several authors describe their entrance into heaven by their experience with this grass.

When Jim Woodford looked down and saw he was standing on "the most incredibly beautiful, perfectly manicured green grass anyone could ever imagine." He was also amazed that light rippled out from the grass when he stepped on it. (Woodford, 54)

Betty Upchurch (now Malz) died of a ruptured appendix after many efforts on the part of the hospital staff to save her. Sometime around 5:00 A.M that day, her body functions stopped. This had happened earlier, but at that time, some of the hospital staff were there and got her heart going again. This time there was no one at her bedside to call for the emergency equipment, so she transitioned into death in a way that was serene and peaceful. She found herself walking up a beautiful, green hill that was steep. Even though the hill was steep, it took no effort to walk up it. As she walked, a deep ecstasy flooded over her. Despite three incisions in her body from the operations, she stood erect without pain, enjoying her tallness, something about which she had always had inhibitions. She said she seemed to be barefoot, but the complete outer shape of her body was a blur and colorless.

She saw the grass was the most vivid shade of green she had ever seen. She said each blade was about one inch long with a texture like fine velvet. The grass was moving so that as the bottoms of her feet touched the grass, something alive in the grass was transmitted up through her whole body with each step. Someone she thought was an angel also accompanied her. To the left, and a little behind her, was a tall masculine-looking figure in a robe. She tried to see if he had wings, but she couldn't. (Malz, 84-85)

When Mr. Ledford arrived in heaven after his travel through the long corridor, his first encounter with heaven was of the grassy hill. He landed on a rolling green meadow that was slightly uphill. He saw his brother alive and remembered when he had died. His brother was very glad to see him. They strolled arm in arm up the meadow. Their walk was uphill a bit. Soon they came to what appeared to be a white split-rail fence. (Rawlings, 102)

When Dr. Gary Wood approached heaven, an angel with a sword granted him access to heaven. He was standing outside the city on a lush, green carpet of grass on a hill. He started walking up the hill. He felt the grass come all the way through his feet, and when he looked, there were no indentations in the grass from where he had stepped. (Roth, 100; Wood, 24) This is just one more instance that nothing is harmed in heaven. You will see more of these as we go along.

Rhoda "Jubilee" Mitchell also experienced the grassy area outside the city. Sid Roth tells her account of flying over the walls to the outside of the city where she stood on a grassy area looking toward the city. (Roth, 49)

Dale Black arrived in a meadow outside the city in view of the massive wall with a huge, ornate gateway. (Black 2018, 16)

Dawn Cypret stepped off the escalator into a beautiful green meadow filled with colorful flowers having a wonderful fragrance. She took a deep breath and it was the most cleansing breath she had ever taken. A gentle breeze made the flowers sway as if to be greeting her. She noted that as beautiful as portions of the Earth are, heaven was much more beautiful. (May, 21)

While Mary Neal was recovering in a hospital in Jackson, Wyoming, she had two more visits to heaven. In the second she was sitting on the ground at one end of a long field of wild grasses swaying in a soft breeze and bathed in a beautiful golden glow. (Neal 2017, 47)

Summary

The first encounter with heaven was different for different people, but a common theme was the peace, acceptance, and love they felt and saw everywhere in heaven. They usually see a whiter brightness than is possible on Earth, and the colors are richer and more numerous. Beyond that they may see the gleaming golden city or the wall of brilliant gems. Arriving on a green grassy hill or meadow seems to be very common. In any case, the visitors are overwhelmingly impressed and have feelings of joy, love, and hope they have longed for on Earth, and desire to stay.

CHAPTER 3
Biblical Features Of Heaven

Some of the attributes of heaven we learn from Revelation are the wall with twelve rows of precious jewels, the pearly gates, and the streets of gold. Different people have witnessed each of these. I have already reported the grassy hill as the first sign of heaven some have experienced. Here I discuss their encounters with the items mentioned in Revelation.

The Wall

Rhoda Mitchell, after she stood on the grassy area looking toward the city, described the wall. She saw an amber jewel the size of a football that was rounded on each end embedded in one section of the wall. She stooped down to approximately one foot off the ground and looked more closely at the amber stone. It was transparent, and she could look directly through it into the city. She said it was as if it were a huge bejeweled window. The jewels were absolutely flawless as if they were hand-cut by a master jeweler and inlaid into the walls. The jewels were different sizes, but many of them were very large. Because the jewels were transparent, the light of the city spilled through them, creating rainbow-colored light on the outside of the walls that cascaded to the ground. The jewels shone on the grassy areas leading up to the city walls, creating rainbow pathways of iridescent splendor. These pathways guided people into the city on their designated journey based on their particular birthstone color. She thought this may be one way God separates each person out on his/her own path through heaven. (Roth, 49-50)

While Betty Malz was walking up the grassy hill, she saw she was walking beside the wall with precious jewels. On her right was a low stone wall that became higher as they went along. She said it was made of many multicolored multitiered stones. A light from the other side of the wall shone through a long row of amber-colored stones several feet above her head. She thought it resembled topaz, her birthstone. (Malz,

86)

Richard Sigmund also saw the wall when the angel walking beside him pointed out the wall. It was tall, and he said it looked as if it were a mile away. Suddenly, they were at the wall, as travel in heaven seems to be at the speed of thought.

He saw that the wall was filled with many types of precious jewels: jasper, sardonyx, diamonds, yellowish-gold emeralds, bloodstone diamonds. He said the wall was made of some type of stone material that gave off a sensation that caressed his fingers when he touched it. (Sigmund, 26, 27)

In a vision Matthew Payne saw the great wall. At the time, he was not familiar with the wall around the New Jerusalem as described in Revelation. He said the wall rose a hundred feet into a mist. He couldn't see how high the wall went in the mist. It appeared to be miles long. Jesus told him to reach into the wall. So he did and pulled out a precious stone the size of a soccer ball. Jesus told him the stone is a diamond, and terms of Earth's resources, this diamond is worth enough to pay all the U. S. Government's expenses for 200 years. Jesus told him the whole wall is made of diamonds like that. He believes God showed him this to show him that money is irrelevant in heaven, and on Earth we should not place its value above the things here that are relevant in heaven, such as love, forgiveness, relationships, compassion, etc. The real worth in heaven is someone with a pure heart, someone with a heart that is sold out, someone with a heart that doesn't consider the wealth and possessions and things of this world, a heart that only wants God's ways and desires and only wants to do what God wants. (Payne, 13-15)

Dale Black said the wall was made of huge, translucent, colored stones, which would weigh tons on Earth. The light of the city shone through the stones giving beautiful dancing colored lights outside the wall. (Black 2018, 16) He, too, said it was very large. It was made of seven layers, each twenty-five to thirty feet thick and forty feet tall, with each layer stair-stepping up against the inner wall, making the whole thing about as thick as it was tall. Multiple colors with many hues shone through the stones in the wall and made dancing colors on the area outside the wall. They were dancing because they were alive and changed according to Dale's movements. They responded to his every move and filled his heart with joy. (Black 2018, 20-21)

It is not a single wall but a series of three outer and three inner walls. Between the outer and inner walls is a higher wall. The outer layers of the wall were about forty feet high. They got progressively higher toward the center. The highest point was about two hundred feet or so tall and about that thick also. It was massive and went as far in each direction as he could see. The outer wall was greenish with a hint of blue and black. It was made entirely of multi-colored translucent stones in layered rows. A strong light permeated the wall and caused all the colors of the rainbow in it to change as he moved. (Black 2010, 105-106)

David Taylor said the walls around the City of God were beautiful translucent golden walls, which he could see through. (Taylor, 164)

Dr. Gary Wood said the colors of the foundation stones of the city are the same as on the breastplate of Israel's high priest's garments. He also saw the twelve foundation stones of the city: there was one layer on top of another as giant gemstones. The bottom layer was of jasper, standing for the glory. He said it is the foundational stone of the city. Each additional layer consisted of sapphires, carnelian, beryl, topaz, emeralds, and rubies. Each layer had different beautiful colors and different precious gems. He said a certified gemologist told him it would take seven of this world's total wealth just to garnish one of the stones in the foundations. (Roth, 101; Wood, 25) He said the wall was so high he could not see the top and it seemed to go on forever. (Wood, 25)

It is not clear if Colton Burpo actually saw the stones in the wall, but he was obsessed with the many beautiful colors of heaven, which could include the stones. (Burpo, 107)

Sid Roth tells, in *Heaven Is Beyond Your Wildest Expectations: Ten True Stories of Experiencing Heaven,* the story of Michael McCormack who, at ten years old, was sitting in church praying and suddenly was taken to heaven. Michael arrived at heaven's golden gate, and beyond the gate, he could see a massive palace and a town. He said a golden-colored wall surrounded them. (Roth, 80)

The Gates of Heaven

Colton Burpo did see the gates, though. He said the gates of heaven were made of gold and pearls. (Burpo, 105)

Mary K. Baxter said the magnificent gate was made of a solid pearl. (Baxter, 22)

Dr. Gary Wood saw the twelve gates, for the twelve tribes of Israel, each gate made of one solitary pearl. (Roth, 101; Wood, 25) He said the solid pearl gate was the most excellent work of art he has seen, studded with sapphires, rubies, diamonds, and many other previous gems. (Wood, 25)

Oden Hetrick saw the twelve gates. They look like pearl in that they are white but the white is not on the surface, the color comes from deep within. He said as you approach the gate you see the light and then you can see right through the light into the light of the city itself. He said the gate is never shut and never open; you just walk right into it. He said there are three gates on each side, just like it says in Revelation 21:13. There are colored decorations around the gates. He didn't identify them as gems. He said they change colors.

Above the gates are the names of the tribes of Israel, one each above each gate. This, too, is described in Revelation 21:12. The name above (one of) the eastern gate(s) is Issachar. He said we enter by the eastern gate because God's throne faces east.

Inside the gate is a long hallway with an angel at the end to greet us and welcome us to heaven. He said Saint Peter is not sitting at the gate. That is a myth. By the time we get to the gate we are in. (Doucette 2013-1)

But some other authors mention an angel at the gate with the Book of Life to check to see if our name is there. The ones without their name in the Book of Life seem to report going directly to hell as reported in the Appendix, The Bad News.

Betty Malz describes a gate about twelve feet high that was a solid sheet of pearl. It had no handles but had a Gothic structure with some lovely scrollwork at the top. The pearl was translucent, and she could almost see inside.

When the angel pressed his palm on the gate, an opening appeared in the center of the pearl and slowly widened and deepened as though the pearl were dissolving. Inside she saw a street of golden color with an overlay of glass or water. The yellow light that appeared was dazzling.

The angel asked if she wanted to go inside. She did, but she thought of her dear father who, at that time, was grieving beside her hospital bed. She said she would like to sing a little more and then go back to her father. After she said this, the gate slowly melted back into one sheet of pearl. Her angel escorted her back down the same beautiful hill with the jeweled wall on her left this time. (Malz, 87-88)

Richard Sigmund's view of the gates was different from that of Betty Malz. For him the gates were huge, seeming to be twenty-five miles high, in his words. And there were three tongues of fire on each gate, representing the Father, the Son, and the Holy Spirit. The gates were made of gold like wrought iron, curved on the top, with vertical stringers and filigree between the stringers at the bottom. He said the gold represents the great mercy of God. He saw thousands of individual pathways coming to the gates. (Sigmund, 27)

I noticed, in several places, Richard Sigmund's estimates of size were considerably larger than what other people estimated.

Dale Black approached an impressive opening in the wall that was an archway forty feet high and thirty to thirty-five feet wide. A tall majestic angel stood to the right of the gate. He appeared very strong and masculine. His hair looked white but could have been the bright white light radiating from him and illuminating his whole being. His face was lighted with love and joy.

The gateway was opalescent as if made with pearls that had been liquefied and then solidified into the gate and coated the entire inside of the opening. There was ornamentation with phenomenal detail surrounding the opening. There were large gold letters above the entrance that seemed to quiver with life. He didn't recognize the letters but knew the message they communicated was important. There were other letters in honey-colored gemstones around the entrance. A pure white light filled the opening. There was music all around filling him with music, light, and love. He was excited in anticipation of entering the beautiful gate. This was the place he had been searching for his whole life; he belonged here; he didn't want to leave. (Black 2010, 106-107)

The gate was astoundingly beautiful. It was intricate, ornate, and gorgeous with an arch forty to fifty feet high and thirty to thirty-five feet wide. It appeared to be open and unobstructed, granting access to the city. Streams of light came through the opening and gave a colorful display of love and energy to everyone it touched. (Black 2018, 21-22) Then he said the gate appeared to be coated in pearl as if the gems had been liquefied and poured over the gate. There were jewels wrapped in gold all around the lining of the gate. The light shone through the jewels making an iridescent rainbow of color that filled the opening. There were large shimmering gold letters inlaid above the opening and others in the pathway that led up to the opening. He didn't know what they said, but knew they were important.

A large angel was beside the opening. He was dressed in a long, flowing white robe with a gold belt with an emblem for a buckle. He had pale hair that flowed to his shoulders. He moved to the center of the opening and held up his hand indicating that Dale was not allowed to enter, but he did this with joy, acceptance, and kindness. Dale was directed to a pillar to the right of the opening upon which was the large Book of Life. (Black 2018, 25-27)

Don Piper in his next moment after death said he was standing in heaven. With joy pulsing through him, he looked around and saw a large crowd of people standing in front of a brilliant ornate gate. (Piper 2004, 21-22)

Marvin Besteman saw an enormous door attached to the gate. It was several stories tall and the wall stretched as far as he could see in both directions. He describes the door as a large wooden door, darker than oak or ash, maybe like mahogany. It had a plain design carved in it and brilliant colored lights danced all over it. He did not see anything he would call pearly. He saw no top to the door. It just ascended upward and disappeared into a mist. It had a large wooden handle about two and a half feet long and six inches wide. (Besteman, 73-74)

The gates he saw were not pearly. The gate he saw was made of heavy, dark wood, covered with twinkling lights. (Besteman, 82)

He estimated the gate to be about seven feet high. There was something like steel beams in a giant X shape embedded like a ribbon in the glassy surface of the gate. It had a faint multicolored, mostly red, outline. (Besteman, 119)

Jesus flew Rhoda "Jubilee" Mitchell over the walls into the city. She was told that no one can enter through the gates without having an Earthly death. Anyone who enters through a gate cannot return to Earth and will be permanently dead from this life. She was only allowed in as a visitor. (Roth, 48) See the experience of Betty Malz above where the angel asked if she wanted to go in after he had opened the pearl gate. She declined, but if she had chosen to enter, she would not have been miraculously resuscitated in the hospital.

The Streets of Gold

Colton Burpo saw the streets of gold. He said that the heavenly city itself was made of something shiny. To him it was like gold or silver. (Burpo, 105)

Betty Malz peered through the open pearl gate and saw what appeared to be a street of golden color with an overlay of glass or water. (Malz, 87)

Willie Agnes Chennault saw a winding road of thick gold that was yellowish and shining. (Chennault, 57)

Richard Sigmund said he was standing on a golden pathway, which was like a guided tour. It led him in a direction he had to go. It took him to things he was supposed to see and to his appointment with God. He said the pathway was about six feet wide, and it had thickness. He also said the path took him through a garden that stretched as far as he could see in either direction. (Sigmund, 12-22)

When he saw the golden pathway led to buildings further ahead, he was suddenly there. The pathway came to a street made of a clear substance, like a jewel intermingled with strands of gold. (Sigmund, 28-29) He saw people walking up and down beautiful golden and crystal streets. They appeared to be made of diamonds or one big diamond with layers of gold and silver. (Sigmund, 37)

Rhoda Mitchell said when she stepped barefoot onto the street, she saw her foot out from under her flowing white robe. Stepping onto the street was like standing in four inches of water. In addition, the street emitted a beautiful glow and made it look like she was stepping onto a golden mirror. Since the street looked like water, she quickly pulled her foot back under her robe, but she tested the street again and found it was perfectly solid but so transparent that it looked wet, even though it was dry. She continued strolling down the golden street barefooted. (Roth, 50-51)

Dawn Cypret said there are streets of gold, but there are also streets of marble, pearl, and other precious coverings. They are all very beautiful and clean, as if someone is on cleanup patrol all the time. But she did not notice anyone doing any cleaning of the streets. She thought maybe they clean themselves. (May, 30)

I think the people in heaven do not litter like people on Earth do and there is no dirt in the air, so the streets never need cleaning. I lament that too many people of Earth do not appreciate the beauty of this Earth enough to treat it with respect and not litter it with trash.

Kat Kerr said the streets are transparent to reflect the glory of God. They are made of gold. God made them the best for us on which to walk, and so they have a beautiful golden glow. Sometimes the streets move you toward your destination. Kerr 2010, 41-42)

Oden Hetrick said there is a golden street beside the Trees of Life on each side of the River of Life. He talked about the golden street becoming grass and flowers and then becoming gold again. In some places it seems to be the bed of a river. He also said it starts at the Throne of God and winds around through the city to the Eastern Gate where it ends. (Doucette 2013-1)

Dr. Gary Wood said the streets are alive with a glittering palette of colors with the brilliance of Jesus shining on it. The streets are crystal clear yet pure gold. (Wood, 31)

(In the chapter on the physics of heaven I describe how it appears that heaven is not made of atoms and molecules like Earth is. As a result things there are compared with similar things on Earth but are not the same. Hence the gold there is not atoms of atomic number 79 and whatever it is made of can be both clear and gold-like.)

A patient of Dr. Maurice Rawlings reported that the streets seemed to be made of wonderfully beautiful, shining gold. (Rawlings 76)

Another patient reported the angel set him down on a street in a fabulous city with buildings made of glittering gold and silver. He also noted it had beautiful trees. (Rawlings, 78)

Michael McCormack said the Lord took him outside the town, which was lined with golden roads. There were many houses, all different. (Roth, 82)

The Light of Heaven

Everyone talks about it always being light, and the light comes from the Father and Son directly. They light heaven, and it is brilliant, too bright for Earthly eyes.

Willie Agnes Chennault said she "stepped into the light. There is nothing dark there." (Chennault, 56, 181)

Crystal McVea said the light was everywhere with no beginning or end, not originating from any one point but just a pervasive whiteness, whiter than any white on Earth. It was a trillion times whiter than the best whiteness you have ever seen. So she calls it a brightness rather than light. (McVea, 13)

Steven Musick saw bright "sunshine" everywhere. He said the light is "brilliant, beyond description." He never mentions, though, that there is no sun nor that the light is from the glory of God. (Musick, 37-38)

Betty Malz said as she walked beside the wall that there was no sun, but light was everywhere. As many have said, heaven is illuminated by the glory of the Father and the Son. (Malz, 85)

Jeanne Enstad noticed it was never dark there; there was no division into day and night. The angel told her people don't rest or sleep there; there is no need for sleep. (Enstad, 89)

Jim Woodford said all the light of heaven is the light of God. Everything is infused with the light of God; it comes out of everything, grass, flowers, waters, angels, everything. Because the light comes from within everything, there are no shadows; there is no darkness anywhere. Because there are no shadows in heaven, everything is revealed in perfect optical clarity. There is no blazing sun and no foul weather from which to hide. There is no weather, and it is like a constant 72 degrees. The light is the warmth of God. There is no night and no need for sleep and rest. There are no worries or stress from which we have a need to recover. Our spirit bodies are perfect and need no recovery sleep. (Woodford, 84)

Dale Black said the light of heaven is God. It is not in God, from God, or by God, it is God Himself. God is the light, and it doesn't shine on things, it shines through them. The light, even though brighter than the sun, was not hard to look at. In fact it drew him in because it was warm and loving. As it flowed through him, it gave him life and energy, and bathed him with love. (Black 2018, 18)

He said the light of heaven that emanates from the throne in the center of heaven is also love and life, and rolled together into one. For him it embodied 1 John 4:8b, "*God is love,*" 1 John 1:5b, "*God is light; in Him there is no darkness at all,*" and John 1:4, "*In Him was life and that life was the light of men.*" Seeing how the light of heaven is also completely love and life was transforming for him, transforming his understanding of creation, Earth, heaven, and God, in ways that have changed his life and attitudes forever. It is foundational to life. When he first arrived in heaven this light was brighter than the sun and beams arched hundreds of miles overhead in amazing radiance and glory. This light blanketed heaven going into everyone and everything, giving the person or thing satisfying and rejuvenating life, energy and love. The love in the light is perfect, complete, pure, and true. (Black 2018, 172-173)

He said there was "a great phosphorescent display of light." It had weight and thickness, something he had never experienced with light. As brilliant as it was, he had no trouble looking at it and, in fact, enjoyed looking at it. The glow and energy radiated in all directions. He said it was warm and inviting, almost hypnotic. He knew that light, life, and love were all interconnected. This light did not shine on things; it shone through them, through the grass, trees, walls, and people. (Black 2010, 100)

Colton Burpo's comment best sums up the idea of God being the light of heaven. Todd, his father, tried to trick him and asked what he did with Todd's grandfather when it got dark in heaven. He looked serious and couldn't believe his dad thought it got dark in heaven. He said it never gets dark in heaven because God and Jesus light up heaven. (Burpo, 104)

The City

As a professional airline pilot, Dale Black has had the privilege of seeing many of the world's largest cities from the air. At the center of heaven from which the light emanated, was a massive city far larger and grander than any city he had ever seen on Earth. The light from this city radiated out for miles and miles. Even when he was not in the city, he was still awed by the grandeur he saw. The city was surrounded by an enormous wall outside of which were lush colorful gardens. The city was architecturally perfect, a masterpiece. Throughout the city were communities that looked like small happy colorful towns. Each one was park-like with colorful gardens, fountains, lakes, and streams. (Black 2018, 164-166)

Jim Woodford was also a former airline pilot who was given a pilot's eye view of the City of God. The walls around the city were quite thick. The absolutely beautiful countryside is referred to as Paradise or "walled garden." In his overview, they would occasionally go in for a close-up of some aspect of the city. It looked to him like parkland where the buildings blend in with the beauty of the landscape. The city of heaven is huge and from his highest point of view it was like concentric circles of golden boulevards separated by other circles of greenways. It was interspersed with occasional sparkling crystal waterfalls and meandering waterways. The streets were not like the gold of Earth but a softer muted gold with all impurities removed. There were cross-shaped intersections among the gold and green circles with smaller walkways.

He saw many buildings, some with columns and arches. They were not made of hewn stone like Earth buildings, but of some material exhibiting a soft glow and the love and warmth of God. The buildings served different purposes. This included halls of great knowledge, halls of learning, halls of healing, halls for music of many kinds. The music blended with all other sounds into a symphony of the love of God. Everything flowed to a brilliant light that appeared to be the throne of God. As the streets drew nearer the throne they became more transparent as a kind of crystal. (Woodford, 108-110)

Richard Sigmund floated up in the air and could see the whole City of God. It was centered around the Throne of God and seemed to be the capital city of heaven. He had seen other cities, too, including one on a peninsula out into an ocean. There were many clean beautiful villages around the city, some hundreds of miles from the city. (Sigmund, 82-83)

Oden Hetrick said the city was a huge cube, matching the description given in Revelation 21:16, being about 1500 miles in each dimension. (Doucette 2013-1)

Summary

The testimonies about the wall, the gates, the streets, and the brilliant permanent light from the glory of God the Father and the Son are all like the Spirit revealed them to John 2,000 years ago. God is the same yesterday, today, and forever, because in heaven, there is no time. It is always *now*. But God has allowed these visitors to see more than was shown to John, so we have an even more complete picture of those details in Revelation. All of these things John described and more are going to be there for you and me to be awed and amazed at the awesome love and glory of God.

CHAPTER 4

Personal Appearances

Bodies

Richard Sigmund saw that as each person stepped into heaven, he/she was immediately transformed into a whole and healthy person in his/her prime of life. (Sigmund, 18-19)

Everyone Mary K. Baxter saw was glorified, radiant, and handsome and without any scars. (Baxter, 76)

Marvin Besteman said in the hospital he was as weak and uncomfortable as he would ever want to be, but when he was in heaven in the waiting line to get in, he felt no weakness and was awake, alert, and strong and healthy as a horse (his words). He felt fantastic, better than he ever had as a young man. No one he saw there had crutches, damaged bodies, missing appendages, Down's syndrome, or any other special need. (Besteman, 78)

In heaven, his vision improved immeasurably beyond what his glasses had done for him. His eyes, ears, brain, and body were performing far above par. He likened it to going from a broken down old jalopy to a sleek racecar with a high performance engine! No one there was wearing glasses or hearing aids. (Besteman, 127)

Crystal McVea was suddenly aware she had left her physical body behind and was now in her spiritual body. She didn't examine it, she just knew. It didn't have defined edges or shape. She had the stunning realization she was the "me" that had existed since before she was born on Earth. She was a far more complete representation of her heart and being without any of the uncertainty she might have on Earth. She had a more complete representation of her spirit and heart than was ever possible on Earth. She had a deeper self-awareness than all the hopes, fears, dreams, and scars of her earthly life. She met her real self! She marvels that the first person she met in heaven was herself! (MaVea, 12)

Mary Neal said the people she saw had shape but without any distinct edges. The edges of their bodies were blurred, but they were dazzling and radiant with a blinding radiance. Their presence encompassed all of her senses, sight, hearing, feeling, smell, and taste, all at once. They simultaneously communicated thoughts and emotions and understood each other perfectly even though there was no audible speech. (Neal 2012, 69-70)

They appeared ageless, neither young nor old, neither fat nor skinny, neither dark nor light. Their radiance was generated from within; they cast no shadows. They were wearing robes made of a fabric woven from millions of shimmering filaments. They appeared solid but were also translucent. She had on a similar robe, but could not feel it moving against her skin, if she had any skin. She seemed very much to be herself but without any flaws or limitations. She thought she was the perfect self; the way God sees her. There was no sense of weightlessness or gravity. She just existed in space. She embraced others but she had no memory of brushing the other garments or what they felt like. (Neal 2017, 97-98)

When she left her body, she gained a greatly expanded view of everything around her, her senses were sharpened, especially her sense of God's deep love in everything. She never felt more alive than she did when she was absent from her body. (Neal 2017, 30) The reality of her experience apart from her body, gave her the sense that we are in reality a spiritual being temporarily housed in a physical body. More than the flesh and bones that make up our physical bodies, our spirits are the very essence of who we are. (Neal 2017, 33)

Dale Black said his spirit body looked just like his Earthly body. He had arms and legs, eyes and ears, but his senses were all heightened above what they are on Earth. He had the same size and reach, but had some new awesome capabilities. (Black 2018, 156) He experienced sensations deeper and more profound than any he had on Earth. The colors were prominent, striking, and super enhanced. (Black 2018, 142) When he moved about, he could not detect any change in his feet or ankles. He moved by his mind rather than his feet or sometimes by a force outside himself. (Black 2018, 130)

He had always worked hard to stay healthy in excellent condition, but he never felt as strong and healthy as he did then. He felt as though he could accomplish anything. (Black 2010, 102)

Betty Malz said she seemed barefoot and the outer shape of her body was a blur and colorless. (Malz, 84)

Oden Hetrick thought he would get his shoes wet when he stepped into the water, but then saw that he was barefoot.

He also described our body and soul by how our hand fits a glove. The glove fits our hand perfectly and without our hand the glove is lifeless. Our soul fits our body like a hand fits a glove. And when our soul is in our body the body is alive, but when the soul leaves, the body is lifeless.

He said that men are masculine beings in a male body and women are feminine beings in a female body. In heaven we will be masculine and feminine beings but not male and female. We will have a relationship with our spouse with better companionship than we have here but without the maleness and femaleness that is part of our bodies here. He will be fully masculine and she will be fully feminine. Here we have to reproduce because things die, but in heaven nothing dies so reproduction is not needed. (Doucette 2013-1)

As I mention later in the chapter on children, does the fact that there is no reproduction in heaven, mean there will be no more babies and children in heaven when the Earth passes away even though Jesus loves children?

Dr. Richard Eby, as a physician, was interested in inspecting his heavenly body. He noted that his heavenly body looked like him, felt like him, and reacted like him and was the same shape all the way down to his feet as his Earthly body. He was the same size and shape as the image he had seen in a mirror that he had always known himself to be, but now with a cloud-like body that had no pain and had the presence of a peace that he never knew on Earth. (We never get to see our whole three-dimensional selves, only flat two-dimensional photographic images or reversed front view mirror images. George Ritchie in *Return from Tomorrow* talks about this problem when looking for his "solid part".) As his robe was translucent, he could look through it and through his translucent body to the white flowers behind and beneath him. This did not seem strange to him but perfectly normal in his heavenly outlook on things now. (Eby, 203) He could see his feet as he was no longer near-sighted and had unlimited range of vision. It was sharp and clear no matter the distance, ten inches or ten miles. (Eby, 204)

As he looked through his transparent abdomen and chest, he could see no bones, ligaments, vessels, organs, or blood. Also he had no genitals. His mind was sharper and he immediately knew that Jesus supplies all the energy we need, so no food or air is needed. (Eby, 204) Unlike our carnal body with lungs, stomach, intestines, and heart, in heaven we need no food to digest and eliminate or air to breathe. Without lungs where would our breath go? Without a stomach, where would food go? In the chapter on fruit, people said the juice ran down their throat with exquisite taste. My guess is at that point it just vaporizes like it does on their hands and faces there.

Willie Agnes Chennault had dentures but in heaven she had all her original teeth. She went to heaven as a very sick person, but in heaven, she was young, about thirty, and strong with no sores, weakness, or pain. Her mother wore glasses, but in heaven she did not need glasses. (Chennault, 115, 117)

Hair

We apparently have hair there like we do here. Rebecca Springer was concerned about her hair when she came out of the water, only to find it was still dry and smooth as it was before going into the water. (Springer, 14-15)

Colton Burpo described Jesus as having brown hair on his face. (Burpo, 65)

Akiane Kramarik's painting Prince of Peace shows Jesus with a light beard and hair.

Richard Sigmund told of a girl who had beautiful hair, which she had lost on Earth due to cancer. There she had a full head of hair, and she showed Richard that she could shake it up and it would return to a beautiful perfectly arranged state. (Sigmund, 30)

Minds and Senses

There our minds will be capable of far more than they are here. Many report that they cannot describe what they experienced because much of it is beyond our Earthly minds to comprehend or express. Our minds will be sharper and faster. Similarly, our senses will be sharper. We will touch, taste, and feel things better than here. (Kerr 2007, 28)

Richard Eby said his heavenly mind functioned at the speed of light.

(Eby 203) He said talk is mind to mind, no voice or sound or ear involvement. He and Jesus communicated rapidly in his mind with clarity and full comprehension. (Roth, 171) He also said that when he thought of picking a bouquet of flowers, he immediately found that he had done it. To think an action is simultaneous with doing it. From this he understood that all God had to do was think Creation and it happened. (Eby, 205) Conversation is mind to mind with voices primarily used for singing praises.

Several people report that they could understand all languages there. There is even a language of heaven that corresponds to our experience of speaking in tongues as the apostles did that first Pentecost day. Khalida Wukawitz, a former Palestinian Muslim, said after her return from heaven she continued to speak in the language she heard there, which she later learned is described in Scripture by Luke in Acts and by Paul. (Roth, 92-93)

Richard Sigmund said that there everyone can understand and speak all languages. There is also a heavenly language that everyone knows. (Sigmund, 64)

Rhoda "Jubilee" Mitchell found her heavenly mind very sharpened. She immediately started receiving heavenly knowledge flooding her mind at an incredible rate, sorting through her mind at lightning speed. Her knowledge was perfected as she gained answers to questions that had plagued her for years. Everything made sense. She experienced a myriad of sights and sounds in her travels through the Universe. (Roth, 46)

When Jesus was bringing her back to Earth she began to lose the perfect memory she had. The answers she received were fading from her and the unanswered questions stuck in her mind. Just as others have reported, our Earthly minds cannot contain the knowledge of heaven. God told her it would be "unlawful" for her to remember all that she knew in heaven. (Roth, 59)

While the knowledge she gained while she was in heaven was taken from her, she retained enough of the memories of her journey to change her life and ours, too, as she shares the story of her time in heaven. This is true of every author I have read. No one visits heaven (or hell) without being changed dramatically, and their lives afterward are never the same as before. They are more focused on what is of eternal importance, including love, relationships, praise of God, and the awesome gift of Jesus.

Eben Alexander said when he thought a question the answer burst into his mind in an explosion of "light, color, love, and beauty." His questions were answered in a way that did not require language. He said thoughts there are solid and immediate, not vague and abstract like here. He was able to understand concepts instantly that would have taken years to grasp fully here. (Alexander, 46)

Crystal McVea describes having other senses besides those we have on Earth. First she was not only in the presence of God (the Father, Jesus, and Holy Spirit together), she could feel Him. She could not only see light, but she could taste it also and touch and feel it. There was another sense that was neither taste nor touch but a more amazing and rewarding way of connecting with something than any of our earthly senses allow. (McVea, 90)

Steven Musick said heaven is more real and physical than anything he had known on Earth. All his senses were brilliant and deep there. (Musick, 40)

Willie Agnes Chennault said she did not have to breathe in heaven. (Chennault, 57)

Mary Neal doesn't remember any feeling of breathing or swallowing, and never needed any nourishment. She smelled the intense fragrance of the flowers, but doesn't remember any other smells. But all her senses were expanded over those on Earth. She said all the senses intermingled so she could "hear" color and "smell" sunshine. (Neal 2017, 98, 99)

Jim Woodford said the most unexpected thing about heaven's landscape was that the sounds had colors and the colors had sounds. It created a sensory spectrum that overwhelmed him. (Woodford, 80)

Vision

Jim Woodford said he had 360-degree vision. He could see up and down, forward and back, right and left, all with perfect clarity. He had no limitation of depth or distance. He could see a flower on a distant mountainside as clearly as one right in front of him. His vision was simultaneously microscopic and telescopic. (Woodford, 80-81)

Clothing

We know that when we die our spirit leaves our body but the clothes stay here. We therefore leave our bodies and go to heaven naked. But no one is naked in heaven, at some point we acquire heavenly clothes, usually robes but sometimes other clothing, all provided instantaneously and automatically.

Richard Eby said he was clothed in a translucent pure white flowing robe. (Eby, 203)

Mary K. Baxter "saw families dressed in beautiful robes." (Baxter, 61) She saw saintly men dressed in beautiful, glorious, white robes. (Baxter, 72)

Richard Sigmund reports seeing a missionary coming through the veil dressed in a beautiful robe. He grabbed his clothes and excitedly noted their beauty and exclaimed that he was not in rags any more. (Sigmund, 38) There are new clothes for us there. Richard Sigmund reported seeing some dressed in pants and pullover shirts, some in suits, some in flowing robes, all made out of some heavenly material. (Sigmund, 65)

In keeping with everything else, I presume these clothes never fade, never wear out, and never get holes or worn places. Maybe they never get soiled either.

Richard said no jewelry is worn there. It is not necessary; the glow of God's presence is what makes people beautiful. (Sigmund, 66)

Marvin Besteman saw many different styles of clothing on the people waiting to go through the gate. They were all wearing clothing like they would have had in their native land. Marvin had a golf shirt and khaki pants. A couple of the people apparently came from a primitive African tribe as they were wearing loose flowing robes and toga-like garb with sandals. The Middle Eastern man in front of him in line wore a baggy, brown caftan, slouchy loose pants, and a headpiece or hat on his head. He said the men in the line were between fifty and seventy and the women between seventy and ninety. Apparently they had not yet been transformed into the youthful appearance others have reported. (Besteman, 75-76)

The clothing of heaven apparently doesn't include shoes, although sandals were mentioned. As Betty Malz was barefoot walking on grass, she felt it as well as saw it. (Malz, 84)

Rhoda Mitchell stepped on the street in bare feet and felt the smooth-as-glass street. (Roth, 50-51)

Eben Alexander said the people wore simple but beautiful clothes that had the same warmth as the trees and flowers. He was with a girl who escorted him who he also said had simple clothes but with vibrant living colors, blue, indigo, and orange-peach. (Alexander, 39, 40)

Dawn Cypret said when she met her mom and dad her mom was wearing the same dress she wore at her husband's funeral, which Dawn remembers as her mother's prettiest dress. Her dad was wearing a white robe like most other people. (May, 23)

Willie Agnes Chennault said the men she saw working in the wheat field were wearing fieldwork clothes with belts tied around their waists. On their feet they wore sandals and scarves or rags around their heads. The women had very long hair and wore scarves on their heads also. She said the women had on sandals and shawls. Some had clothes for working in the fields while others were elegantly dressed. One she saw had on a long white dress that went down to her ankles. She had pretty, long, brown, wavy hair. (Chennault, 59)

Richard Sigmund saw clothing stores that seemed to be specific for the person who walked in. He was in one store which had clothing tailored just for him. Some had clothing that had been made before time and was being kept in pristine condition for the person for whom it was intended. He saw a jewelry store that had diamonds for a specific woman, but he also said no one in heaven wears any jewelry. It isn't necessary; the glow of God's presence makes everyone beautiful. He saw many different types of clothing, white pants with white pullover shirts, outfits of many different colors, suits like we might wear on Earth, and long flowing robes. (Sigmund, 64-66)

Dr. Gary Wood noticed three different textures of clothing in heaven. A soft velvet garment is worn for everyday activities over the linen garment fitting the body. Outside of that is a garment made of linen that fits to the body and is known as the robe of salvation. Outside of that is the "robe of righteousness," worn in the presence of God. He said this is the "garment of praise" mentioned in Isaiah 61:3. It has on it many jewels and decorations that indicate what you did on Earth. (Roth, 108-109)

Kat Kerr saw Jesus and someone named John in tunic tops and loose pants. She said that citizens of heaven only wear gowns and robes at important meetings and in the Throne room. (Kerr 2007, 62)

Oden Hetrick said we have three garments. The first is our garment of humility. It is a soft white garment that fits very neatly. The second over that is our robe of righteousness. It is like the garment the priest wore when ministering in the temple. It is a long shining garment and is frequently the one described in visions of heaven. Over that is the garment of praise, which is a sleeveless coat that comes down to just below the knees. It is set with sparkling diamonds, rubies, and other jewels. (Doucette 2013-1)

Summary

Our bodies in heaven look like our bodies here on Earth as they were in our prime. But they are translucent without internal organs. We still have all the senses we had on Earth, but they are much sharper. Our minds in heaven grasp things much faster and more permanently than here on Earth. As a result, when people returned to Earth, they lost some of the knowledge they gained in heaven that was beyond the capabilities of our Earthly minds.

We do wear clothing in heaven, but it is not always robes. Sometimes we wear clothing similar to what we might wear on Earth. We will have different clothing for different occasions, just like we do on Earth. There are even places where there is new clothing tailored just for us that has been waiting for us. Everyone is beautiful in the radiant love of God, and clothing and jewelry are not required for beauty. But the clothing we will have is nevertheless beautiful.

CHAPTER 5

Heavenly Music

One of the first experiences of heaven is the heavenly music that abounds. Here is what several authors have said about their experience with the heavenly music.

Heavenly and Choral Music

Mary K. Baxter said heaven is "saturated with beautiful music." It is the result of joy and expresses the happiness and joy of heaven. She heard choirs and ensembles, whose splendor and beauty cannot be compared with anything on Earth. It is a fantastic symphony. Stringed instruments and trumpets accompanied the music. All the voices, pitches, and tones were perfect. She said that there were unbelievable anthems coming in waves of praise across the landscape. (Baxter, 61-62)

While Betty Malz and the angel were walking up the hill before encountering the gates, she heard her father's voice calling, "Jesus, Jesus, Jesus." His voice seemed a long distance away. She considered turning back to find him but did not because she knew she had to move ahead for whatever awaited her. She came to a structure like a magnificent silver palace. Then she heard voices, melodious, harmonious, and blending in chorus. The singing included the word "Jesus". There were more than four parts in the harmony, and she joined in. She said she has always had a low boy's voice, but there she sang in high, clear tones. Soon the chorus began a new song. The multiple parts were in other languages, with richness and perfect blending of the words. The amazing thing was that she could understand the words for each of the languages! (Malz, 86-87)

Rhoda Mitchell said the music in heaven was incredible! It was a wonderful expression of praise to the Father. The music had great diversity, and the intriguing melodies and their magnetic refrains played over and over in her spirit. The words of the songs were clear and meaningful. They spoke of honor, covenant, majesty, goodness, mercy, and truth. Although people sang, shouted, and talked with their voices, they often communicated non-verbally with just thought.

Everything was directed toward God, Jesus, and the Holy Spirit.

This includes every song, every poem, and every dance. All were expressions of the love of the people and the heavenly creatures for their God. The music was very captivating. Everyone froze when the heavenly choir began to sing songs that were so beautiful that no one wanted to miss a word or a note being sung. The singers hit notes that reached octaves above the highest pitches sung on Earth. There was much diversity in the heavenly choirs made up of people and/or angels. Sometimes there were other creatures all praising and adoring God. She found the sights and sounds of the celestial city to be magnificent! (Roth, 54, 58)

Richard Eby described the music as more beautiful and melodious than any on Earth. Unlike Earth music it was not instrumental, nor vocal, nor mathematical. It didn't originate from anywhere; it just emerged from everything and every place. It had no beat, no tempo, no major or minor key. (Eby, 206) There is no time in heaven so there is no time in music. Compare this with the other testimonies, and you see that some do hear Earth-type music, while some hear music of a completely different sort. But whatever it is, it goes beyond the music we experience on Earth in its beauty and glory.

When Mary K. Baxter entered the gate, she was surrounded with beautiful music coming from everywhere and penetrated her being. Waves of beautiful music, including singing, surged across the landscape enveloping everything. Even the flowers seemed to participate in the music. The music continued to swirl around her and she seemed to be a part of the music. (Baxter, 23,25)

Don Piper was in a terrible auto accident on a bridge returning from a camp in the rain. He died instantly, but ninety minutes later miraculously came back to life. *Ninety Minutes in Heaven* is the account of his experience. His most vivid memory of heaven is the sounds. One of his favorite sounds was a holy swoosh of wings. He found it impossible to explain the effect of that sound in heaven. It was the most beautiful and pleasant sound he had ever heard, and it went on forever. He was awestruck and only wanted to listen. When he heard the music of the swooshing, more than just hearing the music, he became part of it, and it played in and through his body as if the sounds were embracing him. The joyous sounds and melodies so permeated every part of his being that he found it impossible to be distracted. Yet at the same time, he could focus on everything around him. Our mental capacities and our attention spans are apparently greatly enhanced in heaven.

He never saw what produced the sound but sensed that it was just above him. He didn't look and asked no questions, never wondering about anything. Everything seemed perfect, leaving him with no questions to ask. There were so many sounds that filled his mind and heart that he finds it difficult to explain them. The sound of the angels wings is still, however, one of the most amazing to him, a beautiful holy melody with a non-stop cadence of swishing as if it were a form of praise.

The second sound that is his single most vivid memory of his entire heavenly experience is the music. It is different from any music on Earth with its melodies of praise, nonstop intensity, and endless variety. The praise expressed in these songs was unending, but the most remarkable thing he experienced was that hundreds of songs of worship of God were being sung at the same time. He heard them from every direction and knew that each voice and instrument praised God. Musical praise, comprised of melodies and tones he had never experienced before, was everywhere. The music rang out with words such as "Hallelujah," "Praise," "Glory to God," and "Praise to the King," in the midst of all the music. He was awestruck and caught up in the heavenly mood. He experienced the deepest joy of his life. Even though he wasn't a participant in the worship, his heart rang out with joy and exuberance.

He said if we played three CDs of praise at the same time here, we'd have a cacophony of noise that would drive us crazy. But he said that in heaven, every sound blended and each voice or instrument enhanced the others. He could clearly distinguish each song, and it seemed to him that each hymn of praise was meant for him.

The songs he heard included old hymns and choruses he had sung in the past, as well as hundreds of new, unfamiliar songs. There was much variety, including hymns of praise, modern choruses, and ancient chants. They brought a deep peace and the greatest feeling of joy he had ever experienced.

He didn't hear songs that were about Jesus' sacrifice or death such as "The Old Rugged Cross" or "The Nail-Scarred Hand." There were no sad songs; there can't be sad songs in heaven. All music was praises about Christ's reign as King of Kings, for what He has done for us, and how wonderful he is.

Thousands of songs were sung simultaneously, and they surpassed any he had ever heard. But in spite of all this different music being sung simultaneously, there was no chaos. He could hear each one and clearly discern the lyrics and melody.

He marveled at the glorious music and knew that if he sang too, it would be in perfect pitch and harmonious with the thousands of other voices and instruments. He said that even though on Earth he didn't have a great singing voice, there he could have sung in ways he never could on Earth.

Even as he wrote his book, he could sometimes hear faint echoes of that music. Especially when he was tired and lay in bed with his eyes closed, he would drift off to sleep with the sounds of heaven in his heart and mind. The memories of the heavenly music bring peace in every part of his being. When he has flashbacks, they are flashbacks of the sounds rather than the sights.

Above all else, he cherishes the memory of those sounds. He looks forward to being able to hear them again in person. He wants to see everybody there and everything else about heaven, but what he wants most is to experience those never-ending songs of praise. (Piper 2004, 29-32)

Dr. Gary Wood is another who died suddenly in an auto accident two days before Christmas. He said the most beautiful singing surrounded him. He remembers angels singing, "Worthy is the Lamb who was slain, who is worthy to receive dominion and power forever more. Wisdom and power be given unto Thee, O Lord. Amen and Amen." He said the singing to the Lord of trillions of angels is far beyond anything you have ever experienced, and it meant a lot to him especially since he had a music degree. He was overwhelmed by the effect of the surround sound of the songs of angels. He does not have mortal words to be able to describe the music and its effect. (Roth, 100-101; Wood, 24) He heard people of every tribe and nationality singing, "All hail the power of Jesus' name, let angels prostrate fall." The angel explained to him that all songs of praise originate in heaven and then are given to someone on Earth to put into writing. Satan was the director of music before his fall, and when he fell he took the music with him and perverted the words of praise into something else that worshiped that for which he stood. Christian songs that are based on rock tunes are merely the result angels enabling people to bring back the words of praise to the original heavenly music. (Wood, 29) He said people in heaven are always dancing joyfully and singing praise celebrating Jesus. (Wood, 30)

Richard Sigmund noticed that in heaven music is everywhere. People in the villages and cities were singing songs of praise to God. One village would sing one song and another village would sing a different song. He went up in the air and could hear many different villages at the same time, and they were all singing in concert! The higher he went, the more villages he could hear. He heard everyone from every village singing the same song in perfect harmony. He considered it "the song of heaven."

He saw choirs at a distance and then up close. They had been singing in the background. He also saw smaller groups singing. The choirs were sometimes groups of angels, or choirs of people, or both. Apparently, one of the songs was specifically for him. He knew what it was while he was there, but back on Earth, when he was writing his book, he did not understand the song or its meaning, nor remember the melody or the lyrics. It was apparently for him only while he was there.

The songs the angels sang related to ministry and to something God was saying to people in heaven.

The songs that people sang were different. Singing groups varied from two or three people to large groups. There was a large group in an amphitheater that seemed to be standing on air, but it looked like risers. Their songs were similar to what we sing on Earth.

He remembers them singing "The King Is Coming,'" but there it was "The King Has Come." The song went through the whole story from heaven's point of view, and it was a most beautiful song. He remembers hearing it, but now back on Earth, he can't recall all the words.

He found that when you leave heaven, you lose the ability to understand some of the things you heard there, maybe because there aren't Earthly words to express it. Perhaps because our mind and attention are much enhanced in heaven; when we return to Earth, we must return to our former mental ability and attentiveness.

The size of the choirs seemed to increase the closer he came to the throne of God. There was one he remembers of perhaps fifty or sixty thousand. They sang with the deepest bass and highest soprano. They sang beyond the ranges common on Earth, and their music could be heard in the background all over heaven. It was pleasant music in the language of God. (Sigmund, 62-64)

While standing on the banks of the Celestial Sea, Rebecca Springer describes hearing child voices singing "Glory and honor!" Then the vast multitude answered with "Dominion and power!" She and her friend Mae joined in the refrain. A singing cherub band floated further away. In the distance, they could hear the faint melody of the cherub choir's sweet voices accompanied by the stronger cadence of the response from those below.

Then later, while they were floating in the sea, she was also attracted by the sound of distant music. She turned and looked at her friend, Mae, who smiled back but did not speak. Presently, she heard the words, "Glory and honor, dominion and power," and knew it was the cherub choir, although they must now be miles away. She heard the soft sounds of a silver bell with a silver tongue. As the last notes died away, she asked Mae why she could hear the sounds from so far away. Mae described how the water transmits musical sounds for a great distance.

On another occasion, she asked her brother-in-law Frank what they did in heaven when they want to pray. He said they praise, so she asked that they pray right then. So standing there with clasped hands, they lifted their hearts and voices in a hymn of praise to God. Frank was leading with his clear, strong voice, and she followed. She thought the roof echoed the notes they sang, but soon realized that other voices blended with theirs, until the whole house was filled with unseen singers. It was a hymn of praise beyond anything on Earth. In the singing she recognized many voices from the past joining in the hymn of praise. There was the distinct tenor and exquisite soprano of two friends of the past she recognized, and many other voices from her past. Then she heard the cherub choir again, there in that room, and her heart was flooded with joy. (Springer, 36,47,57)

Dean Braxton, in Sid Roth's *Heaven Is Beyond Your Wildest*

Expectations, describes another type of singing: God himself singing before the throne. He heard God the Father singing back to each and every being, and each one in turn giving praise to Him. His was an individual love song to each of His creations, and it had an aliveness that made it go into each intended being. What he saw was like the Song of Songs in the Bible; there was an exchange of love words between God and each person expressing his/her love for one another. He was expressing His love for each being, who was in return expressing his/her love for God. God's love song was not limited to those in heaven, but He sings His song of love out to every human being on Earth and nothing stops His love from reaching us. (Roth, 38-39)

Betty Eadie heard music when she visited a garden with a stream flowing from a waterfall. She heard a melody of majestic beauty that carried from the waterfall and filled the garden she was in, beside the River of Life. This melody eventually merged with other melodies of which she was only faintly aware. The music came from the water itself, and each drop produced its own tone and melody, which mingled and interacted with every other sound and strain around it. She sensed the water was praising God for its life and joy. This was beyond the ability of any symphony or composer here. In comparison, our best music here would sound like a child playing a tin drum. We simply don't have the capacity to comprehend the vastness and strength of the music there, let alone begin to create it. (Eadie, 80)

She even saw a rose that stood out from all the other flowers in the garden, and it was swaying to faint music. It too was singing praises to the Lord with sweet tones of its own. The rose swayed to the music of all the other flowers, creating its own music, a melody that perfectly harmonized with the thousands of other roses joining it. She said the music in her flower came from its individual parts. Its petals produced their own tones, and each petal was adding to its perfect notes, each working harmoniously to the overall effect. Her joy was absolutely full again! She felt God in the plant, in her, his love pouring into them. She and the flowers were all one! (Eadie, 81)

Then when Betty Eadie decided to return to Earth, thousands of angels surrounded her with love and began to sing. No music in her life, even the music in the garden, had ever been as magnificent as this. It was

49

grand, glorious, awesome, and meant especially for her. She was overwhelmed. The flowers sang spontaneously, with notes instantly known, instantly felt. Their voices were pure and each note was clear and sweet. (Eadie, 120)

Richard Sigmund said when he put his ear up to anything solid, he found that it hums beautiful songs. Some of the songs were ones we sing on Earth, but others were not. Everything in heaven gives praise and glory to the Lord. (Sigmund, 37-40) *"Some of the Pharisees in the crowd said to Jesus, 'Teacher, rebuke your disciples!' 'I tell you,' he replied, 'if they keep quiet, the stones will cry out.'"* (Luke 19:39-40, NIV). In heaven they apparently do cry out, everything does! (Sigmund,40) In the chapter on flowers that follows, Richard said that the flowers hum and make music.

Dawn Cypret was in a courtyard with a fountain in the center, surrounded with people listening to an angel choir concert. The angels were wearing brilliant white robes, and they had soft downy-looking white wings. They were singing Breath of Heaven, a Christmas song to which Dawn had been listening just days before she died. As she listened, it was the most amazing choir she had ever heard. Their voices blended in such rich and layered harmonies that each word was heard distinctly and every note was clear. The acoustics in the courtyard were incredible and the sound was glorious. (May, 30-31)

Steven Musick said heaven is full of song. It is in the background as if it were an integral part of the environment. The music swells, supports, envelopes, and complements and is deep and resonant. It is not a specific tune and has no apparent source, although he did hear voices even though he couldn't tell the source of the voices. (Musick, 38)

Dr. Gary Wood saw musical notes floating in the air. They would go into a person and that person would burst forth in song, singing in the spirit. He also saw musical notes go over the mountains that surround the city. (Roth, 110)

Mary Neal said the music sounded like the rustling of a gentle breeze and a harmonic of some sort to her untrained musical ear. (Neal 2017, 99)

Robert Misst saw strange but beautiful shapes and objects that emitted color and sound. He hummed a short tune and was amazed at how well the sound produced by these objects matched the tune he hummed and added improvisations to it. (Roth, 122)

In the throne room he heard amazing seven-layered multiple chorus choirs with a huge number of voices. This, combined with the object producing colors and sound, lightning, and thunder, made the worship there bathe him with beauty and joy, but it also made him more conscious of his sin. (Roth, 123)

Dale Black said the music in heaven calibrates everything. Everything happened right when it was supposed to happen. Nothing waited for you because you were never late or early. Everything was in sync with the music and the worship. Nothing was ever hurried or stressed or late. He said time was evident and perfect. It was relaxed, comfortable, and natural with no limitations as we have here. The music was in perfect timing with beginnings and endings to the songs and hymns. (Black 2010, 100-101)

He said music was everywhere. Worship of God was at the heart of all of it, and the joy of the music permeated everything. His heart so resonated with the music that he wanted to be a part of it forever. It was an endless blend of vocals and instruments, each enriching the other in perfect harmonic order. It gave him the feeling he was made for the music; each muscle was like a taut string of a finely tuned instrument. He felt part of the music and was in complete harmony with it. He thought he might burst with exuberance! The music passed through him making him like a tuning fork. The music and the light both existed in everything with no discord. It seemed "all of heaven knew the beat, the tempo, the words, the pitch, [and] the tone." It was all united in one song that everyone was singing simultaneously. It was more beautiful and blissful than anything he had ever heard and gave him an overwhelming sense of peace. (Black 2010, 102-103)

William Smith saw wheels like those seen by Ezekiel. Only these wheels had to do with the spinning of the universe and out of them came a symphony of glorious sound. He said all sound joins together as the wheels create a musical expansion of sound. God's glory and greatness is seen in the music. The experience of the heavenly music was totally exhausting in that he was overwhelmed with the glory and majesty of it. (Roth, 156-158)

Everything in heaven sings praises to Jesus and the Father, even things that don't make music here.

Instrumental Music

Not only are there choirs, but there are also instrumental sounds. Richard Sigmund said God makes use of all the talent and skill He has given people on Earth, including how He has helped them develop that talent through their lives. In heaven that talent is multiplied far beyond what we have on Earth.

He saw and heard Johann Sebastian Bach performing on a huge organ. It had notes above and below organs on Earth. Richard was able to hear all of the high and low notes. The choirs of heaven accompanied his playing in praise and worship. Everyone joined in with glorious musical praise.

He reported seeing a boy about seven or eight playing a piano and a harp at the same time. (Sigmund, 31-32)

Chimes and Bells

Richard also heard chimes and bells in the distance. (Sigmund, 41,42) The chimes were huge and had a deep full sound that could be heard from large distances. He said there were seven large towers with chimes in them, chimes that were very loud and beautiful and looked like diamonds, and the chimes would sound when saints went into the towers and prayed for revivals on Earth. After some revivals on Earth, he was able to hear the chimes mingling with the praises being sung on Earth. He was told the chimes sound by angels rubbing them whenever someone on Earth is saved. (Sigmund, 68-69)

He also heard distant chimes coming across the crystal sea. He wanted to go see, but was not allowed to. He asked why and the only response was a stern glance indicating it was not his business to know. That was all he needed to know about it! In addition to the chimes there was a bell system that with the chimes was playing beautiful music. Choirs of people and angels were singing from above. This all caused him to weep with adoration and joy. (Sigmund, 41, 42)

Dale Black heard the delicate ringing of bells, reminding him of wind chimes. While some wind chimes on Earth are not pleasant, these were the most joyful and captivating sounds he had ever experienced, unlike wind chimes here. He also heard choral and instrumental music with many perfectly balanced harmonies. There was no direction from which the sound was coming; it was everywhere. He also said there were notes above and below the ranges we experience on Earth. The music had substance and power and seemed alive and full of love. He heard many voices and instruments, including some he had never heard before. All music was directed at worshipping God. There were colors like the aurora along with the music that danced with the music. (Black 2018, 166-169)

Rebecca Springer also heard sounds of distant bells. (Springer, 41)

Summary

One of the most common features of heaven is the abundance of wonderful music, vocal and instrumental. We will sing in heaven whether or not we can sing on Earth. All of the music is songs of praise for what God and Jesus have done for us, no popular Earthly music there. I have never cared much for popular music, preferring music that honors God, and now I know why. Without knowing the reason, I have always been inclined toward heavenly music. An amazing feature of heavenly music is that different groups of people can be singing different music, but it all blends in perfect harmony. No matter the language of the song, in heaven we can understand all languages. Even the instruments seem to be superior to what we have on Earth. They are like some Earth instruments, such as pianos and harps, but are superior. There are bells and chimes, too, which give more beautiful sounds of praise than their Earthly counterparts. Everything in heaven is going to amaze and bless us, and the abundant music will be a glorious part of that blessing, so much so, it is Don Piper's favorite memory of heaven.

Heaven Is Beyond Imagination

CHAPTER 6

River Of Life, Lake, And Sea

Jesus took Michael McCormack to a door with a ruby on the handle and had him open it. The door opened into a beautiful garden—the New Earth. It was filled with wildlife, lakes, waterfalls, and rainbows. Deer and other animals were drinking from a lake. It was like a colorful rainforest full of life. (Roth, 83)

Dean Braxton, in Sid Roth's *Heaven Is Beyond Your Wildest Expectations*, said there was something like water between the throne and the people and other heavenly beings that were around the throne. It resembled a crystal sea. Another liquid was under the throne of God, and the throne hovered over it, but it was not water either. Both liquids were alive and had a personality to them. They had different densities. These two liquids flowed through each other, but stayed separate, not overlapping, blending, or bleeding into each other. He could not effectively describe the beauty of these water-like liquids. He saw other water-like liquids that were also alive and had delightful personalities. (Roth, 37)

The River

Dale Black said the river started from the gathering area [before the throne] in the center of the city and flowed toward the wall. From there it just seemed to him to disappear. It was clear with a bluish-white hue. The light didn't shine on the water; it shone out from within it. (Black 2010, 105)

Oden Hetrick described the River of Life as starting at the throne of God then flowing through all the mansions coming to the garden of fountains. The water is collected in a basin and from there flows out in an ever widening river. It flows in twelve circles around the holy place and then out the Eastern gate down to Earth. It is the flowing of the Holy Spirit and so we can't see it here because we can't see spiritual things. We experience it as the love of God in our hearts. (Doucette 2013-1)

Jim Woodford said there are streams and brooks in heaven. They are three or four feet wide and not deep. The water was a brilliant blue and had golden pebbles on the bottom. Light came up from the bottom of the stream and created patterns of rippling light on the surface. The water also made sound. It was a tinkling musical offering, praising God just like everything else that made music in heaven. The angel described these streams as "the living water of life." These brooks flow into a larger river that flows beneath the sixth gate of joy into the city of heaven. (Woodford, 82)

When Rebecca Springer reached the brink of the River of Life, a few steps away, the lovely field they were passing through came to the water's edge. In some places, there were flowers blooming placidly in the depths of the River of Life, among the many-colored pebbles at the bottom of the river.

Her brother-in-law, Frank, stepped into the water and invited her to step in also. She was afraid it would be cold, but he assured her it would not be cold. Then she was concerned about getting her beautiful heavenly gown all wet, and he told her not to be concerned. So she stepped into the gently flowing River of Life. She was surprised to discover that the water had the same temperature and density as the air. They stepped out deeper and deeper until she felt the soft sweet ripples of the water around her throat. Frank encouraged her on, but she was afraid the water would go over her head and she would drown. He simply said they don't do things like that there, so she walked on. Her head indeed went under the water, but she discovered she could still breathe. She could do everything in the water that she could above it: breathe, laugh, talk, see, and hear just as naturally. She sat down on the bottom of the river and filled her hands with the multi-colored pebbles that were on the bottom, much like a child would do. Frank lay down on the bottom and laughed and talked joyously.

He rubbed his hands over his face and ran his fingers through his dark hair. He told her to do the same and experience a delightful sensation. She rubbed her arms and throat and ran her fingers through her long, loose hair, imagining how tangled it would be when she got out. Then she wondered what they would do for towels and if her gown would have been damaged by the water. But when they got out, everything was immediately dry, soft, and fresh. No towel was necessary, nor did she need a brush for her hair. (Springer, 13-15)

She marveled at the water and air and wondered if all rivers here are like that. Frank said they are similar but not the same. The water had given her a different feeling, as if she could fly. Frank said it had washed away the last of her Earth-life to prepare her for life in heaven. (Springer, 15)

Richard Sigmund had a similar experience at a place called the meeting place. It was an amphitheater with a wall-sized window in front from wall to wall and floor to ceiling through which you could look out over all of heaven. No one could talk there but just behold the beauty of heaven. He said this is where one experiences heaven's cleansing glory, and all the cares of Earth are cleansed away. He felt such peace there his spirit cried out, "Holy, holy, holy!" (Sigmund, 85)

Richard saw four rivers flowing from the throne coming out of the glory cloud and washing over the coals from the altar of God. The water did not extinguish the coals, and there was no hissing sound. The rivers came out from the throne as one, flowed across the pavement, and then divided into their separate streams to go on to the destinations prepared for them. The streams were small and seemed to be about half a mile wide. As they flowed through heaven, they appeared bottomless. The flow of one of the rivers was the mercy and grace from God. (Sigmund, 110)

Dr. Gary Wood saw the magnificent River of Life with crystal clear water flowing from the throne room of God. He stepped into the body of water and it rose up until it totally covered him. He found, like others, that he could breathe under the water. He interacted with the water and it vitalized him, invigorated him, and gave him strength. He drank some and it was very refreshing, sweet, and rejuvenating. (Roth, 109; Wood, 27-28) He picked up large golden nuggets, diamonds, and other precious gems from the bottom of the river. Light shone upon them producing indescribable colors. (Wood, 27)

Oden Hetrick stepped into the river and found it not to be cold and wet but rather found it to be exhilarating and refreshing. He stepped deeper and deeper into the river until it was over his head, but he was still breathing. He understood that this was the flowing of the Holy Spirit. The blood of Jesus has cleansed us from our sin but the memories and scars of the sin remain. The Spirit flowing in the river washed away the memories and scars of our sin so that in heaven there will be nothing bad in our memories or our experience there. This takes away any thought or feeling that we are unfit for heaven because of the memory of our sins. We know we are fit for heaven entirely because of God's redeeming love. (Doucette 2013-1)

Willie Agnes Chennault lay on her back in the water of the river. She did not sink and she felt her whole body healed from the water. It felt warm and smooth like Jell-O. She spread both hands out in the water but cannot explain the feeling. It was a dark blue and shiny. She can still remember the wonderful feeling of the water. The water of the river is different from water on Earth. (Chennault, 55) She said there was shining gold on the sides of the streams. (Chennault, 57)

Michael McCormack came to a river, the River of Life, which was crystal clear and fast-flowing. It flowed out of the Tree of Life. Jesus dipped his cupped hands in the water and poured it over Michael's head. It caused him to feel power coming into him. (Roth, 82-83)

Betty Eadie saw a beautiful river running through the garden nearby and was drawn to it. A cascading waterfall of the purest water fed the river. The river then flowed into a pond, and it dazzled with clarity and life. There was life in the water too. Each drop had its own intelligence and purpose. A melody of majestic beauty came from the waterfall and filled the garden. (Eadie, 79-80)

Jeanne Enstad saw the beautiful river of Revelation 22:1 with colors of gold, bdellium, and onyx. The river was lined with fruit trees. (Enstad, 31)

Dawn Cypret also saw a waterfall. The one she saw was so tall she could not see from where it came. The water from the falls shimmers and sparkles with the colors of diamonds and opals. She scooped a handful of the water from the pool at the base of the falls and drank deeply. It was the best tasting water she had ever had and it was full of life and vitality. It was tingling through her body. (May, 22)

The Lake

Richard Sigmund also visited a lake. It was a small lake, and there were people in the water and even floating below its surface. The lake had no waves, and the water was crystal clear, clearer than the air, and beautiful.

The lake appeared bottomless to him, and there was a glow coming from the interior of it. He didn't know what caused the glow, but it was glorious. He saw too that the water was alive.

He didn't enter the water but did dip his hand in it. He found the water had texture to it. It caressed his hand like the wall of stone had done when he touched it. The water was refreshing. He compared it to putting your hand in chilled, but room temperature, 7-Up. He found it to be a glorious experience.

People had no fear when they came to this water. He said he saw millions of people in the water, walking, floating hand in hand, or even swimming. He saw that they could breathe under the crystal-clear water. And when they came out of the water, they were instantly dry just as Rebecca Springer experienced. (Sigmund, 27-28)

Richard observed the same things with the water in the lake that Rebecca observed with the water in the river. That must be the nature of heavenly water.

Since there is no death in heaven, no one can die, no one can drown. Children can play in the water without fear of drowning. He also said there are no dangerous bugs or snakes in the water. Nothing in heaven can harm you.

He learned this lake is fed by one of the rivers from the throne of God. The river from the throne is hundreds of yards wide and very deep in some places, but shallow in others. The water begins to multiply as it flows out from the throne. (Sigmund, 28)

Rebecca also visited the lake. Her friend Mae took her there. (Springer, 33)

When she saw it, it was divinely beautiful to her. The scene at the lake was beautiful and glorious. It was smooth as glass but had a golden glory from the heavens. She likened it to a sea of molten gold. Blossoms and fruit-bearing trees grew down to the border of the lake. In the distance, across its shining waters, arose the domes and spires of a mighty city.

She saw many people resting on its flowery banks. There were boats of wonderful structure on the surface of the water. They were filled with happy souls. It was not clear what power propelled the boats. Little children and grown persons were floating upon or swimming in the water. A band of singing cherubs floated high overhead and drifted across the lake. They sang songs of joyful praise with their sweet voices.

Mae led her into the water, down into its crystal depths. She thought she was hundreds of feet beneath the surface. They lay down in the water and began slowly to rise. At some point, they no longer rose but floated mid-current, still many feet beneath the surface.

As she was floating in the water, she saw perfectly prismatic rays surrounding her. She saw a more vivid and delicate coloring than she had ever seen on Earth. Instead of the seven rainbow colors of Earth, the colors there blended in such an unusual gradation of shades, making the rays seem infinite.

They were rested and soothed by the gentle undulation of the waves. She rested as peacefully as a child on its mother's bosom. When she came up from her rest, she had a strange sense of invigoration and strength. It was different from the feeling she had had in the river. She could not explain how. Mae told her the River of Life takes away the last of the Earth-life and prepares her for the heaven life, as Frank had said earlier. Mae said the lake fills us to overflowing with a shower from the Celestial Life itself. (Springer, 34-37)

Marvin Besteman saw a huge shining blue rippling lake or sea. (He couldn't see the other side to determine if it was a sea or just a lake.) There were many old well-used fishing boats pulled up on a sandy rocky shore. (Besteman, 116)

The Sea

There is also a sea in heaven. Both Richard Sigmund and Rebecca Springer saw the sea. Richard Sigmund said he was taken to the Sea of God's Glory, which was crystal clear and seemed to have no bottom. He saw what looked like millions of people in the water and under the water. Since no one could drown, people were playing under the water. He saw a man who had built a castle out of rocks on the bottom of the ocean.

He saw conveyances on the oceans, the seas, and the four major rivers, just as there are conveyances in the air and on the land. He likened them to boats in the water. (Sigmund, 82-83)

Rebecca Springer eventually emerged from a forest she was

traveling through and stood before the overwhelming glory of a golden beach sloping downward toward the shore of a glorious sea. The beach was many hundred feet wide and extended on either side far beyond what she could see. The beach caught and radiated the light, making it glitter and glimmer like diamond dust and other precious stones. The waves came and went in ceaseless motion, caught up this sparkling sand, and took it to their crests. The sea was spread out before her in a radiance that was beyond description. She said it was like the white glory that shone through the windows of the temple. The waters of the sea had a blue tint, and there was no limit to its depth or bounds.

She too saw boats in every direction. She said the boats represented all nations, and their beauty far surpassed anything on Earth. They were like great, open pleasure barges and were filled with people looking eagerly toward the shore. Many were eagerly standing erect and gazing expectantly at the faces of those on the shore that were waiting for them.

The people on the shore stood as far as the eyes could see. The great throng was dressed in the spotless garments of the redeemed. Many of them had golden harps and various instruments of music. When a boat touched the shore, the glad voices and tender embraces of their loved ones welcomed its passengers. Then the harps would be held up, and the vast multitude would break forth in a triumphant song of victory over death and the grave. She wondered if these people always stand here like this. Someone standing near her told her it isn't always the same people, but there is always a crowd of people here who are expecting friends from the other life. They assemble to share in their joy. Some of the heavenly characters are always here, but not always the same ones. He said that their friends, and many others who are constantly joining the multitude, quietly lead away most of those who arrive. (Springer, 107-109)

Fountains

Richard Sigmund reported fountains everywhere. The fountains had statues of stone that were animated. Many had statues of Jesus doing something such as pouring out a cup of glory. The water was like H_2O but different. It could turn into ice that was not cold; it could change colors. (Sigmund, 74-75)

There was one fountain Richard called a mountain-sized fountain because it was so huge. It was very high and a long way around according to Richard. On top was another living statue of Jesus suspended in midair above the fountain. He was lifting an altar cup of what looked like his blood toward the throne of God. The empty cross of Calvary was there, too. Below that were seven layers of living scenes carved in white, translucent stone. The scenes were all about the price paid at Calvary for the redemption of all mankind. The scenes were alive playing over and over the complete life of Christ on Earth. The glory cloud of the peace of God's presence was there. It was a fountain of peace and was the third most beautiful and glorious place in heaven after the God's Throne and the Lord Jesus. It continues to give Richard peace when he thinks of it. (Sigmund, 77-79)

Oden Hetrick saw beautiful fountains, some spraying water high in the air. His daughter Lois also visited heaven during a prayer time at youth camp at which time she saw a magnificent fountain falling all over her. It was loud and rushing. The base was clear like crystal or cut glass. The water was flowing up and over her and felt soft, warm, invigorating, and comforting. She saw the head and shoulders of Jesus in the water of the fountain. He stepped out of the water and came toward her. They had lunch or tea on the grass; she doesn't remember what they ate. (Doucette 2013-1)

Rhoda "Jubilee" Mitchell saw a small water fountain at the end of a street. Its jet sprays were perfectly aligned and it spouted up in perfect uniformity. (Roth, 51) It exhibits the perfection that characterizes everything in heaven.

Summary

The water of heaven looks and acts like water on Earth, but it is very different. One cannot drown in heavenly water. Heavenly water does not make one wet or soil ones clothes. The water has a living, tingling sensation. The water has healing and restorative power. The water is always clear. I have always enjoyed swimming under water. This is partly due to having never learned how to breathe in the crawl (freestyle) stroke. I must soon come back up, eager for breath. There, I will be able to swim under water all I want.

River Of Life, Lake, And Sea

The water of heaven is in the River of Life as well as lakes and seas. There may be two different kinds of water-like liquids under the Throne, which flow through the City into the River of Life. There are wonderful fountains with amazing animated statues.

CHAPTER 7

Trees, Fruit, Flowers, Grass

Heaven has plants like we have here on Earth, but they are not the same. I have already discussed the grassy hill in chapter 1, as it is commonly one of the first things seen in heaven. In this chapter, I will tell more of what the witnesses say about the grass and about the trees, their fruit, and the flowers.

Dale Black said the countryside is filled with natural wonders to please us. He said there are "thick living forests, vibrant colorful gardens, crystal clear lakes, all types of animals, and majestic mountains." (Black 2018, 173)

When Betty Malz was walking up the grassy hill, she saw off to her left multicolored flowers blooming, as well as trees and shrubs. (Malz, 86)

Ian McCormack saw the new Earth with fields, a crystal river with trees on its banks, rolling green hills, mountains, blue skies, and meadows with flowers and trees. It looked to him like a Garden of Eden or paradise, a place where he belonged and one that he had always been seeking. (Roth, 72)

Eben Alexander was flying over trees, fields, streams, waterfalls, people singing and dancing, children playing. (Alexander, 39)

Dawn Cypret mentioned the trees, grass, and wildflowers of heaven look a lot like those of Earth, but are much more beautiful. Everything there is much more beautiful than the corresponding thing on Earth.

Jeanne Enstad said there were no brown leaves and no rotten fruit anywhere. The grass was always a beautiful green and always looked like it had just been mowed. (Enstad, 89)

Colors

Everyone reports that there are more colors in heaven than we have on Earth and they are brighter. They also come from within and are part of the character of whatever it is rather than being reflected light. Most authors talk about the colors in conjunction with other things, such as the flowers, the grass, the sky, etc.

Marvin Besteman has a section on colors in general. (Besteman, 55-57, 60-61) He describes the colors as the deepest, richest, lushest, most glorious colors he has ever seen. In some ways the colors are indescribable because they go so far beyond anything we have here with which to compare. He says the most common color there is white followed by blue, but many colors are commonly swirled together.

Dale Black said every color imaginable existed, more than he had ever seen, and they were pure and innocent. They seemed to be alive, dancing in the air. It was breathtaking. (Black 2010, 99) He said a million jewels gathered into one place in the brightest sunlight couldn't begin to describe the colors he saw. Heaven is filled with more hues than is any rainbow. (Black 2010, 105)

Oden Hetrick said the primary colors of heaven are gold, red, purple, violet, and wine tone, maybe blue or green also. Gold is the sky color and the leaves and the ground were gold. (Doucette 2013-1)

Mickey Robinson said the colors there are unlike earthly colors. Everything is like translucent jewels with flowing colors that he could see through. The incredible colors and shapes were like an orchestra of visual harmony. (Robinson, 106)

Trees and Their Fruit

Richard Eby gazed at a valley with forests of symmetrical trees on the foothills on both sides of the valley. There were no brown spots or dead leaves. Each tree was tall, graceful, unblemished, perfect, and a duplicate of all the others. He thought they looked like Giant Arborvitae Cedars (Thuja plicata, also called Western Red Cedar). (Eby, 204) He said the huge trees were not exactly like anything on Earth, as they are made of a heavenly indestructible material, not like the molecules of Earth. (Roth, 173)

Richard Sigmund was taken to a beautiful countryside in a wooded area where people were having reunion parties, and the people had tears of joy flowing from their eyes. (Sigmund, 80)

In another place he saw a beautifully manicured park containing many huge trees. He said the trees seemed to be two thousand feet tall. There were many different varieties of trees. Some were like those on Earth; others were very different from anything he knew on Earth. He knew they were tall and strong and had no dead branches or leaves. Again, this is because nothing dies in heaven, not even leaves. Some of the leaves were huge and shaped like diamonds.

One tree he saw was crystal clear and huge. He thought it to be miles and miles across. (It always seems that Richard Sigmund describes things in dimensions greater than anyone else tells.) He was told that it was a Diadem tree. Each leaf was shaped like a crystal chandelier teardrop. As the leaves brushed against one another in the gentle breeze, it made a continual beautiful sound of crystal chimes. As the sound emanated from a leaf, there was a glow when he touched it.

Each leaf, each limb of the entire tree gave off a tremendous glow with all the colors that were in the glory cloud, causing the tree to glow with sound and light, aflame with glory. The flame started in the root and went all the way up the tree and out through the branches to the chandelier-like leaves. The tree exploded in a beautiful lighted cloud of glory and an unbelievably beautiful sound. He said the Diadem tree was glorious, and there were tens of thousands of people worshipping God under it. As he continued on the path he saw more trees as glorious as the Diadem tree.

He saw a tree that was like a walnut tree on Earth and was told to take one of the fruits, which was pear-shaped and copper-colored, and eat it. As soon as he picked it, in its place, another fruit grew instantly. When he touched the fruit to his lips, it evaporated and melted into a delicious juice that was like honey, peach juice, and pear juice. It was sweet, but not sugary. He said it was the most delicious thing he had ever tasted. His face was filled with juice from the fruit, and it immediately ran down his throat like honey. The beautiful, wonderful liquid juice that had covered his face all over, in that atmosphere of heaven, was also instantaneously gone. He points out that nothing can defile a person in heaven. It was a wonderful experience, and he said he can still almost taste that delicious juice years later.

He saw trees whose leaves were shaped like hearts and gave off a beautiful aroma. He was told to take a leaf and smell it. When he did, the moment he smelled the beautiful fragrance, he was strengthened. (Sigmund, 23-25)

Rebecca Springer saw that in a wonderful field of perfect grass and flowers equally wonderful trees were growing. Their drooping branches were laden with exquisite blossoms and fruits of many kinds. She remembered John's vision recorded in Revelation 22:2, *"On each side of the river stood the tree of life, bearing twelve crops of fruit, yielding its fruit every month. And the leaves were for the healing of the nations"* (NIV). (Springer, 11)

The fruit-laden branches of the trees could be easily reached. She noticed seven different types of fruit. One kind was like a Bartlett pear, but larger and more delicious. Another fruit was in clusters that were also pear-shaped, but smaller than the previous one. It had a consistency and flavor similar to the finest frozen cream. A third fruit was shaped like a banana and was called a breadfruit. It tasted like a dainty finger-roll.

She perceived that food for an elegant feast was provided there without labor or care. She tried some of the varieties with, as she says, much relish and refreshment. Once, the rich juice from the pear-like fruit ran out profusely over her hands and down the front of her dress. She thought she had ruined her dress! But to her amazement, not a spot could be found, and her hands were clean and fresh, as though just from a bath. Her brother-in-law, Frank, explained that no impurity could remain for an instant in that air. Nothing decays, tarnishes, or in any way ruins the universal purity and beauty of the place. As fast as the fruit ripens and falls, all that is not immediately gathered evaporates, not even the seed remaining. She had noticed no fallen fruit remained beneath the tree. (Springer, 27-28)

Jeanne Enstad said that many of the fruit trees that lined the river she saw bore large fruit, and there was no fruit lying on the ground. (Enstad, 31) On her second visit to heaven Jeanne saw another beautiful river and it also had fruit trees along the sides of the river. They branched out over small creeks. (Enstad, 88)

She saw no brown leaves or rotten fruit anywhere. She said everything is perfect in heaven. (Enstad, 89)

Willie Agnes Chennault said the trees are beautiful. Their bark is deep chocolate brown, thick, and shiny like gloss. The leaves are a very bright spring green. The trees are tall, huge, and wider than any tree she had seen on Earth. (Chennault, 56-57)

Oden Hetrick said the tree of life, or trees of life, grow along the

River of Life. He describes the fruit he tasted as being like a pear smooth and juicy. When he took a bite the juice ran down his arm and dripped off his elbow. He thought it would stain his garment; but there was no stain. He also said a new fruit grows when one is picked and every month there is a different fruit. New flowers are on the tree when the previous fruit is ripe. The flowers produce an excellent fragrance. (Doucette 2013-1)

Michael McCormack said the Tree of Life had loads of fruit on it. He knew that each day the youngest children came and took some fruit to share with their families. He said everyone in heaven is part of a big family, and the families live on that fruit for the day. He saw different varieties of fruit on the tree. These included pomegranates, apples, grapes, oranges, bananas. And all these different varieties of fruit were growing on the same tree. The tree was like a big, strong oak tree with a thick trunk. (Roth, 82-83)

Dr. Gary Wood said the crystal river was lined with orchards of fruit-bearing trees. He said the fruit represents a gift and when you eat the fruit you receive the gift. If the gift is knowledge, after eating it you have perfect understanding. The Tree of Life had a golden trunk and its long branches were covered with fruit. (Wood, 28)

Mary K. Baxter saw fruit trees loaded with all kinds of beautiful fruit. (Baxter, 61,86)

In addition to the fruit, there are fields of grain. Richard Sigmund spoke of the grain but he didn't give any details. (Sigmund, 92)

Willie Agnes Chennault saw a large field of wheat with people gathering it. She saw men with satchels around their waists and knives with them were tying up the bundles of wheat and barley and placing them in a wagon pulled by two oxen. (Chennault, 58-59).

Kat Kerr said that although one does not need to eat in heaven, there is lots of delicious food. It is not made from animals but from light she said. The food tastes and smells much better than its counterpart on Earth. There are things like steak, chicken, pizza, vegetables, fruit, cinnamon rolls, and desserts. If your gift is that of a chef, you will have a restaurant there and make delicious food for anyone who wishes. There is no money in heaven; everyone uses his/her gifts for the benefit of everyone else out of love, not for compensation. (Kerr 2010, 36)

Flowers

When Richard Eby arrived in heaven, he landed in a valley in heaven and saw thousands of different kinds of flowers. (Roth, 173) He said, viewing the gorgeous valley floor, the perfect blades of grass were interspersed with white flowers with four petals around gold centers and stems that were two feet tall. The white was a brighter white than any white on Earth. White on Earth is a combination of the colors of the spectrum, but the white in heaven is the white of God's glory that lights heaven. Each flower was identical to the others. As he stood there in the flowers, he saw that the flowers and the grass came up through his feet and legs and he left no footprints. (Eby, 204-205)

Rebecca Springer already mentioned the flowers in conjunction with the field of grass, which was thickly studded with fragrant flowers. She added that many of the flowers were ones she had known and loved on Earth. She remembered noticing heliotrope, violets, lilies of the valley, and mignonette, and many similar species wholly unfamiliar to her. She observed how perfect each plant and flower was. She said the heliotrope, for instance, on Earth often runs into long ragged sprays, but there, it grows upon short smooth stems. Each leaf was perfect and was smooth and glossy, instead of being rough and coarse-looking. The flowers peeked up from the deep velvet-like grass, with sweet, happy faces, as though inviting admiration. (Springer, 10-11)

Richard Sigmund said there were flowers of every imaginable size and color along the path. He saw banks and banks of flowers, and some were the size of a dinner table! There were roses that looked about four feet across and might have weighed fifty pounds on Earth. (Here again, Richard Sigmund's measurements seem greatly beyond anyone else's.) The flowers faced him as he walked. The air was filled with their aroma, and they were all humming. He picked one, and it was wonderful. Then when he put the flower down, it was immediately replanted and growing again. Again, there is no death in heaven; flowers never wilt or die. (Sigmund, 22)

Betty Eadie reported that the garden was filled with trees and flowers and plants. It was as if they were *meant* to be exactly how and where they were. She was filled with awe by the intensity of the colors.

We have nothing like them on Earth. Here, colors are the result of reflected light that gives off a certain color. Thousands of shades are possible, but light in the spirit world doesn't reflect off anything. She said it comes from within and appears to be a living essence. A billion colors are possible.

The flowers she saw were so vivid and luminous with color that they didn't seem solid. The intense aura of each plant's light made it difficult to identify where the plant's surface started and stopped. Each microscopic part of the plant was made up of its own intelligence. (Eadie, 78-79)

Jim Woodford said each flower's color merged with the next one beneath it. This was possible because the petals seemed to be translucent, like stained glass. A red flower would have a yellow flower beneath it and below that a blue flower and then the green of the stem, creating something like a multi-faceted stained glass window.

The flowers not only had amazing colors, they also had sounds. The petals emitted sounds as they moved in the gentle breeze creating an original infinitely flowing melody without cadence or conclusion. He asked the tallest of his angels, the Guardian angel, about it, and he said the flowers are happy to see him and are singing to him filled with joy. The angel then described joy as "living on the edge of a huge laugh motivated by the constant awareness of the presence of God." (Woodford, 81-82)

The flowers also had fragrance. As he bent toward a flower, a wonderful fragrance would come up. He had trouble finding words to describe it. The best he could find was to say it was like being surrounded by sweet smelling jasmine flowers. He said it was just another of the pervasive fragrance of love that was everywhere around him. The angel told him it was the scent of sanctity. Jim said everything in heaven, the sights, the colors, the sounds, the fragrances, the light, the waters, the people, the angels, and everything, reflects the love and nature of God. (Woodford, 83)

Dr. Gary Wood was taken to an area that looked like a school playground except it had fountains and benches. There were flowers everywhere producing sweet-smelling fragrances. The flowers had brilliant colors and every one was different from all the others. He was amazed with delight when he heard the flowers singing a sweet melody of praise. They were vivid and alive, so much alive he could see expression in each one as it was singing. (Wood, 30)

Dale Black saw that the endless grass was sprinkled with colorful flowers. They were like a chorus caught up in praise. He smelled the flowers and found they have a sweet gentle aroma that permeates heaven. (Black 2010, 101)

He said he saw people planting and nurturing flowers for their enjoyment. And every time someone touched a plant it gave off light and a melodic vibration. He said when he touched a leaf, micro tornados of life swirled in concentric circles. He said this illustrated the symbiotic interdependent relationship of the people and all plant life. (Black 2018, 175) Each flower and plant continually vibrates with melodies that glorify God. Everything in heaven is infused with God's life and energy. God is the source of all life. (Black 2018, 178)

He was fascinated with the flowers. They were diverse and unique but all blended into a whole. Every petal and leaf gave forth the glorious light and added just the right splashes of color to the velvety green grass of the meadows. (Black 2010, 105)

Mary K. Baxter said there were clusters of flowers of every description in the greenest grass she had ever seen. The flowers had the appearance of roses and were "splendid." Each plant had at least one bloom and the petals were beautiful. The flowers appeared as though they were singing. (Baxter, 62, 86)

Jeanne Enstad said there were many types of colorful flowers on the mountains. There were more colors than she had ever seen before. (Enstad, 31)

Colton Burpo said the flowers and trees in heaven were beautiful. (Burpo, 105)

Seven-year-old Kurt said it was a beautiful place with flowers and rainbows. Everything had its own white light. (Morse, 35)

Dawn Cypret said a gentle breeze made the flowers dance and sway as if greeting her. (May, 21)

Aromas

There are wonderful aromas in heaven. Richard Sigmund, upon his arrival in heaven, smelled an aroma, and it had a taste like strawberries and cream. (Sigmund, 16) He saw leaves on the trees that gave off a beautiful aroma. (Sigmund, 23) When he was viewing the mansions he saw roses that gave off a beautiful aroma. (Sigmund, 42)

Dale Black smelled the flowers and found they have a sweet gentle aroma that permeates heaven. (Black 2010, 101)

When touring the mansions, Rebecca Springer smelled vines that had the fragrance of a delicate perfume. (Springer, 18)

Steven Musick said the smells are piercing and pungent. Every aroma had an indescribable vibrancy. (Musick, 38)

Richard Eby called the aroma that pervades all of heaven the sweetest revelation of all. This wonderful perfume was everywhere, in the flowers, in the grass, in the air. It was exotic, refreshing, and fit for a King. He considered it one of the unsearchable joys prepared for us in the Father's house. (Eby, 26-27) He said it was a sweet-smelling aroma and it came from the prayers of the saints who are in heaven. The prayers of those who were saved in heaven are so sweet smelling that God has allowed them to smell the aroma of their prayers. (Roth, 173)

Grass

The grass in heaven looks like the grass here, but it is different. It is a beautiful green grass and makes a luscious carpet. And it never dies; a plucked blade of grass continues to grow and, if dropped back on the ground, continues as part of the heavenly carpet. It is alive in an animated way that grass here is not. It gives a warm tingling sensation to one's feet as he/she walks over it.

Richard Eby and Dale Black both said the blades of grass were not broken when they walked on them. (Roth, 173, and Black 2018, 174)

Dale Black said it was like a living carpet of rich green velvet. He stopped frequently to appreciate the grass and enjoy the visible life in it. All of heaven looked perfectly designed and maintained without the careful attention of anyone. (Black 2018, 174)

He said the grass was the purest most perfect grass he had ever seen, the most vibrant iridescent green he had ever seen. It stretched endlessly over rolling hills. It was precisely the right length and no blade was bent, damaged, or out of place. It was alive (in a sense beyond what it means here for grass to be alive.) It was slightly transparent and emitted light and life from within each blade. (Black 2010, 101)

Ian McCormack said the grass gave off the same light he had seen in the presence of God. There were no disease spots on the grass and it would spring back if you stepped on it. (Sharkey, 32)

Marvin Besteman said the greenest surface he had ever seen was the flawless emerald-colored carpet at the Master's Golf Tournament in Augusta, Georgia. But the grass in heaven is far greener and more deluxe, a greener green than you can imagine. (Besteman, 56-57)

When Betty Eadie was in the garden, she walked on the grass and found it to be crisp, cool, and brilliant green, and it felt alive under her feet. (Eadie, 78)

Mary K. Baxter said the grass was the greenest imaginable. (Baxter, 62)

Jeanne Enstad said the grass was always a beautiful green. It was like it had just been mowed, except the grass there is always like that and never needs mowing. (Enstad,89)

Betty Malz was walking on grass that was the most vivid shade of green she had ever seen. She said each blade was perhaps one inch long and had texture like fine velvet and was moving. As the bottoms of her feet touched the grass, something alive in the grass was transmitted up through her whole body with each step she took. (Malz, 84-85)

Dr. Gary Wood was standing outside the city on a lush, green carpet of grass on a hill. When he started walking up the hill, the grass came all the way through his feet, and there were no indentations where he had stepped, since nothing is harmed in heaven. (Roth, 100)

Willie Agnes Chennault said the grass was beautiful and looked like plastic. The dirt glowed a light brown. (Chennault, 57)

Rebecca Springer says she was sitting in a sheltered nook made by flowering shrubs and was resting upon the softest and most beautiful turf of grass, thickly studded with fragrant flowers. She felt it was a beautiful scene as she rested upon the soft, fragrant cushion, secluded and yet not hidden! This wonderful field of perfect grass and flowers stretched as far as she could see. (Springer, 10, 11)

Richard Sigmund was walking on a pathway on either side of which was the richest turf-green grass he had ever seen that was moving with life and energy. Supernaturally, he knew that if he picked a blade of grass and then put it back down, it would just keep on growing since there is no death in heaven. Not even for a blade of grass. (Sigmund, 22)

He also saw a park with park benches everywhere that were made of gold but looked like wrought iron so that people could sit and talk and praise together. (Sigmund, 23)

Summary

The trees, flowers, and grass of heaven are similar to those on Earth but are different in significant ways. Some are like specific species on Earth; others are completely new. The trees are bigger, the fruit more delicious, the fruit never spoils but just evaporates. Other things grow and provide food that is very delicious, even though one does not have to eat in heaven. The flowers are more beautiful, and they also hum with melodies that give praise to God. The grass transmits feeling back up into the person. The flowers even turn their heads toward someone. And nothing dies—leaves never turn brown, flowers never fade, and fruit never spoils. The light of God gives life to everything in heaven. He is the source of all life.

All the colors of heaven have brightness and luster beyond any we know here. There are colors we can't now imagine. And all of the colors come from within and are not reflected radiance as they are on Earth. Marvin Besteman said the dominant color in heaven is white (second is blue) and the white is a whiter white than we have ever seen. There are brighter whites and lighter whites, all gorgeous. (Besteman, 60)

CHAPTER 8

Landscapes and Sky

Landscapes

Jesse Duplantis in his audiotape of his experience in heaven described seeing mountains with snow on them.

Ian McCormack saw mountains and rolling green hills. (Roth, 72)

Oden Hetrick said there are very high mountains and lakes. The topography is very much like Earth. (Doucette 2013-1)

Dale Black saw a range of majestic mountains that brought out reverence rather than a goal to climb them. (Black 2010, 101-102)

The hills and mountains towered before Dr. Gary Wood, and he saw many people on the hillsides. They were watching things taking place on Earth, and whenever someone on Earth would accept Jesus as his/her Lord and Savior, all the people on the hillside, on the mountaintops, and in the city, would jubilantly break out in applause and praise. The mountains would sing and the trees would clap their limbs together. (Wood, 29)

Jim Woodford said the landscapes of heaven are punctuated with mountains, trees, flora of all kinds, streams and brooks, and a blue sky deeper than any blue he has known. It all has a bedazzling array of colors and sounds. He walked a pathway surrounded by lush green grass and bordered with flowers of many varieties and colors. The trees had iridescent leaves that hung over everything. The flowers were pearlescent and their petals were translucent like stained glass. (Woodford, 81)

Dawn Cypret saw mountains and hills in the distance. (May, 21)

Dean Braxton said the mountains praised the Lord, so he testified to there being mountains in heaven. (Roth, 28)

Rhoda "Jubilee" Mitchell saw hills and mountains. She didn't describe them but said heaven is huge and some of it is countryside. (Roth, 50)

Richard Sigmund saw mountains he said were fifty thousand feet tall. Because his measurements in other areas seem to be exaggerations from what others observed, I can't be sure of this estimate. However, they are clearly better then any we have on Earth. He also said there was snow on them that never melted even though the temperature was just right. (Sigmund, 82)

In other chapters I have reported the green, grassy hill that can be climbed effortlessly and has been seen by most when they arrive in heaven. I have also mentioned above the meadows with vibrant green grass with flowers of multiple different colors.

Richard Eby saw a valley with hills on each side covered with forests. (Eby, 204)

It appears the landscapes of heaven are much like those on Earth but much grander. Things not mentioned by anyone were features like Yellowstone or the impressive and beautiful canyons of Yosemite, Utah, and Arizona. But everyone only had glimpses of heaven. Who knows all that is there awaiting our joyful discovery?

Sky

Rebecca Springer said there was a golden and rosy color everywhere, and the sky was like the afterglow of a Southern summer sunset. (Springer, 12)

Marvin Besteman said the sky on his way to heaven and the one there are the wildest blue you could ever imagine. The atmosphere was filled with color and light and the blue was not like any tint we find on Earth. He compared it with a tropical ocean bay, like in the Caribbean or Hawaii, on a bright day. Imagine the bluest tropical ocean bay and the blue in heaven is far beyond that. (Besteman, 57)

He also saw something like fireworks in the sky. He saw many shapes and formations and a huge array of colors. Occasionally there was a gigantic color-ball in motion with different shades of color going all through it. (Besteman, 65-66)

He said the colors were profoundly beautiful and the lights in the sky were like 10,000 silent fireworks all going off at the same time. (Besteman, 79)

Ian McCormack saw blue skies. (Roth, 72)

Eben Alexander saw big, pink-white puffy clouds in a blue-black sky. (Alexander, 45)

Dawn Cypret said the sky was a soft blue. (May, 21)

Michael McCormack saw clouds above the throne that were like the Northern Lights only more colorful. The clouds were dancing and angels were dancing in them. He went up into them and danced, too. (Roth, 82)

Dr. Melvin Morse wrote of an eleven-year-old patient named John who returned from a trip to heaven and said the sky contained many beautiful colors, more than here. (Morse, 61)

Dean Braxton said the sky is far more gorgeous than even the best sunset on Earth. It is bright because of the brightness of God and is golden, yellow, and white, with more colors going through it, resembling curtains moving in a breeze. (Perhaps the aurora on Earth resembles the sky in heaven in terms of the colors and the movement like curtains.) He even said the atmosphere bowed when Jesus spoke to him. (Roth, 27) My Earthly mind finds that hard to imagine.

Richard Sigmund said the sky was rosette-pinkish in color but also a crystal blue. There were what looked like clouds in the sky, but they were bunches of angels or people strolling the sky singing praises. (Sigmund, 23)

Kat Kerr said the sky was a soft blue with peach and gold streaks in it. (Kerr 2007, 84)

Jim Woodford said the sky was a deep blue, a deeper blue than he had ever seen. (Woodford, 81)

Willie Agnes Chennault said the sky was bright and it almost seemed like you could reach up and touch it. It was much closer than the sky on Earth. There was no sun or moon, and she didn't see any stars.

Summary

There are beautiful landscapes like those on Earth. The sky in heaven appears to be like a beautiful sunset all the time. Different people observed different colors in the sky: blue, different shades of blue, sunset colors of pink and orange, and colors like the aurora.

Mary K. Baxter said the brilliance of the light of the Son of God, the jasper walls of the city, the gates of pearl, the amazing mansions, the beautiful River of Life, [the delicious fruit, the brilliant colors, the radiant flowers, the hills and mountains, forests and meadows], the absence of any decay, withering, or crumbling, is a scene no artist could ever adequately depict. (Baxter, 27)

CHAPTER 9
Things, Work, Recreation

Conveyances

Richard Sigmund saw conveyances floating in the air when he was at the base of a mountain. He said they were made of carved wood and metal. People sat in them and talked as they floated around. Angels ministered to them there. (Sigmund, 82)

He also saw conveyances on the oceans, the seas, and the four major rivers, just as there are conveyances in the air. He likened them to boats in the water. He saw some that were very large and some with hand-carvings of Biblical sayings on them. Angels guided some. He also saw land conveyances, which traveled on golden roads. Their purpose seemed to be to allow people to sit together and enjoy one another's companionship. It seemed to him that these vehicles were the pastime building projects of someone who enjoyed making conveyances. (Sigmund, 82-83)

Kat Kerr also saw various types of transport vehicles that transported groups of people by air, land, or sea. They were powered by light or, on the seas, by wind-blown sails. Occasionally she saw individuals piloting one of these vehicles alone. (Kerr 2007, 29) She also reported seeing chariots, antique cars, trolleys, motorcycles with "hyperdrive," and high tech star cruisers. She saw children on hover boards. You can also step into a Transportation Kiosk that will instantly take you where you wish to go on beams of light. All these conveyances are powered by either wind or light. There is no other fuel in heaven. (Kerr 2010, 42)

No other author reported all these kinds of conveyances.

Oden Hetrick said the primary mode of transportation is by thought. If you need to go somewhere, you just think of it and you are there instantaneously. But there is also a mode of moving slowly allowing you to enjoy the countryside as you move along. It is not walking as we know it; it is just gliding along gracefully. This mode enables you to learn as you move along. Sometimes we just float in the air like birds, but without wings. He said there are little chariots that are like servants. Some are two-seaters, some are the size of buses. They can move on the land, the river or through the sky. The Spirit of God is their power. We don't direct these vehicles, we are yielded to the Spirit of God and the vehicles are under His direction. (Doucette 2013-1)

In the process of her angel showing Mary K. Baxter the glory of God, she saw his chariots. The wheels of the chariot were so large, she couldn't describe them. They were studded with many precious jewels: diamonds, rubies, and emeralds. There were two wheels on each side, and it was low and open on the front like a sleigh. It appeared to be on fire but the fire never consumed it. (Baxter, 76)

Tools

Rebecca Springer reported that her brother-in-law Frank told her some boys came with tools to embed roses in the marble floor of the house that was to be hers. No description of these tools was given. (Springer, 20)

There are several reports of musical instruments, including an organ that Johann Sebastian Bach was playing and a young boy playing a piano and harp. (Sigmund, 31-32) Bells and chimes have been reported.

People were seen sewing and weaving, but no tools were mentioned. Instead the work was done simply by thought and the spirit that was in the threads and fabrics.

Houses are built there, but again no tools were mentioned.

Richard Sigmund reported seeing conveyances made by someone whose pastime was making conveyances. But again no tools were mentioned.

Willie Agnes Chennault saw garden tools, including pitchforks and rakes. She saw two huge oxen that were off-white with light brown stripes running down their backs. The wooden wagon they were pulling was made of light brown wood and also had the same color stripes. Their eyes shown with God's glory. The oxen had hooks across their heads so they could pull the wagon. She said there were twelve spinners inside the wheels. (Chennault, 58-59)

In fact, it appears work is done there largely through the spirit and not through tools. And the tools that are mentioned are never described except the musical instruments and are probably unlike any tools we have on Earth. Also there appear to be musical instruments unlike those we have on Earth.

Work

We will each have work to do there. Those who were just visiting weren't assigned any work other than to tell the world when they return about Jesus and the Father and how they don't want anyone to miss heaven. But some of the residents reported having work to do, e.g., Rebecca Springer's brother-in-law, Frank. He built Rebecca Springer's house there. (Springer, 19) And when he left her, he said he had other work to do. (Springer, 29)

Some boys came and inlaid roses in the marble in her house. (Springer, 20)

Kat Kerr said everyone does what they can as free gifts to others there. There is no money in heaven, nothing is sold or bought, but given away to any who want out of love. (Kerr 2010, 34-35)

Colton Burpo reported that Jesus gave him homework, but the homework was not irksome. (Burpo, 71-72)

Richard Sigmund reported that the older children all had schoolwork, but he was not allowed to see what they were studying. However, he could tell the children were all extremely capable and could routinely study things geniuses on Earth would struggle to understand. (Sigmund, 35)

Jeanne Enstad said everyone was very happy doing his or her job there. She was told everyone has a special job to do and keeps very busy. (Enstad, 89)

Mary K. Baxter said we will be happily occupied in something of service to God. She couldn't say what that service will be, but from others we can tell it will be in keeping with the gifts and talents He gave us from the beginning. (Baxter, 29) She did say that we will not be idle and will enjoy the work we do. The work will be stimulating and exhilarating. It will fulfill some useful purpose in heaven and will glorify God. Some of the work will be of kinds no one has experienced on Earth. (Baxter, 71) The work is always done thoroughly and excellently. Nothing was ever done poorly nor was mediocre. Everything was always the highest quality in glory to God. (Baxter, 72) After all, God spared nothing to create heaven as a perfect place. He paid the perfect price for us to be there. How could we do anything less than perfect out of respect for Him?

Money is not needed there because everything is free. Whatever work anyone does is based on that person's gifts and is a free gift to bless others. God provides everything one needs, and we have the joy and blessing of being able to participate in God's providing for others. (Kerr 2007, 30)

Richard Sigmund saw stores. There was a jewelry store that had diamonds for a specific woman in a man's life. He saw clothing stores where women with piles of fabric were telling them what to do to make garments without thread for people coming. (Sigmund, 64-65) He saw people building houses and putting blessings there. (Sigmund, 54)

Richard saw a woman weaving a tapestry in a large picture window of a beautiful home off the street on which he was walking. It was the most beautiful tapestry he had ever seen. He went inside and saw that the tapestry was just hanging in midair. The woman had a large ball of yarn-like material ("yarn-like" because things in heaven are not made of the same stuff as similar things on Earth). All she had to do was speak softly to the ball of yarn and tell it what to do, and it would form itself into the tapestry. Then Richard noticed the tapestry was an image of everything that was visible outside the window. It had depth, and it seemed like you could just walk into it. Amazingly, everything that was going on outside the window was going on in the tapestry, people were moving and tree leaves were blowing. Some people were standing in groups and singing. Richard could hear them singing in the tapestry. He even saw himself in the tapestry moments before when he was standing outside the window! He asked when did she weave this into the tapestry. He was told she did it the day he was born. (Sigmund, 44-45)

Richard saw that angels were at work and people were at work creating homes and putting everything in them needed to bless their occupants with every blessing. (Sigmund, 54)

In another place he saw a building like a community center where thousands of women were creating garments for people who were coming. They were not sewing with needle and thread, they merely told the pieces of cloth what to do to make the garments. (Sigmund, 65)

Matthew Payne reported that some paintings in heaven become interactive when you approach them and begin to show a three-dimensional video of the scene. It starts before the scene in the painting, goes through the image of the painting, and continues on past the scene. (Payne, 54)

He reported from his book, *Great Cloud of Witnesses Speak*, a person named Rahab has three signature restaurants in heaven where she cooks meals for guests. (Payne, 46)

His sister Karen is a ballerina in heaven and gives performances and lessons. His sister Talitha, who died in a miscarriage, is a painter with an art gallery. She has a five-story gallery of her paintings of scenes, people, her family, and Matthew. He said everyone in heaven does fun activities they enjoy and for which they are gifted to help and bless other people. (Payne, 50, 52)

Kat Kerr saw all kinds of shops for work in heaven, matching many different people's gifts. She saw LPP, Little Papa's Productions studio, a jeweler, and a perfume shop. (Kerr 2010, 38) People's work was always a labor of love; his/her work was given to whoever wanted it out of love.

Jeanne Enstad said everyone was kind and they were all working together and enjoying each other. (Enstad, 31) Everyone has a special job and is very happy keeping busy with his/her work. It is always daytime and no one needs to sleep or rest there. (Enstad, 89)

Willie Agnes Chennault saw a large field of wheat with people gathering it. She saw men with satchels around their waists and knives with them were tying up the bundles of wheat and barley and placing them in a wagon pulled by two oxen. (Chennault, 58-59).

Recreation

Kat Kerr said there is lots of fun in heaven. There are no classes on holiness because we have been made as holy as we can get through the blood of Jesus. There is lots of praise and worship of the Father and Son in heaven, but God has also provided many ways for His children to have fun. She reminded us that Jesus said we must be like little children. Well, children like to play, and God wants us to play in heaven. (Kerr 2010, 103)

I heard an atheist say he would rather be partying it up with friends in hell than sitting on a cloud playing a harp all day. He has been very deceived by Satan. There is no partying in hell except for the demons partying at the expense of the humans that are alone there, whom the demons are torturing for amusement. On the other hand, heaven is going to be a lot of fun, beauty, love, togetherness, and wholeness. Some of the fun activities for children are mentioned in Chapter 12 on children.

Mary K. Baxter saw entire families together going places, doing things together, and having happy times with glowing faces. (Baxter, 29)

Richard Sigmund reported that the children he saw played hide and seek; they climbed trees and jumped out floating down like cotton balls; they made a ring with one child floating above the others and being pushed by them. They jumped two hundred feet in the air and floated down; they ran faster than horses. (Sigmund, 33-35)

Kat Kerr described a surf park called Wipeout near a large mountain. Water comes down the mountain and creates 75-foot waves in a blue lagoon that is associated with the Crystal Sea. The waves race across the lagoon onto the beach. People who like surfing are going to have a lot of fun. Keep in mind that in heaven nothing can hurt you. The surfers cannot get hurt by the waves or anything and can never drown. There were also whales and other marine animals with which one can interact and play. (Kerr 2010, 104-105) (Swim with dolphins anyone?)

There is also a Remember When Gallery in which you can sit in your own theater and review funny, fun-filled, hilarious things that happened in your life. But since nothing bad or negative can be in heaven the scenes from your life do not include anything sinful, tragic, or sad. It will also include all the rewarding moments in your life. You can invite friends and family to your theater and entertain them. Kat Kerr looks forward to seeing scenes from her mother's life and especially things her mother never told her. (Does her mother have to invite her to the viewing?) She mentions several family events from her childhood she will enjoy seeing. (Kerr 2010, 105-106)

Kat Kerr saw a girl with her great-grandfather approaching an amusement park with a huge roller coaster. (Kerr 2007, 50) She also visited the park herself and was astounded by what she saw. The roller coaster cars had no wheels and zoomed faster than their counterparts on

Earth. She did not know how they stayed on the track without wheels. At one point the cars leaped through the air to the next part. The people riding the roller coaster were thrilled and there was no fear, motion sickness, or any other negative experience with it. There were many other things there that God made for the happiness of His children. There was no security because there are no thieves or vandals in heaven and everyone respects everyone else. Also there are no fees to ride anything. She saw a place where people can learn to fly without wings. She said beginners looked like Peter Pan wannabes! (Kerr 2007, 83-86) When I was a young child many times I had dreams that I could levitate and fly if I thought about it just right. It looks like when I get to heaven, I will be able to fulfill those dreams!

There are also "reality theaters" in heaven where Earth movies are shown if they satisfy heaven's criteria: no graphic violence, no profanity, no sensuality, and no spiritual darkness. Kat went with a family into a theater to watch *The Sound of Music*. She was surprised that the mother was the lead character in the movie. As she questioned how this was possible, she was taken to a place where she saw the action occurring and everything was real, not staged. She was amazed that in heaven you can be a part of a movie. (Kerr 2007, 87-91)

At another place there were pedestals with a mirror/monitor in front of them. When someone stepped up on the pedestal and pressed the up arrow, a beam came down, and he/she was transformed into the dress and appearance of someone from another culture. She saw an Asian boy become Bahamian. Then he pressed the down arrow and went back to his original Asian appearance. She then stepped on several of the pedestals and saw herself as an Aborigine, then Native American (which tribe or nation was not identified), then Asian, Dutch, Italian, and finally Scottish. She said that is just one of the many supernatural sources of entertainment God has prepared for us in Heaven. (Kerr 2007, 93-97)

She also saw a man playing golf on his personal golf course in his backyard. In front of his house was a royal-looking deck facing a sea and boats were arriving with people wanting to play golf with him on his golf course. She said his wife told her that he had always wanted to take golf lessons and play golf but they could never afford it. God had granted his deepest desire. (Kerr 2007, 61-62)

Sports are played in heaven but as worship. There are three score boards, one for each team and one above them for Jesus, who gets all the points. Each team tries to get as many points for Jesus as possible. The winning team gets to carry Jesus across the field or court and celebrate with him. Kat has seen all kinds of sporting games except ones that require abusive contact such as boxing. She mentions golf, football, basketball, fishing (How can there be fishing when no animal ever gets hurt?), water sports, and horse riding sports. There is no protective equipment because it is not possible to get hurt or injured in heaven. (Kerr 2010, 123-124)

Summary

We will definitely not be bored in heaven. We will have work to do in keeping with the gifts God has given us that we exercised on Earth, or even if we did not get to exercise those gifts on Earth. The work we do will be for the blessing and pleasure of others. Everything we need is provided to us and therefore no wages or financial compensation is given. We will be able to enjoy wholesome entertainment and familiar sports, although they may be played differently or for different purposes than here. Some of our entertainment will be based on supernatural things for which there are no Earthly counterparts. (However, note that only one person reported all of these interesting entertainments.) This is all in addition to enjoying the constant and ubiquitous songs of praise.

CHAPTER 10

Meeting Jesus

Heaven is all about God the Father and Jesus the Son. Worship and praise of the Father and the Son for all they have done is constant in heaven. The light of their love permeates everything in heaven. Meeting Jesus is very common in these stories. Books could be written on the stories of meeting Jesus; however, I will tell about some of the testimonies I have read to give you a general idea of what it is like to meet Jesus in heaven.

Former Muslim Meets Jesus after Jihad's Bomb

First is Samaa Habib who was instantly killed by a Jihad's bomb. She was nearest to the third bomb. It was in a fire extinguisher cabinet next to which she was leaning. Suddenly it exploded, throwing her ten feet into the air and smashing her against the opposite wall. She called out to Jesus silently in her agony, "Jesus, help me!" Then her spirit left her body, and she died. Her body was burned, and her head split open. Friends told her later they could see inside her skull.

She said the next thing she saw was a brilliant white light illuminating Jesus. His face was brighter than the sun. In an Earthly sense, His unapproachable light was blinding but in heaven our eyes can take in His glorious radiance. She describes His light as glorious and transcending. Everything around her was bathed in golden light. She trembled in awe at His mighty presence and felt the fear of the Lord. Seeing the majesty and indescribable beauty of the Lord made her speechless. Every fiber of her being exclaimed, "Holy, holy, holy is the Lord God Almighty" as she worshiped Jesus, the worthy Lamb of God.

She fell face down, prostrate at His feet, trembling under the weight of His glory. She was terrified, and completely undone, fully aware that she was unclean. She didn't see how she could stand in the presence of such a holy, awesome God. She refers to Isaiah's experience in Isaiah 6:1-6 and John's in Revelation 4:8.

Then Jesus touched her as she was lying on her face before Him and said, "Do not be afraid." He reminded her His precious blood was shed for her and washed her clean as white snow, making her clean and pure, because He loved her.

As was stated in Chapter 1, this is like John's experience recorded in Revelation 1:17, *"When I saw him, I fell at his feet as though dead. Then he placed his right hand on me and said: 'Do not be afraid'"* (NIV).

She sensed that Jesus could see through her, reading all the thoughts of her heart. Her whole body was shaking. She felt so unworthy to be in His presence. She was amazed that He was revealing himself to her—a woman. She did not know whether she would be judged or whether He would say, "Well done, good and faithful servant." But He showed her His mercy, which surrounds His throne and triumphs over judgment. Knowing her thoughts, He spoke to her heart and reminded her of His character—that He is gracious and compassionate, slow to anger and rich in love. He radiated an amazing love that contained acceptance. She felt neither condemnation nor shame. This is the same as others who come face to face with Jesus; they feel neither condemnation nor shame nor guilt, but only total acceptance, peace, and joy.

She couldn't bring herself to look at Him, but He raised her up so she was standing before Him and as He smiled at her, relief poured over her soul. She says He said in a sweet and gentle voice, "Welcome home, Samaa," yet His voice was also powerful, like the sounds of many waters. He opened His arms to her. His beautiful eyes were like blazing fires of consuming love that overwhelmed her. Like a magnet, His love drew her in, melting her heart and transforming her from the inside out. Embraced by His love, she started to weep.

Do You Want to Stay or Go Back?

He asked her, "Do you want to go back or stay here in heaven?" and showed her the life she had lived as if seeing snapshots of a movie. She saw her childhood and all nineteen years of her life. She saw the choices she had made and realized she had been living for her own agenda, and repented.

She said to him, "Oh, Lord Jesus, I'm so sorry. Please forgive me. All my life I have been living for myself—my ways, my dreams, my desires, my plans. But it is not about me. It's all about you. As I died for you, I want to live for you. Please give me another chance to live for your will alone, Jesus." She was shaking so much she couldn't verbalize these words; they just formed in her mind, and she immediately knew they were formed in Jesus' mind also. He had heard her heart.

He then showed her another scene—her whole family, some of whom weren't saved yet. And she saw herself, dead from the bomb blast, and her parents', siblings' and other relatives' reactions. It broke her heart to see their pain.

"Oh no, they can't take it," she thought. But Jesus instantly revealed to her that they too would be in heaven one day, reminding her of His promise in Acts 16:31: *"They replied, 'believe in the Lord Jesus, and you will be saved—you and your whole household"* (NIV). She understood He wanted her to go back for their salvation, but also for the salvation of His family, which is multitudes! God is all about family, from Genesis to Revelation. The multitude was His children who were lost on Earth. He wanted her to go back for the nations, which is His inheritance. This was like Psalm 2:8 to her. *"Ask, of me, and I will make the nations your inheritance, the ends of the Earth your possession"* (NIV).

She understood nothing was hers. Her life and future, her friends and family, heaven and Earth—all belong to Jesus. All communication in heaven is heart to heart; no sounds came from her mouth.

In heaven, she experienced such joy, peace, and overwhelming love that she wanted to stay forever. After being there, she knew being in His presence is her real home, He is everything—Alpha and Omega. But He is also a gentleman. He never forced her but gave her the freedom to choose. Her choice was that she would go back to Earth and be a witness for Him. She was motivated by love, not a sense of duty. She knew Jesus is the worthy Lamb who was slain to receive the reward for His suffering. She knew that she had been martyred for Jesus and that her reward would be great in heaven. Jesus is her reward!

But she also wanted to live for Him. She thought He would say no, but He didn't. It was God who put the desire in her heart to fulfill His calling. As it says in Psalm 37:4, *"Delight yourself in the Lord and he will give you the desires of your heart"* (NIV). She confessed that He is her desire!

"All right, see you soon," He said. And immediately a fresh wave of love washed over her. It was easy to talk to Him, to communicate, like a child speaking to her father. She said that although we make our relationship with Jesus complicated, in reality it is as simple as being childlike.

There all was eternally peaceful, and she no longer experienced the dimension of time. The moment she was with Jesus, she existed in the eternal present. She understood that Jesus himself *is* heaven, and that without Him it is not heaven. He is the center of everything. (Habib, 176-180)

Another Muslim Meets Jesus and Is Instantly Healed

Another former Muslim who saw Jesus was Gulshan Esther. She didn't die temporarily and go to heaven like the others here, but her encounter with Jesus is significant enough that I thought I would include it. As a 6-month old child she became a weak cripple, paralyzed on her left side from typhoid fever. (Esther, 12) She was faithful in the ways of Islam as taught to her by her dear father. She and her father believed Allah would heal her, but all their prayers to Allah went unanswered. When she was fourteen they went on a Hajj to Mecca. She was sure Allah would heal her then when she visited Muhammad's tomb and other sacred sites. But they returned to Pakistan without her healing. As they waited for the plane to Karachi in the Saudi airport her father told her, "God is testing you and testing me. Don't be hopeless. Maybe at some stage in your life you will be healed."

She replied, "All right. I won't be hopeless. I will remain faithful to the Prophet and Allah." (Esther, 34)

But soon after that her father contracted pneumonia, didn't get the medical help he needed, and died, leaving Gulshan an orphan as her mother had died when she was an infant. She was devastated and did not know what to do. She knew suicide is a sin in Islam, but prayed as if talking to One who was listening, "I want to die. I don't want to live any more and that is the end of it." Somehow she knew she was being heard as if a veil between her and some greater Peace was lifted. She sobbed as she continue her prayer more boldly, "What terrible sin have I committed that You have made me like this? As soon as I was born my mother was taken away, and then you made me a cripple, and now You have taken away my father. Now tell me why You have punished me so terribly."

There was deep silence and she heard a low gentle voice saying, "I won't let you die. I will keep you alive." Now knowing that God, the Supreme Being, heard her, she was free to approach Him.

She continued to question Him with "why." Then she heard a low, vibrant voice say to her, "Who gave eyes to the blind, and who made the sick whole, and who healed the lepers, and who raised the dead? I am Jesus, son of Mary. Read about Me in the Quran, in the Sura Maryam."

She did not know how long this interaction had taken, but no one had come to bathe her feet, and she had been left alone for this whole encounter. (Esther, 48)

The Quran is officially only allowed in Arabic, the language in which it was given to Mohammad. But Esther couldn't read Arabic very well and obtained an Urdu version of the Quran. She opened her Urdu Quran and read (English translation of her Urdu Quran), "The angels said to Mary: 'Allah bids you rejoice in a word from Him. His name is the Messiah, the son of Mary. He shall be noble in this world and the next, and shall be favored by Allah. He shall preach to men from his cradle and in the prime of manhood, and shall lead a righteous life'..." Later she read from the Sura Inrams, "By Allah's leave, I will give sight to the blind man, heal the leper, and raise the dead to life." She was amazed at this prophet Jesus who knew her need and could speak out to her as if He were alive. She was sure one day she would find out the secret of this mysterious prophet veiled in the pages of the Holy Quran. (Esther, 48-53)

One day she asked her Aunty if she knew anything about Jesus. She said, "He is the only prophet in the Holy Quran who gives eyes to the blind and who raises the dead and who is coming again." She didn't know where in the Quran it states this, but Gulshan found, "By Allah's leave I shall give sight to the blind man, heal the leper, and raise the dead to life." Now she came to believe that Jesus could heal her, too, something she had never felt from the Quran before. So from then on she added to her regular Islam prayers, "Oh Jesus, Son of Maryam, heal me." (Esther, 58-59)

"Stand up and come to me. I am Jesus"

She continued praying like this until one night she woke up as usual at 3:00 am, and noted that she had been praying this for three years and was not healed. She prayed, "Look you are alive in heaven, and it says in the Holy Quran about you that you have healed people. You can heal me, and yet I am still a cripple." Then she cried out in pain, "Jesus, if you are able to, heal me — otherwise tell me." Then the room became filled with light that came from no Earthly source. She was frightened and covered herself with her shawl. Then she looked around and saw twelve shadowy figures in long robes in the light and a thirteenth in the middle larger and brighter than the others. She prayed, "Oh, God. Who are these people, and how have they come here when all the windows and doors are shut?" Suddenly a voice said to her, "This is the path you have been seeking. I am Jesus Son of Mary, to whom you have been praying, and now I am standing in front of you. You get up and come to me."

"Oh Jesus, I am crippled. I can't get up."

"Stand up and come to me. I am Jesus." She hesitated, so He said a third time, "Stand up." She felt new strength flowing in to her wasted limbs. She put her foot on the ground and stood up. She ran a few paces and then fell at His feet. As Jesus put His hand on the top of her head she saw a hole in His hand from which flowed a ray of bright light that made her green dress seem white. His light made many things clearer to her. He said to her, "I am Jesus. I am Immanuel. I am the Way, the Truth, and the Life. I am alive and I am coming soon. See, from today you are my witness. What you have seen now with your eyes you must take to my people. My people are your people, and you must remain faithful to take that to my people." He told her He will be with her wherever she goes and taught her to say the Lord's Prayer. Through that prayer He became the father she had lost. (Esther, 59-61)

Even though her family was a witness to this amazing healing miracle of Jesus, they still could not accept that Jesus was real and the source of this miracle. She eventually had to leave Pakistan. Her book tells many more details of how God was with her wherever she went.

Jesus Comes to Rhoda Crying in Her Bed

Rhoda "Jubilee" Mitchell met Jesus when she was on her bed crying out to Him. He took her out of her body and into the night sky. Her senses were sharpened and she felt more alive than she ever had. As they were traveling along, she became aware of Jesus and His Father communicating thoughts although to her it was a distinct dialogue. She could sense how much they love one another. She was able to witness the Godhead working together in complete harmony, the incredible ultimate love relationship. She found God's love a tangible presence in the Universe, shining brightly through every twinkling light. His love was shooting through her, His affection surrounded her, flowing over her like waves, loving her like no one ever could. She had never felt so loved as she was then in Jesus' arms as they flew along at an incredible speed. (Roth, 44-45)

Later after she was in heaven being escorted by angels, she saw Him again. She said He was engulfed in an orb of pure white light extending out in a circle about four feet in diameter. The light shone from every fiber of His being and was the glory and anointing of God. Once, when He was coming over a hill, it was like the sun dawning except His was pure white light. (Roth, 56)

Several Experience Jesus' Radiance and Power

Dean Braxton said Jesus spoke to him with words that were alive with power and authority but were life and comfort to him. As with everything else, communication is by thoughts rather than voice, and there is no miscommunication, no misunderstandings.

Jesus' eyes were like flames of fire, just like John said in Revelation 1:14. There were many colors in his eyes that were changing constantly. His eyes were deep, full of life, and had love for each person who looked at Him. He saw love for himself in Jesus' eyes, but, as Dean thought of someone else, he saw love for that person in Jesus' eyes. He saw in Jesus' eyes that He wants everyone alive on Earth to be with Him in heaven. He does not want to lose even one person to hell. As Dean saw the love in Jesus' eyes, he became that love and knew we become that love in order to love others with His love. (Roth, 26-29)

When Rebecca Springer saw Jesus, a radiant glow overspread His wonderful face, as He looked directly at her. She knew it was Jesus! With joy and adoration, she threw herself at His feet, bathing them with happy tears, reminiscent of the woman in Luke 7:38, "*And as she stood behind him at his feet weeping, she began to wet his feet with her tears.*

Then wiped them with her hair, kissed them and poured perfume on them" (NIV). Jesus gently stroked Rebecca's bowed head and then lifted her to His side.

She whispered, "My Savior—my King!" as she clung closely to Him.

He added, "Yes, and Elder Brother and Friend," as He tenderly wiped away her tears. Then He drew her to a seat and had a long conversation with her, unfolding many of the mysteries of life in heaven. (Springer, 43-44)

Crystal McVea said that when she saw and recognized God, she immediately confessed Him as Lord and worshiped Him with all she had. Unlike in church on occasions when she was glad for it to be over, there she was completely surrendered to His greatness and had an overpowering desire to worship Him forever. She had an immensity and intensity of love that she had not known before, and that is what drove her desire to worship and praise God. She experienced a beautiful new way of sending and receiving love. She was infused by God's brightness and love. She said it is true there that " *'As surely as I live,' says the Lord, 'every knee will bow before me; every tongue will confess to God.'"* as it says in Romans 14:11, and in Deuteronomy 6:5: *"Love the Lord your God with all your heart and with all your soul and with all your strength."* She said that is exactly how she felt—that she loved God with absolutely everything she had. She also noted that all the questions she had on Earth that she was going to ask God when she saw Him just evaporated in heaven. She absolutely understood that in every way God's plan is perfect and it made perfect sense. (McVea 89-91)

As she journeyed toward the gates of heaven, she met a three or four year old girl. She wore a frilly summer dress with tinges of yellow and had a white bonnet and a white wicker Easter basket. She was skipping and dancing and dipping her basket in the water to fill it with brightness and then to pour it out. Crystal felt love pour out for this girl, and she want to take her in her arms and shower her with love. Then God took away that feeling and she realized the girl was her and was the way God always saw her. She saw that it said that God had been trying to show her all her life that He loved her. (McVea, 163-164)

The one question she still had for God was, "Why haven't I done more for you?" But it was a question more for herself than for God. However, she felt no regret or feeling bad, since no negatives exist in heaven. There was no answer, just the overpowering presence of God's love and acceptance. It is not that He has love, He IS Love! (McVea, 149-150)

Jesus' Appearance, Compassion, Understanding, and Control

Willie Agnes Chennault saw someone she thought to be Jesus sitting on a rock beside a field where workers were gathering wheat into bundles. He did not speak to her; He just looked at her for five seconds. But that look was transformative to the extent she has thought much about that man ever since. She describes in detail what he looked like and what he was wearing. He was about six feet tall. His eyes were like a watery blue ocean she said. His skin was gray and pink mixed. His hair was thick and bushy, the color of dark chocolate brown, was combed back from his face, and came down to his shoulders. He had a beard. He wore an eggshell color fine linen robe and dark brown sandals with straps on his feet. His legs were straight and hairy. She even described the details of His toenails, His face, and His fingers. There was half a scar on his right hand. (Chennault, 61-62, 102, 132)

Strong arms took Steven Musick in tight hug and said, "Welcome, walk with me." He knew it was Jesus Christ, Son of God. He perceived Jesus as a young man of about 35. He was clearly a male person and not a shadowy figure, figment of imagination, or floating being, but a real person. He had shoulder length dark brown hair, dark hazel soothing reassuring eyes, and a muscular and stocky build. He has strong powerful angular features, but his "mannerisms and movements are the epitome of gentleness." He glows with the light about his countenance. His hands are large, strong, supple, and powerful. He was wearing a white robe with sleeves that fell to His mid forearm, and there was a white rope tied around His waist. He had simple brown sandals on His feet. He had a soothing melodic conversational tenor voice. Then he recognized that the background music was highlighting the words of Jesus, which were not just the foreground of attention; "they *are* the foreground of attention." (Musick, 41-42)

Jesus then walked with Steven with His arm around Steven's

shoulder. They walked through the meadows, the fields of tall grasses, the hayfields that looked like they were ready to be harvested. He noticed that Jesus is compassionate with a kind of fierceness befitting the Lion of Judah. Jesus spent all their time talking about Steven. He reviewed Steven's life telling him everything that happened and why it happened. This included his childhood, his teenage years, his time in the U. S. Navy, and his time at the hospital where he died and came here. Jesus communicated that all was okay and revealed the purpose of it all, the plan that was woven through his life giving meaning to every part of it.

He understood that although he had felt alone most of his life, he had not been alone. God had been there the whole time and had been there with purpose, "guiding, providing, redeeming, protecting." Everything that had happened to him was in the end a benefit. Whenever Jesus mentioned wounds in his life, His words provided a healing over those wounds. Some of the wounds were so deep they were still unhealed. Others were deemed inconsequential until seen from the light of heaven.

He began to see things from a heavenly perspective and saw that things he thought hadn't mattered had had an effect on other people. He began to understand why his mother and father were they way they were. Jesus made everything seem okay. As Jesus revealed the emptinesses of his soul from the things that had happened to him, He filled them up. He saw that what others meant for evil, God was able to turn to good. "Nothing is ignored, no wrong is brushed aside. But His love transforms."

As they talked Jesus showed him the sovereignty of God and His provision but also His giving us complete freedom to choose the course of our lives and the attitudes we will have. But He controls the aftermath; we cannot choose the consequences of our choices. He saw how deep, attentive, encompassing, complete, and astounding Jesus' love is. God knows all that has happened; it has a purpose, nothing is wasted, and He loves us intimately. (Musick, 44)

The angel accompanying Mary K. Baxter disappeared at one point and in his place she saw Jesus. He was tall and wore a robe that was distinctive from everyone else's robe. He had a neatly trimmed beard and thick hair. His beautiful piercing eyes created a tenderness that she found it impossible to describe. His loveliness was exciting and inspired awe. Being in His presence caused everything in her to want to bow before Him and praise Him. (Baxter, 65)

Michael McCormack said Jesus was suddenly next to him in shining white clothing and His face was all light and hard to see clearly, but He had very kind eyes and was tall. Jesus took him and showed him many things in heaven. (Roth, 80)

Jesus' Deep Unconditional Love

On her second visit to heaven, Jeanne Enstad said she always sensed Jesus around her. "His loving presence was everywhere. There were no words to describe how wonderful it was there." She wanted to stay in heaven and asked why she had to leave so soon. Jesus told her He wanted her to tell His people He loves them and how beautiful and wonderful heaven is. He told her to make it known she was there for a short visit to experience as a witness the eternal home God has prepared for those who love Him and have been redeemed. He also told her to tell us that we need to be alert and get ready for His coming. (Enstad, 89)

Then she saw her three children around her bed in the hospital asking God to let her live. Jesus then gave her a choice. She could stay in heaven or she could go back. She was surprised He was giving her a choice. She wanted to stay. What she experienced in heaven is what real life is about; that is where she wanted to be. Heaven is beyond anything we will ever experience on Earth. But she wanted to take care of her children, but to do that she needed to go back. So Jesus said, "It is time for you to go back." He took her in His arms and looked into her eyes. She said she will never forget the look of deep unconditional love in His beautiful glowing eyes. She knew He loved her unconditionally and would take care of her on Earth. He told her, "Your job is to tell my people about their home in heaven, to give them hope, to bring my glory to everyone. And do not forget to express to them how much I love them." (Enstad, 90)

Jesus Has a Beautiful Laugh, Smiles Easily and Often

Dawn Cypret saw Jesus coming in her direction surrounded by people shouting, "Jehovah! Jehovah!" Both adults and young children were circling around Him. She says when you meet Him you know it is Him without anyone introducing you. There was instant recognition when their eyes met, making a soul connection. She said He is just over six feet in height, has a medium build, and his light brown hair comes to his shoulders. He has a soft beard. She said His eyes are green, not brown as you would expect, but it is an unusual shade of green. She could see them sparkle with love and humor. He was wearing a white tunic and sandals.

He called her by name and greeted her with a warm hug, in which she felt His love, peace, and joy. She felt no awkwardness or uneasiness, like He was her best friend. She looked at His hands and saw the scars in the fleshy part of His hands between the palm and wrist. She felt an overwhelming sorrow and regret for what He had to endure to take her shame and sin on the cross. Yet Jesus took away her pain and sorrow and filled her with overwhelming emotion of love. She says absolutely nothing compares with the love Jesus has for us. It was actually easier for Him to go through the agony of the crucifixion than to see us suffer without the hope of Calvary.

Amid all the beauty and love she knew again she had to go back home. Jesus said she is home. She then explained why she needed to go back. She looked in His eyes and saw a twinkle, and then He laughed with a beautiful laugh. He then told her, "You know most people are begging to get into heaven and yet, here you are begging to leave. I may have created you to be short in stature, but I certainly made you spunky!"

He then took her on a walk as her parents smiled and waved goodbye. The first thing that happened is like a wall disappeared and she could see into the hospital. She saw her family in the waiting room. She wanted to comfort them but could not. She was close enough that she could touch them and feel, not just hear but feel, their prayers for her. Jesus felt their anguish and held Dawn close. (May, 24-26)

Later when He showed her the mansions of heaven, she said she has never been with anyone who smiles as easily and as often as Jesus does. (May, 28)

At one point He walked up to a wall and when He touched it, a large portion of the wall just disappeared. After they stepped through the opening, the wall closed up like it was before with absolutely no evidence of having ever been parted or even capable of parting. Dawn noticed that although Jesus was sweet and loving (her words), He was also all-powerful with the ability to create and destroy at will with just the touch of His hand. (May, 29-30)

Jesus Is Rugged But Handsome, His Eyes Striking

When Jim Woodford first saw Jesus, the angels were bowing to a figure taller than the tallest angel with robes brighter and more radiant than theirs. A golden light emanated from Him flowing up and out and onto everything around Him. When the light touched the flowers they bloomed brighter and grew taller, stretching upward toward him. Golden light flowed like liquid from Him. It flowed down the path and pooled around Jim's feet, filling him with the knowledge that this was indeed Jesus the Christ, Son of the Living God. Jim did not initially see Jesus' face, but he saw that His robe was a beautiful seamless white garment with a red sash. The angels bowed to Him and all became quiet. Then Jesus turned to him and he could see face to face with Jesus.

Seeing Jesus' face was the highlight of Jim's trip to heaven. He was ruggedly handsome but nevertheless human. His hair was brown and curled just over the collar of His robe. Jesus smiled at him with a most radiant, beautiful, loving smile. It was beautiful, and Jim felt the warmth of the smile flowing through him. The smile exhibited unconditional love even though Jesus knew everything about him, including all his rebellion and waywardness. The most striking aspect of Jesus' face was His eyes. They flashed blue, gold, and green, and were filled with relentless love for Jim. Even though Jim had squandered his life ignoring Jesus and never giving Him any attention or respect, in His eyes was sadness and sorrow for those who had never acknowledged Him and had spent their lives apart from Him, but His love and acceptance of Jim (and all of us wayward children) was so great it brought Jim to tears. The love was so strong that it still gives him tears years later.

The tall angel took a very thin book from his sleeve and handed it to Jesus. He knew it was the book of the record of his life. There were very few entries of his kindnesses or love he had shown to someone. He had spent his life on himself, ignoring the needs of those around him. The angel turned his face to Jim and with those violet eyes communicated the thought, "James, what did you do with the life my Master gave you?" As he stood face to face with Jesus, he had deep despair, wondering how he could stand in the presence of such love. But Jesus never commented on the thinness of the book but only exhibited love and acceptance, no shame or judgment. The shame and judgment was Jim's own assessment of himself. In the midst of this encounter there flowed from Jesus joy! It was His heart's desire to impart joy to Jim. As Jesus read the pages, the scenes of Jim's life appeared before him, scenes from his childhood to the recent present. After He finished reading he said, "James," and held out His hand to him palm up. Jim tried to move but couldn't, he was frozen in awe. Jim then saw the radiant light from His garment shine out through a hole in his wrist, the wound from when Jesus took the nail to the cross to pay for all Jim's sin and waywardness. He was filled with an overwhelming sense of profound sadness, guilt and shame. It was so personal an experience that Jim could almost feel himself hammering the nail into Jesus' wrist. But Jesus just looked at him with compassion and love!

Then Jesus spoke to him by name, called him His son, and told him it is not his time. He was to go back and tell his brothers and sisters the wonders He had shown him. Jim's whole perspective had been changed from only being interested in himself to now wanting to fulfill his new commission and live out the love of Jesus in the rest of his life for all to see and be changed themselves. But he had to depend on the grace of God for this task, as he was totally unprepared to fulfill it on his own. Now he carries heaven in his heart and recalls Jesus' eyes when he looks into the eyes of others. Jim did not want to leave Jesus' presence and tried to follow Him, but the angels held him back. Soon he found himself traveling back through the tunnel and back into his earthly body. (Woodford, 123-130)

So if you haven't read or heard Jim's message to his brothers and sisters, I am sharing with you the wonders Jim had been shown so your heart can be transformed also.

Jesus Is Unconditional Love

When Betty Eadie went to heaven, she approached a pinpoint of light that grew in intensity until she was standing in the presence of

Jesus. As her light merged with His, she felt as if she had stepped into His countenance and felt an explosion of love.

She felt the most unconditional love she had ever felt. She went to Him as she saw His arms open to receive her. She received His complete embrace and said over and over, "I'm home. I'm home. I'm finally home." (Eadie, 41) She then spends the next thirty-one pages writing about what Jesus explained to her, mysteries no one else I have read has repeated. At the end of her encounter with Jesus, she says, "I'll never forget the Lord's sense of humor, which was as delightful and quick as any here—far more so. Nobody could outdo his humor. He is filled with perfect happiness and perfect goodwill. There is a softness and grace in His presence, and I had no doubt he is a perfect man." (Eadie, 72-73) It is good to see an actual observance of Jesus' good sense of humor.

When Ian McCormack, an atheist until the last minute of his life, came into Jesus' presence, he wanted to turn away because he realized he didn't deserve to be there. He understood that Jesus knew his name, knew all his thoughts, and could see everything he had ever done. He wanted to hide or go back down the tunnel. But wave after wave of pure light and love started flooding over him, love that was pure, unadulterated, clean, uninhibited, and undeserved. It was filling him up from the inside out making his hands and body tingle. He began to weep uncontrollably as the love became stronger and stronger. Everything he thought was love on Earth was nothing compared to the love he was feeling. He didn't see how God could love him after all the sins he had committed. As God's love poured over him with each thought of his sins, he stood there weeping in God's presence. He learned his forgiveness was assured when he asked for forgiveness seconds before he died. As he stood there the waves quit and he was bathed in light and love. He pondered stepping into the light, thinking if he could get closer to God he would know the truth he had been seeking all his life. No one said he couldn't so he stepped through the light and the light continued to heal the deepest part of him, his broken inner man, his broken heart. He saw the bare feet of a man with dazzling white garments and light seemingly coming from every pore of His face in brilliance, purity, and holiness. The radiant light was so intense he could not make out the features of Jesus' face. But Jesus held out his arms for him as purity and holiness radiated from Jesus' face and began to fill Ian up with purity and holiness. (Roth, 70-73, Sharkey, 29-31)

"Tell My people I am coming soon. I love them."

Richard Sigmund said that while everything in heaven is beautiful, it all pales in comparison with just the sight of Jesus and His wonderful face. (Sigmund, 40) He would get a glimpse of Jesus many times just a little way ahead as he traveled down the pathway he was on. He saw Jesus talking with people, loving them, and hugging them. They were looking at Him with adoration and worship. It made Richard want to fall at His feet. But the angel who was guiding him told him he had to go a little further down the path. Then he would have an appointment with God and meet with the Lord. He was eager to be with Jesus, but he knew he had to wait. He knew that when it was his turn to meet Jesus, it would be a glorious moment of ecstasy. It seemed like Jesus could be in front of him and also behind him. Jesus could move at the speed of light and seemed to be everywhere all at once. (Sigmund, 29)

He saw an auditorium that was an announcement center. He saw the Lord Himself on stage there, but Jesus was with him also. He could look down and see Jesus as He was with groups of people walking through the air. He could see Jesus in all these places at once. In heaven, Jesus is omnipresent. Jesus was able instantly, at the right moment, to be on the stage of that auditorium, which seemed to have seated ten million people. He was there, always, and right now. (Sigmund, 84)

At one point he saw Jesus coming his way. Richard fell on his face before Jesus, and when Jesus was a few feet in front of him, he noticed the holes in Jesus' feet where the nails had been. A beautiful light shone through them from the inside. Jesus touched him and helped him stand. Jesus told him to look at Him and said, "I love you. Even though you have been disobedient and haven't done what I have told you to do, I still love you, and I desire for you to tell My people about this place called heaven. I desire for you to tell My people the glorious things My Father has made for them, that they might want to come here. I have chosen you and ordained you for this one work … Tell My people I am coming soon. I love them." Then Richard saw His hands with the nail scars. They were open and a beautiful light was shining through. He also saw that his name was carved in Jesus' hands. Then Richard knew what Isaiah 49:16a meant. *"See, I have engraved you on the palms of my hands."* (NIV) (Sigmund, 76-77)

Richard said he was aware of thousands of people listening to what Jesus was saying to him. He told him about people who were currently in his life and those who would later come into his life. He told him some very personal and private things about his life. He told him some of the troubles and heartaches he would have—the things he would go through. Jesus told him that great revivals were about to spring out in His church. He was going to cause revivals to come in small places, and that Richard would be on Earth to see them.

At the end of his book, *My Time in Heaven*, the page "About the Author" has the following: "Over the years, Richard preached the gospel through television programs, radio broadcasts, and speaking engagements. He was in meetings with Kathryn Kuhlman and Oral Roberts, and was interviewed by Pat Robertson. Richard ministered in England, Scotland, Australia, South Africa, Kenya, and many other countries. In South Africa, he followed David Nunn and Morris Cerullo in a special series of meetings. It was Rex Humbard who encouraged him to tell his story of a place called heaven." So what Jesus told him did come to pass as He said. Richard died permanently in 2010.

He also talked to Richard of many other things.

Jesus said his Father wanted him to see the other place. Richard dreaded the thought and did not want to go, but Jesus said there is no disobedience in heaven. So Richard was ready to go. He knew he would be perfectly safe because he was with Jesus. Then Jesus picked him up and carried him like a baby. When he was pressed against Jesus' body there was no give to it; He felt as hard as steel. Richard felt that Jesus has all-powerful arms and is the strongest being in the universe. (Sigmund, 115-116)

Jesus' Overwhelming Love

Just outside the hospital where Howard Storm died he was enticed by some demons to follow them. At first he thought they were legitimate hospital staff, but finally he knew they were deceiving him. They were torturing him until he called out the name of God in prayer. Jesus came to him as a pinprick of light at first. In Jesus presence he experienced a love of greater intensity than he had ever known, an intensity greater than all human love put together. He knew this person of blinding glory loved him with overwhelming power and also completely knew him and accepted him. He cried and cried tears of joy as Jesus held him and filled him with love. As they approached the city of light, the experience of Jesus' love totally changed Howard from the inside out. When he was in the presence of Jesus, he was aware of all the wrong he had done and felt the intensity of God's love. He felt he didn't belong there. He felt like garbage, filthy rags, in the presence of the Holy One. He thought to himself, "I don't belong here!" But Jesus spoke directly to his mind and said, "We don't make mistakes, and you do belong here." (Storm, 26-29)

Jesus summoned angels and together with the angels explained many things to Howard. They told him God knows everything that could and will happen, but everything has to express its own will. Every action fulfills God's purpose by fulfilling its nature. The outcome of its activity from negative to positive will always fulfill God's purpose no matter how long it takes or how impossible it appears. They explained that we do not need to know how or why things happen. We are to discover our part of God's divine plan He wants us to fulfill. They communicated many other bits of knowledge about God and His Creation, will, and plan, that I'll not detail here. (Storm, 38-48)

Endless Kindness and Compassion

While Mary Neal was recovering in the hospital, she visited heaven two more times. In the second of these visits, Jesus was sitting next to her on the rock on which she was sitting. She knew in her innermost being that it was Jesus without asking who He was. In being asked what He looked like, all she can say is He looked like endless kindness and compassion. As to the colors of His hair, eyes, and skin, she said there are not words in English to describe what she saw. The fact that he looks like endless kindness and compassion is natural in the kingdom of heaven in ways we cannot comprehend here. She said He was endlessly patient, endlessly gentle, and mesmerizing. He was light of spirit and had a sense of humor. Others have spoken of Jesus' sense of humor also, including Dawn Cypret and Betty Eadie. She asked Jesus a lot of questions to which He gave answers that communicated a complete understanding of the universe and all our interconnectedness. Everything was logically interwoven and magnificent while she was there. But after returning to her body, a lot of that knowledge was gone, not in the capacity of her earthly mind to comprehend. When she was with Him she did not want to be anyplace else. (Neal 2017, 47-48)

Markers

Colton Burpo said Jesus had the angels sing to him because he was so scared and that made him feel better. From this comment, his father first got the impression that Jesus had been there, and he asked Colton if that is what he meant. Colton nodded and said he was sitting in Jesus' lap. (Burpo, xix)

His dad asked what Jesus looked like. Colton said he had red markers, which was his word for the wounds in His hands and feet. When Todd asked about the markers, Colton pointed to his hands and feet. (Burpo, 67) Later his dad showed him Akiane Kramarik's painting Prince of Peace (Kramarik, 58) and after a pensive pause he said that is what Jesus looks like. None of the other paintings had been acceptable. Todd Burpo added that Akiane said Jesus is pure, very strong, big and masculine, and his eyes are beautiful. (Burpo, 143-145)

Colton referred to Jesus having a beard and said His eyes "are so pretty", and when he said this, he had a dreamy reflection. Todd also asked about Jesus' clothes. Colton described white with a purple sash by giving a gesture of where it was. He also said that Jesus was the only one with a purple sash. Then he described Jesus' crown as a circle over his head with something like a diamond in the middle. (Burpo, 65-67)

"You *are* worthy"

Dr. Gary Wood was completely overwhelmed when he saw Jesus, and he fell at His feet. He said Jesus is about six feet two inches tall and looks Jewish with olive skin. His hair has curls along the side of His face, which matches Akiane Kramarik's painting Prince of Peace that Colton Burpo said looked just like Jesus. He said He wore a pure white robe of righteousness with a purple sash, again matching Colton's description. His eyes were deep, beautiful, blue pools of love. He was wearing a crown, as Colton described. He saw the nail prints in His wrists and the nail prints in His feet, which had been nailed crossed together. The crown of thorns left indentations in His brow. Jesus' wounds He endured for us are the only wounds visible in heaven. All the wounds of the rest of us will be totally healed there.

A radiant beautiful light came from Him. His eyes pierced Dr. Wood with love that went all the way through him. When He spoke, it was the same as the sound of water flowing over Niagara Falls. Jesus said we all have a purpose for being here in this life: a song to sing, a message to proclaim, a missionary journey to take, a book to write. (I am fulfilling that last purpose right now!) Jesus said, "Don't ever believe the condemnation of the devil that you are unworthy. You *are* worthy. You have been redeemed by the blood of the Lamb."

Jesus' words were so powerful, Dr. Wood fell at His feet. Jesus reached down and picked him up and continued talking to him. Jesus said, "I will be your focus in heaven. You will worship and enjoy Me forever. Heaven is My Creation for you. And I will be the center of it all." Dr. Wood said that after being with Jesus, everything else in heaven, as wonderful as it was, pales by comparison. (Roth, 106-108)

In his own book he wrote that Jesus' eyes were the bluest he had ever seen. His hair and beard are white as snow. When Jesus lifted him up, he lifted him up into his arms and Gary felt the most wonderful, joyful, peaceful, powerful love he had ever experienced. He said even though his book is about heaven, it is in reality about Jesus. Heaven is all about Him and His Father. They are the source of all the light and love in heaven that makes it the wonderful, joyful place that it is. "Oh, what glory awaits those of us who know Jesus!" Gary said he wants to spend a thousand years just sitting at Jesus' feet. Jesus told him never to accept Satan's accusation that he is unworthy. Jesus told him he is worthy; he has been bought with the blood of the Lamb. He has things to do here on Earth: a song to sing, a missionary journey to take, a book to write. God has a purpose for him (and each of us) to be here for now and won't be called to heaven until those tasks have been completed. Jesus said his soon return would be accompanied by a Spirit of restoration, a Spirit of prayer, and an outburst of miracles. (Wood, 38-40)

Jesus has Beautiful Eyes and More Love Than You Can Imagine

When Jesus appeared to Mary K. Baxter in her first divine revelation, she saw Him in a glistening white robe, full of light and power. She thought Him to be about six feet tall and His beard was neatly trimmed. His thick hair came down to His shoulders. She said His eyes were beautiful (as Colton Burpo said) and piercing. She said He has more love and compassion for us than we can know. (Baxter, 120)

Kat Kerr said when she met Jesus she was consumed by His glory and everything else faded away. The radiance of His beauty engulfed her. Perfect peace washed over her and wave after wave of love flowed through her entire being. (Kerr 2007, xviii-xix)

"You are in the presence of *the* Son of God."

George Ritchie never made it to heaven after he died in an army hospital in west Texas in 1943. He first experienced confusing out-of-body situations: traveling fast over the ground, above cities, not being able to touch anything, not being recognized by anyone he met, then searching for his body in the hospital barracks. At that point, Jesus came to him.

The light in the room began to change, and he suddenly saw that it was brighter, a lot brighter, than it had been. He looked at the night-light on the bedside table and saw that it could not turn out that much light.

He was astonished as the brightness increased, seeming to come from nowhere but shine everywhere at once. It was so bright all the lightbulbs in the ward, even the world, could not give off that much light. It seemed impossibly bright, like a million welders' lamps, all burning at once. Then he saw that it was not a light but a man who had entered the room or, rather, a man made out of light.

Then the instant he perceived this, he received an authoritative command in his mind. "Stand up!" He stood up and heard in his mind, "You are in the presence of *the* Son of God."

Again, the message just seemed to form itself inside his mind, but not as thought or speculation. It was an immediate and complete knowing. He knew other facts about Him too. One was that this was the most totally male Being he had ever met. He knew that if this was *the* Son of God, His name was Jesus. But this Jesus was power itself, older

109

than time yet more modern than anyone he had ever met, not the gentle, kind, understanding Jesus—and probably a little bit of a weakling he had imagined from Sunday School.

But above all, he knew this Man loved him. Far more than power, what emanated from him was unconditional love, astonishing love, love beyond his wildest imagination. This love knew every unlovable thing about him—the quarrel with his stepmother, his explosive temper, the sex thoughts he could never control, and every mean, selfish thought and action since the day he was born—and accepted and loved him just the same. (Ritchie, 48-50)

Then Jesus took him to see what happens to people who die without Him. All during this experience, he found the presence of Jesus' love was so overpowering, he did not want to leave. However, after showing him all the things he wanted him to see, he took George Ritchie back to his body in a medical miracle of healing so he could tell the world about Jesus and what happens when we leave here. He saw heaven from a long distance, but never got there.

The Light of Jesus

When Betty Malz was walking beside the wall and came to a gate, the angel stepped forward and pressed his palm on the gate. As he did this, an opening appeared in the center of the pearl and slowly widened and deepened as though the translucent material was dissolving. Beyond the gate, through the opening, Betty Malz saw what appeared to be a street of golden color with an overlay of glass or water. Then she became aware of a golden light that was dazzling. She said she can't describe it with human language. She saw no figure, but was conscious of a Person. Suddenly, she knew the light was Jesus.

The light of Jesus was all about her, and there seemed to be some heat in it. It was like she was standing in sunlight, and her body began to glow. She said every part of her was absorbing the light. The rays of a powerful, penetrating, loving energy bathed her. (Malz, 87-88)

This is not like some of the others that met Jesus face to face. But still she met him in his radiant light.

It's in His Book

Richard Eby met Jesus five years after his visit to heaven when the lights went out visiting the cave of the tomb of Lazarus. He described Jesus as a fantastically beautiful human figure, about six feet tall. His face was too magnificent to describe. He was absolute divinity, but both merciful and judicial. He put his arm around Richard so that he was permeated by a hug of love. (Roth, 175)

When Richard was in heaven after his accident, Jesus spoke with him as they walked/flew in heaven. Jesus called him by his name, "Dick," and said He is personal with Richard because His death on the cross for him was personal, and when he accepted Jesus he became part of Jesus' body. Whenever Richard asked a question, which was instantaneous, Jesus' answer formed in him just as instantly. With many of the questions, Jesus said He answered that it is in His book. "Didn't you read My book?" He would say. Space is limitless in heaven, and Richard asked Jesus how large an area is designated for each individual. Jesus said He only gives them the desires of their hearts as He said in His book. He said His book explains everything a child of His needs to know. (Roth, 171-172) (So maybe that means you don't need to read this book, just study Revelation 21 and other passages that describe God's kingdom. But it is my hope that while this book supports all the Bible says, it makes the Biblical description more understandable and fills in gaps that are left out. Yes, you don't need this amplification but in many ways it is helpful and a blessing. Furthermore, God appears to want us to have this testimony because He continues giving people eyewitness accounts of His kingdom for them to bring back to Earth before going there permanently. He told some He is coming back very soon and He wants His people ready.)

A Child's View

On June 15, 2000, four-year-old Kennedy Buettner was at the bottom of a swimming pool for almost fifteen minutes. He was given CPR and rushed to a hospital where he recovered. When he was dead, an angel took him through walls (and people) to heaven. He was able to describe many things he saw, but they were not reported in James Garlow's book. He said he saw Jesus and lots of angels and people, and they were all happy. He saw his uncle Mark. He said he looked like Jesus and all his "boo-boos" were gone. He saw a door with jewels on it and snow on the other side of the door. He was on the edge of a volcano with a Pokemon (dragon) in it. The dragon was happy but growled at him. In the volcano were lots of very sad people. His uncle Mark pushed him back to his body. He told his mom that Jesus is coming back here. Many of these things he said belong in other chapters, but because this story is so brief, I decided to tell all of it here. (Garlow, 37, 41-42)

Diane Komp reports in *A Window to Heaven: When Children See Life in Death* that children frequently report seeing Jesus or angels. A four-year-old Asian boy whose family was not Christian was visited by an angel, and as a result he called the hospital staff, thanked each one, said good-bye, and then lay down and died. Another of her patients, Tom, a nineteen-year-old cancer patient, saw a beautiful garden with a man on a bench whose fingers looked like roses, and the man touched him, and he was able to move for the first time since becoming quadriplegic from the cancer. He did not want to leave the garden but the man told him he could not come with Him yet. He knew the man was Jesus. Diane sang the song *In the Garden* to him, and although he had been unfamiliar with the song, he was excited by the words as they mirrored his experience with Jesus. (Komp, 41-44)

Other Encounters with Jesus

Robert Misst said Jesus' entire being was a radiance of love and mercy. Even though he is the King of Kings, he treated everyone with love, honor, and respect. He went to one of those who came out of the great tribulation and placed a crown on his head, even though the person said he did not deserve it. (Roth, 124-125)

William Smith didn't talk about meeting Jesus in person like these others, but he did have an encounter with Jesus in which he had the sense that Jesus was in him, and he was in Jesus, and that settled everything. As he went inside Jesus, he became a part of His love. He said seeing Jesus was not as important as knowing Him and hearing Him. He saw His radiant sovereign glory, power, and righteousness. He was able to experience the spiritual truth that the Father, Son, and Spirit are all one in a way that is hard to visualize on Earth. (Roth, 158-159)

David Taylor was amazed to see how humble Jesus is. You would expect Him to want center stage, but David saw Jesus allow saints who were present give David a message rather than Jesus Himself giving it. (Taylor, 159)

Dr. Scott Kolbaba relates a story from Dr. Thomas Marshall of a patient named Barbara who at age fifteen began developing symptoms of muscular dystrophy. The disease waxed and waned over the years but kept getting worse. She was eventually blind, unable to use her arms and legs, had trouble breathing, had a collapsed lung, and a tracheostomy. She was under hospice care and expected to die soon. Her church was praying for her, and her story was told on WMBI with prayer requests. The response from the WMBI airing was so great there were bags of mail of letters and prayers. She had friends there with her and in a lull in the conversation she heard a clear, articulate man's voice behind her speak with great authority and compassion, "My child, get up and walk!" Barbara turned but didn't see anyone, but she knew it was Jesus who had spoken to her and knew she needed to respond right away. She called for her parents and jumped out of bed, removed her oxygen mask, and starting jumping about the room on perfectly strong legs. She had been totally healed of all effects of her muscular dystrophy and was perfectly normal. (Kolbaba, 115-122)

Don Piper did not see Jesus because, as he says, he was never allowed beyond the gate and could only peer in. But even outside the gate he was bathed in the glory of the Father and the Son from the throne at the center of the city. (Piper 2018, 132)

Summary

Jesus *is* heaven. Jesus and His Father are what heaven is all about. Their presence, power, love, and grace permeate everything. Everyone who comes to Jesus in heaven is awed, deeply moved, and can't help but praise Him forever and ever. Everything in heaven shows God's and Jesus' creative power and deep love. No one who experiences the depth of Jesus' love for him/her ever wants to be separated from Him. That is true when he/she meets Him as well as in heaven, but in heaven, the love is more intense, constant, and permanent. Those who have had the chance to visit heaven, really look forward to being back there forever.

When Colton Burpo visited a dying man in the hospital with his dad, Colton told the man, "It's going to be okay. The first person you are going to see is Jesus." (Burpo, 119) Jesse Duplantis said of his visit to heaven that the first person you are going to see is father Abraham, as that is the first person he saw there. But from all these accounts I have read, there is no one person you are first going to meet. Samaa Habib and Colton Burpo first saw Jesus, but others had to wait to meet him. It appears that this, just like everything else of your heavenly experience, will be what God has chosen for you. The first person you meet there may be a family member, old friend, Jesus, Biblical figure, or whomever. But it will be the ideal experience for the person God made you to be, who you have been, what life you have lived, and what God has prepared for you in Heaven. It is clear, though, that you will be greeted by your welcoming committee. No one comes into heaven alone; there will be one or more loving persons there to welcome you. But at some point, you will get to meet Jesus and be profoundly affected by His love.

In addition to feeling Jesus love and unconditional acceptance, many are amazed at Jesus' humor, smiles, and laughter. He is apparently a lot of fun to be around on top of his love and acceptance.

CHAPTER 11
Meeting Family & Friends

Don Piper Meets Many

The most extensive experience of meeting people in heaven in the books I have read is that of Don Piper, who had ninety Earth minutes there. As he arrived in heaven, he saw people he had known. As they surged toward him, he recognized that all of them had died during his lifetime. Each one had played a significant role in his life, shaping him into the man of God that Jesus wanted him to be. (Piper 2018, 4) They rushed toward him, full of joy, smiling, shouting, and praising God. He recognized they were his celestial welcoming committee. He got the impression they knew he was coming and had all gathered outside heaven's gate, waiting for him.

He first recognized his grandfather, Joe Kulbeth. With his shock of white hair and big banana nose, he looked exactly as Don remembered him. A grin covered his grandfather's face when he stopped in front of him. His grandfather called out to him, "Donnie!" the name his grandfather always used for him. As his grandfather stepped toward him, his eyes lit up and he held out his arms. His grandfather embraced him tightly. He had regained his strong robustness Don remembered as a child. Don had an ecstatic bliss when his grandfather released him, and Don stared into his face. Don experienced great joy in their reunion. How either of them reached heaven was irrelevant.

He doesn't remember who was second or third. The crowd surrounded him with some hugging him, some kissing his cheek, and others pumping his hand. He felt more love than he ever had before. The love of Jesus and the Father and of friends and relatives is perhaps the most common experience of heaven.

One of those he met was Jan Cowart. She was one of three young people who came to his house and invited him to their church. That was the beginning of his journey into a relationship with Christ and growing in it. (Piper 2018, 35-44)

Mike Wood, his childhood friend, was one of those greeting him. Mike was special to Don because he invited him to Sunday school and had an influential part in his becoming a Christian. Mike was the most devoted young Christian he knew, and he lived the Christian lifestyle he often talked about.

Mike died at age nineteen in a car wreck, and it devastated Don. When Don attended his funeral, he wondered if he would ever stop crying. He was always sad about it and couldn't understand why God would let it happen. But now that he saw Mike in heaven, he had joy, seeing Mike smile more brightly than he ever had. He still didn't know why Mike had to die, but the joyousness of the place wiped away any questions. He said everything felt blissful and perfect.

So many more people reached for him and called him by name, he felt overwhelmed by the welcome to heaven he received. There were so many, and they were all happier than any he knew on Earth. Their faces radiated serenity, and all were full of life and expressed radiant joy.

They included Charlie Dingman, who showed Don how to believe God against circumstances when he stood his ground for a larger church building when membership was dwindling because he had faith in what would come. And it did before Charlie died. Also there was Sue Belle Guyton, the mother of his best friend who always showed him the love, acceptance, and wisdom of Christ. His Grandma Nellie was there. She had lived through poverty and trying times after her husband died but never wavered in her faith. When he saw his great-grandparents, J. R. and Hattie Mann, they radiated a joy and happiness beyond any he had seen, even though they had always been loving, generous, and kind, and an inspiration to him. J. R.'s missing fingers were back and Hattie now had all her natural teeth. They had complete physical healing and wholeness. They beamed with real smiles Don had not seen and were enormously happy and contented. The last one he mentions is his high school speech teacher Charlotte Jaynes, who had a major influence in helping him have the spiritual grounding to stay on course through the temptations of college life. (Piper 2018, 56-110)

He points out that there will always be someone there to meet you who has been told you are coming. When a lady mentioned to him her son did not know any Christians and had only recently become a Christian, Don told her in that case Jesus himself would meet her son. (Probably some angels would be there, too, and there may be people you never knew that had a part in your life.) (Piper 2018, 116-117)

He also saw and heard his great-grandfather, who embraced him, saying how excited he was that Don had come to join them. He saw high-school classmate Barry Wilson, who had drowned in a lake. Barry's hug and smile radiated a happiness Don didn't know was possible. Everyone praised God and told him how excited they were to see him as they welcomed him into heaven and to the fellowship they enjoyed.

He saw two teachers who had loved him and often talked to him about Jesus Christ. Among those that welcomed him there was a wide variety of ages—old and young and every age in-between. Many of them hadn't known each other on Earth, but each had influenced Don's life in some way. Even though they had never met on Earth, they seemed to know each other now. Others have observed that in heaven everyone knows everyone else's name, and it is like a huge, happy family.

His experience of unimaginable joy, excitement, warmth, and total happiness exceeded his capacity to explain it in Earth language. His words seemed weak and hardly adequate. Everyone continually embraced him, touched him, spoke to him, laughed, and praised God. This went on for a long time, but it never became tiresome.

Don's father had ten siblings, and some of them had as many as thirteen children. When he was a kid, their family reunions were so huge they rented an entire city park in Monticello, Arkansas. All members of his family are affectionate, and there was a lot of hugging and kissing whenever they came together. But none of those Earthly reunions compared with the sublime gathering of saints he experienced at the gates of heaven. Heaven has many things, but without a doubt, to him it was the greatest family reunion of all. (Piper 2004, 22-25)

Dale Reppert Meets Many Loved Ones

When Dale Reppert first arrived in heaven, he began to see the faces of loved ones who had passed on in heaven. (Reppert, 53) He met several of his family members who had died. His mother was to his left. She was smiling and at ease with herself, something Dale does not remember her being in this life, having lived for twenty years with the pain of debilitating arthritis. Now she was pain-free and full of peace and happiness. She didn't show her age at death of 71, but instead was in the beauty of youth. The wrinkles and lines of age were gone, and she looked beautiful.

To his right was his uncle Ray. Dale found his smile from his moon-like face to be reassuring and encouraging. He appeared to be in his mid-forties, though he had died in his seventies. He had always been joking and laughing and now he was even more so, looking forward to horsing around with Dale and acting like a kid.

Then he saw his paternal grandmother Katie and then his maternal grandfather Roy, whom he was surprised to see since his grandfather lived a rather questionable, immoral life. Maybe there was a deathbed conversion Dale never heard about.

After that he saw many others but could not discern any facial features because they were too far away. Some were family members; some were complete strangers. Based on the other stories here, all had some part in his Earthly life. The presence of all of them was calming to him. He felt a peace and tranquility from all of them that he had not known before. The brilliant light and the presence of all these family and friends completely ridded him of all pain, fear, and anxiety. (Reppert, 55-56)

Rebecca Springer's Brother-in-law and Others

Rebecca Springer mentioned meeting family and friends individually throughout her book *Within Heaven's Gates*. First of all, her brother-in-law, Frank, met her and escorted her to heaven as described in Chapter 1.

As she was traveling to see her heavenly home, she heard a familiar voice and saw her dear friend, Mrs. Wickham. They met in a warm embrace. She said she heard Rebecca was coming and couldn't wait to see her. (Springer, 17)

Next she met her father and mother. She saw them coming through the long room toward her. Her youngest sister was with them. She eagerly embraced her father's outstretched arms and heard his dear, familiar, "my precious daughter!" Then she and her mother hugged with her sister joining in. It was a happy union of their united love. She never dreamed heaven could hold so much joy. (Springer, 28-29)

Frank left allowing them to enjoy their reunion. He said he had other business to which to attend. This is evidence we will not be bored in heaven; we will have pleasurable tasks to perform. In the chapter on children, you will see children in heaven have schoolwork to do.

Next she met her niece, Mae, with whom she later had other adventures. She thought her niece had grown very beautiful. Rebecca said she was always lovely, but she is simply radiant now. She asked if this is the divine life? She answered that it is, but it is more due to being near Jesus so much. (Springer, 31)

She went on to meet Oliver, the husband of her eldest sister. Then she met Mary Bates, who was told of Rebecca's presence by both the Lord and Mae. This was followed later by her old friend, Mrs. Wickham, again, followed by her friend Mary Green, and then finally her husband. This is a little confusing, because her husband was still on Earth as far as I can tell from the beginning of the story. Perhaps it is because there is no time in heaven; it is always "now." The past and future are "now" in heaven, so I think she was seeing the future. Others have seen something from the future also. Colton Burpo saw his dad as a future warrior in the final overthrow of Satan. (Burpo, 136-139) Michael McCormack saw the future barren and lifeless Earth destroyed by man's sin. (Roth, 83-84). Maybe others have seen the future too. In the realm where time is no longer linear, we apparently can experience past and future mixed up with the present. God is "I Am," and I guess in heaven "we are."

Richard Sigmund Learns His Grandpa Had Been Praying for Him

Richard was taken to a large theater where there was a testimonial service going on that he said was going to last for eternity. He heard someone testify about praying for his grandson thirty-five years before he was born and that he began in ministry at an early age and was a blessing to many people. Richard wanted to meet the person he was talking about. Then he was led to an area like a stage and saw his grandpa was the man who had been speaking. His grandpa pointed to him and said, "There he is now." His grandma was there, too, along with his grandpa's two brothers. They had their families and many more people Richard had never seen. (Sigmund, 46)

Dale Black's Spiritual Family

When Dale Black was at the gate, a group of people in soft white seamless robes gathered to his left in the grass along the pathway. He didn't know who they were or why they were there. Then suddenly he understood they had assembled for him. They were his spiritual family who had traveled from other places to be here to welcome him. They knew his name although he didn't know theirs. They knew the story behind his name. Their faces showed excitement at seeing him and welcoming him. They made Dale feel very special and loved, more loved than he had ever experienced before, and it gave him a deep sense of belonging. Somehow they knew Dale, the real person he is, not the one he tried to project himself to be on Earth. He was unaccustomed to receiving so much love and acceptance. He felt more unconditional love than he ever had in this life. They loved and accepted him even though he had never done anything for them. "They were vessels of God's love, both individually and collectively." When he looked at the crowd, he saw their eyes were more colorful, their smiles were brighter and their countenances more alive, than any he had known on Earth. Each person was a vibrant being exuding the life of God. None were skinny, none overweight, none crippled or bent, none old, none young, no wrinkles, no sagging, no sign of aging at all. They seemed to be about thirty years of age. He said although some form of time seems to exist, it is not like Earth time and no one ages. Their skin tones were different, but he did not notice any racial differences. They were recognized by their spirit, the essence of who they were, not by physical or social distinctions. They were full of pure life and connected to the light, which led to God. (Black 2010, 107-108)

The joy he was experiencing was also due in part to the absence of strife, competition, sarcasm, betrayal, deception, lies, murders, unfaithfulness, disloyalty, or anything contrary to life, light, and love. He said the absence of sin was something you could feel. There was no shame and nothing of which to be ashamed. There was no sadness and nothing about which to be sad. There was no need to hide. Everything was out in the open, clean and pure. Other authors talked about communication being by thought, so I suppose in that case one couldn't hide in thought either. He said here was utter perfection and the absence of sin and all its effects was astounding and exhilarating. He contemplated that sin dominates and infects everything on Earth and its total absence in heaven is a large part of his perception of the perfection there. The best unity he experienced on Earth did not come close to comparing with the oneness he felt in heaven with his spiritual family. The boundless love of God and its affect on everything there was transforming and sacred. He felt so special in the presence of all his wonderful spiritual family with their radiant joyful loving faces. He knew they had something very special for him and he anticipated going through the gate and receiving it. (Black 2010, 109-110)

Meeting Grandparents

Dean Braxton saw Jesus standing to his left at about the ten or eleven o'clock position. While Jesus addressed a half-circle of people, Dean saw his family on the left side of Him. He saw his Grandmother Mary, Grandfather Lewis, Grandmother Ruth, Grandfather Begron, and many of his aunts and uncles. He saw friends some of whom he knew had died and others he did not know had died. He also saw generations and generations of relatives he had never seen on Earth, but he knew they were his relatives and that they had died. He did not know why they were gathered there, but his Grandmother Mary explained to him (communicated by thought) that they came to greet him into heaven. He said every family member with whom he shared DNA was there.

He saw past friends that came to his welcoming party that greeted him into heaven. It would have been a great family reunion if Jesus had not sent him back to Earth, but he did, and that was because others here on Earth were praying that his body would be healed. Now even thinking about that welcoming reunion, brings him great joy. (Braxton, 134)

In front of Marvin Besteman was a long line of perhaps thirty-five people waiting to go through the door. Everyone was smiling and knew where they were. They didn't have a look of shock or awe but of deep, thorough contentment with peace, joy, and perfect happiness. He saw people from many nationalities and tribes, including northern Europe, Asia, Africa, and the Middle East. (Besteman, 75)

Though he was not allowed through the gate, he saw inside his fraternal grandparents, his mother, two friends, and his stepson. They all looked more alive, more whole, healthier, and fuller of energy, than they ever did on Earth. They were all wearing clothes like they would have worn on Earth. His daughter was disappointed Marvin's son-in-law, her husband, didn't seem to be missing her, but Marvin did not get to talk to any of them since he was not allowed through gate. So he had no communication with any of them except a wave. He wondered why these are the only persons he saw and why not his mother's parents. He, like some of the others, only saw persons who had been influential in his life. (Besteman, 142-167)

In her second visit to heaven following an accident with a semi Jeanne Enstad saw her grandma laughing as she put cookies in the oven. She had never heard her laugh like that on Earth. The angel told her she is laughing now and very happy because she is here in heaven where there are no more pressures of life. Jeanne wanted to move closer to see her but the angel would not let her because she was here only for a glimpse. She will see her grandma when she comes back on a permanent basis. Jeanne also saw her Grandma Cole, her maternal grandmother, who was also laughing. She had always been rather solemn on Earth and was never as happy as she seemed to be now. Jeanne was also not allowed to get closer to her Grandma Cole, nor was she allowed to go into any of the rooms. She was told when she comes back to stay she can see whomever she wishes and visit any rooms she likes. (Enstad, 86-87) It was the same when she saw her grandpa in a garden. He was laughing like he never had on Earth, but she was not allowed to get closer to him. The angel told her he is the way he is because there is no pressure, just complete peace in heaven. (Enstad, 88-89)

Three-year-old Paul Eicke drowned in a swimming pool and went to heaven. Over three hours later his heart started beating again. He said, "There was a lot of light and I was floating. I came to a gate and I saw Gramma Emmi [his great grandmother] on the other side. She said to me, 'What are you doing here Paul? You must go back to Mummy and Daddy. I will wait for you here.'" Paul said, "I knew I was in heaven. But grandma said I had to come home. She said I should go back very quickly. Heaven looked nice. But I am glad to be back with Mummy and Daddy now." (Doucette 2013-2)

Abby Cleghorn Meet Her Mother and Sister She Never Knew

Abby Cleghorn and her husband Win were riding a motorcycle when a distracted teenaged driver hit them head on. Win was killed at the scene. Abby was taken to the hospital and was there for five weeks in a coma. During that time she left her body and appeared in heaven, seeing her mother and then her sister who had died in childbirth two years before Abby was born, but in the knowledge of heaven Abby knew her sister right away. Her mother told her this was not her time; she had to go back for her kids and grandbabies. Her sister, Patty Lynn, reminded her of what her mother had said and told her to quit talking and get going. But Abby didn't know how to get back. She turned and saw the same green grass others have seen, the greenest grass ever, and there was Win coming toward her with outstretched arms. He wanted her to stay, but she said she couldn't. He told her if she goes back, it will be hard for her, and she will have to be strong. She said she could take it with God being with her. Then he told her to remember that he loves her with all his heart. After that she was back in the hospital. (Garlow, 28-29)

Others Observed Being Greeted

Willie Agnes Chennault saw her mother standing on the other side of the river. She told Willie she had to go back; it was not her time. She also saw her aunts Essie and Lue who were watching the children playing. (Chennault, 55, 56) They looked the same as they had on Earth but with new bodies that had no sickness. They were much younger, perfectly healthy, and enjoying youthful fun together. Aunt Lue was wearing a two-piece shining blue suit. (Chennault, 89, 181)

Dr. Gary Wood was met by his high school friend, John, who had been decapitated in an accident. Though he had grieved for him for years, seeing him brought Dr. Wood joy. John was as he remembered him but much more complete than before. They hugged and their arms went through each other, but it was a deeper hug than any he had experienced on Earth. He said John was assigned to him to show him around. All of the visitors had guides to escort them through heaven and show them what God wanted them to see to bring back to us. (Roth, 101-102; Wood, 25-26) Some are friends as John was to Dr. Wood, some are family as Rebecca Springer's brother in law was to her, some are guided by angels as is the case for Richard Sigmund, and some are guided by Jesus himself.

Richard Sigmund saw several people coming into heaven and being greeted by friends and family. Just a few feet from where he was standing, he could see two women standing. He knew they were of great age, but they looked beautiful, like they were in their mid-twenties. They were hugging each other and seemed very joyful as they were looking through the veil. Finally, one of them said she saw him coming, the one for whom they were waiting. Apparently, they had been informed that he was on his way. Suddenly, a man with a profound look of confusion came through the veil. He didn't seem to know where he was, but when he looked at the women and recognized them, he realized he was in heaven. They began to hug him and praise and worship God. This was another joyous reunion.

Further to the right, he noticed a group of about fifty people who were worshipping God with upraised arms. They were hugging each other and saying that they could see him coming. It was their pastor who had just died who was suddenly coming out of the veil. When he came through the veil, he looked like a very old man, but as he entered into the heavenly atmosphere, all of the age lines in his face disappeared, and his gnarled little body straightened up. This very old pastor now looked as if he was in his mid- to late-twenties; his youth had been renewed. He was bewildered, but suddenly he realized he was in heaven, and he began to rejoice. His first thought was that he wanted to see Jesus, his Lord, but people began to hug and rejoice with him. He called them by name but still asked to see Jesus. He was told Jesus is just a little way ahead down the pathway on which he was to walk.

Then Richard saw a group of about thirty-five people. They were standing in front of the veil, excitedly and joyously waiting for someone special to appear. The group contained those who evidently had died many Earth years ago, but in heaven, it was only yesterday. He saw people who must have been this special person's closest relations who had long since become residents of heaven: children, sister, and husband.

Finally, she appeared through the veil. One person in the group was carrying a baby, which had full power of speech and was fully aware of all its surroundings. This baby cried in a high little voice, "Mommy!

Mommy! There is my mommy. Jesus said I could remain a baby and my mommy would raise me in heaven."

The moment she appeared in heaven, the old wrinkled woman, all stoop-shouldered and very frail, upon entering the atmosphere of heaven, instantly snapped completely straight—her frail, stooped-over body became just as straight as could be. She was once again the beautiful young woman she had been years ago and was dressed in her radiant, pure white robe of glory, which we are apparently given to replace our Earthly clothes we leave behind on our Earthly body.

The little baby flew into her arms amid everyone's shouts of joy. They had been parted at childbirth. The woman had survived a concentration camp, but her baby had not.

Richard notes that God, in His infinite mercy, sees to it that nothing is lost. God allowed this woman to experience the joy of raising her child when the world she was in stole that from her. The love of God is so beyond full comprehension. He had tears running down his cheeks, even though he was just an onlooker. He shared their joy, and still does.

He understood that no one ever comes into heaven without having other people greet him/her (except of course for Abel, the first person to die and enter heaven).

He noticed there were not only people greeting the pastor who had come through the veil, but also angels in the greeting party. There were always angels for the others who came through the veil also.

It seems you can see through the veil from heaven, but you can't see through it from Earth. We on Earth can't see through the veil to see those waiting for us, but in heaven, you know when somebody is coming through. People in heaven somehow knew they should be at the receiving area when someone was coming. Later, Richard learned about announcement centers in heaven where people are notified that their loved ones are about to arrive there. (Sigmund, 17-20)

Later Richard saw his grandparent's house, their heavenly home, and met them. He fell down on his knees and saying, "Grandpa," but when he stood up and faced them, he noticed that it looked like his grandfather was only in his late-twenties or early-thirties. When he had died, he was ninety-seven! Now, he and Grandma were in perfect health. (Sigmund, 42-43)

Jeanne Enstad heard sounds of praising and rejoicing. The angel told her someone just entered the gates of heaven from Earth. She was told there is always rejoicing when someone arrives. An angel is assigned to give the new arrival a tour of heaven and relatives that are already there are notified and meet him/her and take him/her back with them. (Enstad, 89-90)

When Dawn Cypret arrived in heaven all around her were new arrivals being greeted by loved ones with happy cries of joy and laughter. Parents were greeting children; wives were greeting husbands. But she was not greeted by anyone although she knew of loved ones who had died. (May, 21) This was troubling to her, but then she saw her mother and father coming. Her mother said when she saw Dawn, "Honey! What are you doing here? You are not supposed to be here!" They had a dialogue as Dawn had tears of joy seeing them. They were young and beautiful; her mom smelled like Dawn remembered. Her mom kept insisting that she is not supposed to be here. She said, "Go home, baby, you need to go home." She had a job to do that is not finished and must be finished before she can come to this place she now calls "home." (May, 23)

Rhoda "Jubilee" Mitchell went to a section of the city that was full of people. It was like a big party with people dancing and singing praises to God. All the rejoicing was directed to God on the throne. There was total happiness and no sadness or hurt feelings anywhere. Heaven is full of color and diversity, and she saw this in the people at the party. Some wore beautiful sparkling clothes, while others wore dazzling white robes. There were people of different ethnic backgrounds. The dancing was not the same as we might see here; there was twirling and jumping and praising. All of it was expressing the people's excitement and gratitude for being there.

The city would become quiet whenever anyone offered a song or poem to the Lord. Then when it was finished the whole city erupted with excitement as people, angels, and beasts joined together in praising God. She said it was like a mass Halleluiah chorus. God received praise for everything around Him whatever it was, art, sculpture, song, poem, writing, speech, etc. The people knew that all their creative talents were given them by God for their joy, the people's enjoyment, and His praise.

She said, "Any attempt in Heaven to create something wonderful for others to enjoy blessed the heart of God Himself." (Roth, 53-54)

Colton met two of his family. First was his great-grandfather. He surprised his dad one day by mentioning his dad's grandpa and said his dad's Pop was really nice and that his dad and Pop were really close. It was a life-changing moment for Todd when his son told him about seeing his great-grandfather who had died years before Colton was even born and knew things about his dad's and great-grandpa's relationship. Colton said that he got to stay with Pop in heaven. (Burpo, 86)

Later, Todd showed Colton a photo of Pop, and Colton said that is not him. Todd was confused, but after thinking about it he had his mother find a photo of her father when he was in his twenties. She did and sent him a copy. He showed it to Colton, and Colton said that was what Pop looked like. (Burpo, 121-122)

This next story I cannot tell without getting tears in my eyes. Every single time I have read this part of his story I get tears in my eyes, and I am sure this time will not be an exception. I wish I could share the details as they are written in *Heaven Is for Real* with you, but I can't. So after reading my description, perhaps you can get a copy of the book and read the whole story in detail for yourself, so get yourself a tissue now before you continue reading.

Meeting Miscarried Sister

Colton also met his sister. Sonja, his mom, had a miscarriage at two months and lost a precious baby they desperately wanted. They never told Colton about it, but one day, Colton tried to get his mom's attention by telling her he had two sisters. She asked if he meant his sister and his cousin. Then he mentioned that a baby died in her tummy, and she immediately gave him her attention. She asked who told him about the baby dying in her tummy, and he said she did. She had come up to him and hugged him and told him she died in her mommy's tummy. Then he turned to go back to his play.

But Sonja called him back with an authoritative voice. He slunk back and said it was okay because God was raising her. Sonja asked if he meant Jesus was raising her, and he said it was Jesus' Dad that was raising her. Sonja asked what her name was, and he said she doesn't have a name because they never named her. This was partly because they never knew the baby was a girl. He then described his sister and that she was like a smaller version of his Earthly older sister but with her mom's black hair.

Sonja broke into tears when Colton went back to his play whispering, "Our baby is okay!" They had always assumed their child went to heaven but to have such a firsthand witness was an awesome joy and healed some strong old wounds. Their daughter told Colton she is eager for her parents to get there, so now they are competing to see who gets to go there first and gets to name their daughter. Todd then describes the incredible healing they experienced from Colton's testimony about the daughter they never saw or held in their hands. (Burpo, 94-97)

This one experience has been a source of tremendous healing for many women and some men when the Burpos have shared their testimony. If you or someone you know has grieved over the loss of a child of any age, you can take comfort from what Colton shared here about his miscarried sister. Not only is that child in heaven, but also God himself is taking care of your child. Colton said, "God and Jesus really, really love children." He said this repeatedly and with emphasis.

Mary Neal said we will see our loved ones and definitely know them. She saw familiar people in her welcoming group. (Neal 2017, 95)

Mary K. Baxter said you will know everyone in heaven just as God knows you. Your knowledge will be extensive. (Baxter, 87)

Mary Neal said we will see our loved ones and definitely know them. She saw familiar people in her welcoming group. (Neal 2017, 95)

Mary K. Baxter said you will know everyone in heaven just as God knows you. Your knowledge will be extensive. (Baxter, 87)

Summary

From all of these encounters it is clear everyone in heaven is experiencing a joy that goes beyond anything we experience on Earth; it is the joy for which we were created and a joy that God the Father longs to give us if we will just turn to him and receive his Son.

There is a host of people who have gone on before you that are anticipating your arrival. They will be there at the veil to welcome you. Also keep in mind that not all testimonies are identical because God treats each of us individually in the way He has best prepared for us. Your experience may be like some of these but with a unique twist that is special for you, because God loves you so much.

One final note about the people we will meet there and the people we will enjoy. I see nothing in any of the books I have read about any thought of those who don't end up in heaven. It is like all memory of them is wiped away because no bad thoughts can ever exist in heaven; there can be no unhappiness. Nothing will be allowed to tarnish the joy and beauty of heaven in any way.

This raises an unanswered question in my mind. The Burpos' second daughter is looking forward to seeing her parents in heaven. A child that is killed in an abortion is taken to heaven and raised by God himself. But if the mother never repents and accepts Jesus' forgiveness and doesn't go there, her baby cannot anticipate seeing her mother. Does her baby even know she has a mother? Perhaps we need to pray more for the salvation of women who choose an abortion for the completion of her baby's (and her) joy and the woman's healing.

CHAPTER 12

Seeing Saints Of Old And Angels

Martin Luther and John Wesley

Rebecca Springer tells of going to the grand auditorium to hear presentations by Martin Luther and John Wesley.

She and her brother-in-law Frank entered the filled auditorium and were seated with the melodies of an unseen choir floating about them. Then Martin Luther ascended the steps to speak. She said he was in the prime of a vigorous manhood. His great intellect, spiritual strength, and powerful physique made him a capable leader even there.

After his impressive talk, John Wesley took his place, speaking on God's love, how much God had done for us that even an eternity of thanksgiving and praise could never repay. Seeing and hearing both of them was wonderful.

Following John Wesley, Jesus himself appeared accompanied by a grand chorus of voices singing hymns of triumphant praise. The auditorium seemed filled with praise. Then Jesus spoke. Words fail to describe how glorious it was to be in His presence and hear His words, but most of all, to receive His love. (Springer, 55-59)

John the Baptist

Colton Burpo tells of meeting John the Baptist. He told his dad that Jesus has a cousin and his cousin baptized Him. Colton said John the Baptist was "really nice." (Burpo, 63)

Colton also saw Mary, the mother of Jesus. Todd said Catholic friends have asked whether Colton saw Mary, the mother of Jesus. The answer is that he saw Mary kneeling before the throne of God and at other times standing beside Jesus. He said Colton said she still loves him like a mom. (Burpo, 152-153)

Johann Sebastian Bach

I already mentioned in Chapter 4 Heavenly Music that Richard Sigmund saw and heard Johann Sebastian Bach play a magnificent organ. He also saw evangelist Jack Coe, Sr., in heaven. He was whole and healthy, not sick and heavy as he'd been on Earth. He was teaching a crowd of people with a loud, booming voice. He waved at Richard, who waved back, but didn't have time to talk.

He also saw evangelist William Branham sitting and talking with the Lord. He also waved at Richard, who waved back. Richard said Jesus looked at him and smiled and communicated the thought, "Richard will be back; he is just visiting."

He saw other people who had died and gone to be with Jesus, great preachers from throughout the ages. They were encouraging the people, telling them of the great wonders of heaven and the great things God had done for them. Apparently, no matter how long someone has been there, he/she still wants to keep learning and there is always more to learn. Just like little children, they were soaking up something they wanted badly to learn. (Sigmund, 43)

Kathryn Kuhlman and C. H. Mason

David Taylor saw a tall, slender evangelist he didn't recognize, and along with him was Smith Wigglesworth. David visited with them briefly, and they told him things he needed to know about his future ministry. He also met and talked with Kathryn Kuhlman. Then he also received a message from Bishop C. H. Mason, who, after the Azusa Street Revival, founded the Church of God in Christ, the largest Pentecostal denomination in the United States. (Taylor, 154-159)

Mary, Peter, James, and Paul

Dean Braxton saw Mary, the mother of Jesus, doing something with the living water in heaven. He doesn't know how to describe what she was doing because there aren't words to explain it.

He also saw Peter and James in a half circle before Jesus. They were a part of the heavenly army of God and were commanders of some type, moving with each commandment Jesus gave to the unit around them.

Paul had a part in what goes on with praise and worship here on Earth, but Dean does not have the English words to describe it. He knew it had something to do with dancing and praising the Lord down here on Earth. He saw Abraham's awesome place before the throne of God. He was taking living light and lifting it up to the throne of God. God would take it in His hands and toss it in the atmosphere. (Braxton, 139-140)

Mary Magdalene

Marvin Payne saw Mary Magdelene. (Payne, 53, 56)

Simon of Cyrene

Willie Agnes Chennault believes she saw Simon of Cyrene, who carried Jesus' cross. He was tall and skinny. His skin was milk chocolate in color. His hair was a natural afro. He wore brown pants and boots and a plaid shirt. She also saw a woman she thought might be Mary. She had on a long white gown and a scarf around her head. Her hair was wavy and long. Willie thought she was extremely beautiful. (Chennault, 59-60) She also believes she saw Peter, James, and John. (Chennault, 89)

Peter

Marvin Besteman met Peter at the gate of heaven. He had a strong, confident handshake, and his grayish blue eyes were warm with a really nice smile. He had a "good-sized strong normal nose." His dark wavy straight hair hung down to his neck. He was a humble "down-to-earth" kind of guy and wore a dark grayish robe tied with a knotted fabric belt round his waist and sandals. He looked to Marvin like he thought a fisherman of the first century would look. Marvin said he seemed to be about fifty-five years old. (Besteman, 87-89)

Angels

When Betty Malz arrived in heaven and was ascending the grassy hill, she realized she was not walking alone. To the left and a little behind her walked a tall, masculine–looking angel in a robe. She didn't see his wings but sensed that he could go anywhere he wanted and very quickly.

They didn't speak; it didn't seem necessary. Soon she became aware that he knew her, and she felt a strange kinship with him. She didn't know why. She thinks he was her guardian angel.

With the angel she sensed they could go wherever they willed and be there instantly." (Malz, 85,87)

Accompanying Angels

Crystal McVea was met by two angels when she was suddenly in heaven, one on her left and one on her right. They were her welcoming committee to heaven. She somehow knew they were her angels. It felt like they had been a part of her existence forever. They radiated a brightness and had humanlike forms, that of a long slender human body. Instantly she felt love, a great love sweeping over her. She knew they were her protectors, teachers, mentors, strength, heroes, and most of all her best friends. They had been with her through every tear, every decision every year through all eternity. She had instant communication with them, she knew instantly everything they thought and they her thoughts. It was a profound connection and eternal bond. There was no secrets, shame, misunderstandings, or anything negative, just a wonderful, beautiful, nourishing sense of knowing between them. There was also a being to her right, before whom her spirit crumpled and fell. She knew she was in the presence of God. (McVea, 37-38)

Richard Sigmund was always accompanied on the pathway by at least two angels: one on the right and one on the left. The angel on the right was there to explain things, and the one on the left mainly just reminded him frequently that he had an appointment with God. He thought that angel was his guardian angel. He said we all have guardian angels assigned to us at birth. He sensed that these two angels had separate jobs, but they worked in perfect harmony. (Sigmund, 21)

Sigmund refers to these angels off and on through the rest of his journey.

Dale Black was accompanied to heaven by two angels in long, seamless, white garments with silver threads woven into them and a gold band around their waists. They had no gender but seemed masculine and were larger than him. Their skin tone was golden brown and their hair fairly short. They had a golden glowing aura that emanated from their bodies. Their perfectly trimmed hair was like shiny brass. They were taller than Dale. They had wings, but they didn't flap them. They used them to express worship or emotions. When they folded them next to their bodies they blended in and seemingly disappeared. Light radiated from their faces in an expression of joy and delight. Love radiated from them, and he felt safe and at peace in their presence.

Then at the entrance to heaven, he met a larger, majestic, more powerful angel that exuded strength. He was dressed in a seamless white robe also, but he had a golden belt around his waist with an emblem where the buckle would be. He had a bronze complexion and pale-colored hair that fell to his shoulders. Though he seemed very powerful, Dale felt love and acceptance from him. The angels looked masculine, but in reality they were neither male nor female. (Black 2010, 98-99; Black 2018, 17, 25-26, 159-161)

Other Classes of Angels

At one point Richard Sigmund saw a group of fourteen warrior angels coming toward him from the Throne. He said they were twenty feet tall and ten feet across their shoulders. Their eyes were like fire, their swords were flames of fire, and the ground shook when they passed. His accompanying angels bowed in respect as they passed. Richard thought to himself that no demon could stand before them, and they could destroy an entire army of demons. He was told they were being sent into his future and would be there when he needed them. (Sigmund, 47)

He has a chapter on angels in which he describes different classes of angels. First were record-keeping angels, who wrote in God's record book. He saw one off to the side that was writing in Richard's record book.

Next were warring angels. They were huge muscular angels, maybe twenty feet tall and weighing nearly a ton with flaming swords, spears, and hands. They were not friendly like the other angels but were sent by the Holy Spirit to do warfare against Satan's army to protect God's children (us). They were lined up in file, waiting for commands to go and do battle. There were thousands of them. They and all angels only obey Jesus and the Father. They are sent to us when we speak Jesus' name and ask for divine help.

There were wisdom-giving angels. They go to the libraries of God's wisdom and take wisdom to God's children when they need wisdom. The Holy Spirit directs any of these angels to our aid when we speak in the name of Jesus.

Protecting angels are in charge of protecting us and have control of weather and other matters. While everyone has protecting angels, those who have been born again have legions of protecting angels. When we seek their help in the name of Jesus, they are there with power to do whatever is necessary to protect us. God has millions of angels that He dispatches for whatever need we have. (Sigmund, 95-102)

Other Angels

When Howard Storm was with Jesus, Jesus with a musical tone summoned some of the angels that were above the city. They came with a radiance that was brighter than the brightest light he had ever seen, but it did not hurt his eyes to look at them. Their radiance had a range of colors and an intensity he had not seen before and in fact says there are not words that can describe the colors of their radiance. It is somewhat like looking into the radiance of a diamond. He could feel their radiance in him and through him. It gave him a feeling of ecstasy and made him feel wonderful. They knew everything he thought or had thought; he could not surprise them. He was embarrassed and relieved at the same time. They each had a unique personality and voice, which was communicated directly to his mind and his to theirs. (Storm, 28-29)

He has a short chapter on angels, which tells of angels visiting him and people he knew in the appearance of humans. He said the best word to describe angels is compassion. They carry God's compassion to us and help us have compassion for others. He said there are uncountable kinds of angels. They have different attributes and functions. One may accompany a person or a child; others may be responsible for a whole city. Some are protecting us from evil. They are everywhere and are constantly with us. They know what we think and feel. They have the Spirit of God and want to help us have faith and follow God's will in our lives. They know they are servants of God and their desire is to serve Him. They do not want to be worshiped or have attention called to them. They are serving God and want all the recognition and credit and praise to go to Him. As God's servants, they do not make mistakes. As His servants, they take their direction from Him not us. If we need the help of angels, we can ask God to send them to help us. It does no good to try to command them ourselves. (Storm, 135-141)

The three points of light that came to Jim Woodford when he asked for help when the demons were trying to tempt him into the abyss were angels. He said they were indescribably beautiful with brilliant colors. They were tall, ten feet, twelve feet, and fifteen feet. The tallest one seemed to be the one in authority and appeared to be a warrior angel. They wore elegant white robes woven of light and were glorious representatives of the light and love of God. Each was different from the others and were neither male nor female. Their faces were majestic and their hair light and brilliant. But their faces, hair, and robes were not just white; they were a fullness of glory for which a color description is inadequate. The shortest angel put his hand warmly on Jim's arm giving him a warm feeling of comfort and assurance. He then said, "Fear not James, we are your constant friends." He later learned they had been assigned to him since he was born. They didn't have wings as we normally think of wings. Instead they had two spires of golden light coming from their shoulders creating an arc of gold above them. Jim thought the most outstanding part of their appearance was their eyes. They were a deep violet consisting of colors from both earth and heaven that were both describable and indescribable. Their eyes conveyed a calm that was deep in love and compassion.

The largest angel had a commanding presence and his robe was more regal. As he moved "the light of his robe rippled like moonlight on water." The hem of his sleeves was gold with purple threads in intricate and beautiful detail. He had a sash and belt of gold and wore a scabbard, which contained some sort of weapon of light. He commanded authority and the other two angels deferred to him. He wore a horizontal crescent shaped medallion around his neck that was a piece of battle armor. He said this warrior angel came to fight darkness for him and he had won! But Jim was astonished when the angel bowed to him. Jim was humbled and perplexed why this commanding angel would bow to him, a sinful human who had spent his life serving himself. The angel told him it was because he was made by the breath of God in God's image and the light of God's essence is in him. He was bowing to honor the light of God in Jim. (Woodford, 65-70)

Colton remembers angels singing to him in the hospital. They sang "Jesus Loves Me" and "Joshua Fought the Battle of Jericho," he said, but they wouldn't sing "We Will, We Will Rock You." He said one of them looked like Grandpa Dennis, but without glasses. He said no one has glasses in heaven. He said the angels sang to him because he was so scared. They made him feel better. (Burpo, xvii-xix)

He said in heaven everyone kind of looks like angels because they have a light above their heads. (Burpo, 73)

He also saw the angel Gabriel and said he sits on the left side of God and is "really nice." (Burpo, 101)

Dean Braxton observed that angels showed God great awe and respect, never turning their backs on Him, and quickly being dispatched according to our prayers to fight Satan's army on Earth. (Roth, 31) He said he observed prayers going past him very fast as he was on his journey to heaven, even though he was in heaven only an instant after leaving Earth. The prayers went directly to the throne, but the throne IS God, so the prayers were going into God and becoming a part of Him. The answers come directly from Him and the angels bring them to Earth and activate them. (Roth 32-33)

Angels' Appearances

While Jesus took Rhoda "Jubilee" Mitchell to heaven, angels took over when she got there and took her around. Those angels did not have wings, but some did. The cherubim angels had two wings, and the seraphim angels had six wings. There were other beings there that we do not have on Earth. She said we would call them beasts because they look so different from animals we have here. (Although I think some insects and crustaceans look pretty gross, we are used to them). She said some of them are part human and part animal, and, although they seem gross to us, they are not frightening at all. We see these same type of beings reported by John in Revelation. (Roth, 49)

Some angels look like men, but they have round faces and an ageless quality, while men's faces are not perfectly round and show a particular age. (Roth, 55)

Oden Hetrick said angels appear about seven feet tall and most do not have wings. He said they are very friendly and want to serve us under the direction of God. He said the angels all know our names and our character, including that we have been saved by the blood of Jesus. (Doucette 2013-1)

Dr. Gary Wood saw many angels taking care of the books in the massive library. Some had wings but others did not. He did not comment on what made the difference. He said they appeared strong and sexless, not feminine, but like strong, virile muscular men. Some had long beautiful hair. They were all forty or more feet tall and were very busy taking care of the books. (Roth, 102)

Angels and Worship

An angel took Mary K. Baxter to Earth and showed her a small country church and the angels there. There was a large mighty angel that was in charge of all the angels assigned to that church. This is the situation at every church. Two angels with books were outside the door of the church but I didn't see anything that said what their duty was. There were four angels beside the pastor at the altar. There were also angels at the front, middle, and back of the church. When the offering was taken, the angels recorded whether the giver enjoyed the giving as an act of worship or gave it begrudgingly. She saw a host of heavenly beings in the church that were rejoicing as the pastor spoke. A man came into the church wanting to be saved and freed from alcoholism. Two angels with scrolls appeared and wrote down all the man said. She was then transported back to heaven and down a golden pathway to the records room. The record of this man's life was retrieved and everything that had just occurred was recorded there, including the pastor's message, the offering, the records of people's attitude, the exact time this man was born again, and so forth. Then she witnessed all his sins being erased by the blood of Jesus from the book of the record of his life. Then amid trumpets sounding, bells ringing, multitudes saying "Glory to God! Halleluiah," thunder and lightning, a hand came out of the cloud of Shekinah glory and wrote the man's name in the Lamb's Book of life that was lying on the altar. (Baxter, 49-58)

She said angels always have work to do. They are always happy and joyful, never sad (there is no sadness in heaven) or tired. They are always praising God. (Baxter, 71)

She saw angels doing many kinds of tasks, always efficiently and orderly. Some seemed to be coming from Earth with papers or books in their hands on which they had been writing. They would take these reports to the [archives] where the reports would be logged into books to keep a record for someone's later rewards. When you get to heaven you will be rewarded for all you have done for Jesus' sake as recorded in these books. (Baxter, 114)

Robert Misst saw very large angels flying around a center of worship singing "Holy, Holy, Holy is the Lord who was and is and is to come." He was told they are cherubim and are the guardian angels for the mercy seat of God. It was difficult to stare into their holiness without being conscious of his sin. He wanted to leave, but the angel guiding him would not let him. The cherubim had more than two pairs of wings, but he couldn't count the wings with the cherubim flying around. (Roth, 119)

At the throne room, Michael McCormack saw big angels with white robes and wings that were folded down. They had faces that were like men but their faces were happy and very bright. (Roth, 81)

Eben Alexander saw angels flying high overhead with a loud, booming, glorious chant. He saw other angels who accompanied him. He called them "orbs." (Alexander, 45)

After Dawn Cypret returned to her body, she was in a coma but could see and hear. She saw four large over-seven-feet tall angels like NFL linebackers guarding her room, presumably keeping the spirit of death away. She continued to see more angels with different functions in the hospital, although no one else could see them. At one point three comforting angels spread their wings over her making a tent. She heard a nurse say they were having trouble keeping her oxygen levels up. Her angels made an oxygen tent for her! (May, 33-35)

James Garlow in *Encountering Heaven and the Afterlife* gives several stories of people on Earth seeing angels.

Kat Kerr visited the Headquarters of the Host. This is the place of heaven's armies under the command of Michael, the archangel. This is a place of power that looks like a large castle. She described it as being the largest, most amazing castle hundreds of feet high, disappearing into the sky. It was filled with the Glory of God and mystical smoke surrounded it. The angels were huge, some the size of the Earth. The warring angels have a power and appearance that would eliminate any doubt about them being able to protect you from Satan if you saw them. Some were like transformers and could turn into a ship that could streak to the site of the conflict. They didn't have weapons because they *are* the weapons. They have eyes all around so demons cannot sneak up on them.

There are Scribe angels that deliver or collect messages from people on Earth. There are Courier angels that are present in meetings to collect prayers and worship and take them to the throne room as incense. She mentions Cherubim with six wings and eyes all around, who stand at the four corners of the Throne crying, "Holy, Holy, Holy" and others who roam the Earth to see what is going on. Some can become as thin as paper and pass over a congregation to release fire from heaven. (Kerr 2010, 118-122)

Summary

We have seen a sampling of the saints of old that are there and whom you might meet. Whomever you do meet will be someone that has in some way been a part of your life or whom you have wanted to see. It might be just someone God has prepared to meet you for your growth or edification. No one person here met the same saints as anyone else. Your experience will be no different.

There are many different kinds of angels for different purposes. Some are very strong and powerful angels who war against Satan and his kingdom. They protect you when Satan would like to destroy you; so be sure to ask for their help as the Psalmist did. We each have a guardian angel that accompanies us in life and goes with us to heaven. Then there are scribe angels that write in God's books and courier angels that take our prayers and worship to the Throne Room and bring back knowledge and instruction we need. There are many more types of angels that we have yet to hear about. Some look like people and have been seen here when someone has needed supernatural help. James Garlow gives some of these testimonies.

I read of a navy pilot who took off from Honolulu with his squadron toward San Francisco. He lost sight of them and then saw a plane upside down over him with the pilot looking at him. He looked at his instruments and saw he was the one upside down and was headed for the ocean. He righted his plane and climbed back to altitude and just barely made it to San Francisco. He spoke to air traffic control, and they said there was never another plane in his vicinity. In another story, two women had their vehicle break down on a remote road in western Texas. A pickup came along, and two guys got out and fixed their car. As the women got in their car and were prepared to leave, the pickup was nowhere to be seen. I think these were angel sightings.

CHAPTER 13
Children and Animals In Heaven

Children

Colton Burpo said there are lots of kids in heaven. For the next year or two after his experience in heaven, he could name a lot of the kids he saw in heaven. But years later, he doesn't remember their names and neither do Sonja or Todd.

Todd asked what kids look like in heaven, and Colton answered that they have wings, and he apparently thought his wings were too little. (Burpo, 72)

The most constant theme of Colton's testimony was that Jesus really loves children. He said this constantly, in the morning, over dinner, before bed. He did this with both Todd and Sonja. He did it so much that at one point, Todd told him that is enough; he got the message. When he gets to heaven, he will tell Jesus Colton completed his assignment thoroughly! (Burpo, 105-106)

Babies and Toddlers

Rhoda Mitchell also tells of the children in heaven. She saw babies there who had died in infancy. She saw aborted babies who were completely happy and free. She saw that the children forgive their parents, and they want the parents to forgive themselves. She said the children would be hurt to know that their parents and grandparents carry guilt all of their lives. In heaven all the children are extremely warm and loving. The children she saw were full of fun and had the inquisitiveness of children, but they also had the knowledge of the Kingdom packed in their little brains. She said they could have argued down Socrates on his best day. They were full of the knowledge and insight of the adults in the Kingdom. She met six-year-olds with superior intellect that still wanted to sit in her lap.

She saw a baby boy walking around who looked like he was about four or five months old at his death, but he had full intellectual thinking capacity and was able to talk. He was a little over a foot tall, but he was able to walk. Along with the baby boy, she also saw an elderly couple that had been married on Earth. They were Christians who were now happy residents of the city. The baby boy walked up to the older woman and jumped into her arms. They cuddled and loved the baby. After the child patiently and eagerly received the love of the couple and they were finished, he jumped down out of the granny's arms. The little boy went on his way praising God. Things like that do not happen on Earth. She found it to be an amazing spectacle! She remembers the Lord's words in Matthew 19:14: *"Let the little children come to me, and do not hinder them, for the kingdom of heaven belongs to such as these."* (NIV). She found it comforting to see how much love the little ones receive in the Kingdom, where there is no death, no sickness, and no sadness. (Roth, 51-52)

Jesus took Dawn Cypret to a long building where inside she saw toddlers of every race. There are several women bustling around taking care of the toddlers. One went past her chasing after a rambunctious little girl. They all had bright happy smiles. Light was coming through the stained glass windows lighting the room. She saw a woman coming toward her holding the hands of two small curly blonde toddlers boys. "These are Jamie's babies," Jesus said to her. Dawn's daughter Jamie had been told she was infertile and would never have any children. Dawn was ecstatic and saw they even looked like Jamie. They apparently knew she was their grandma, but she told them anyway as she hugged them and said, "I love you soooo much!" Imagine Jamie's surprise and hope, although initially skeptical, when her mom told her she had seen her babies. Later Jamie did give birth to the two boys. (May, 39, 83) She saw many women taking care of the toddlers, some holding them in rocking chairs. She saw all sorts of balls and colorful toys and decided that is the job she wants to have in heaven. (May, 27)

As Marvin Besteman stared through the gate he was not allowed to pass through, he saw children of all ages, all healthy, whole, and contented. He saw babies as small as tiny fetuses as small as his little finger up to toddlers who could jump and play and older children. (Besteman, 119) He saw them grouped by ages from early fetuses, through unborn ones, newborns, small infant, on up. In heaven the unborn are living and growing apart from their mother's womb. They were perfectly safe, entirely happy, and wholly loved. Babies unwanted

144

by their parents here on Earth are highly valued and loved in heaven. He longed to see his own miscarried and lost babies, but he was not allowed through the gate. He knows they are there from what he saw and that they are safe, healthy, happy, loved, and growing normally as they would have been on Earth, or probably much better than on Earth. (Besteman, 123-127) No one was holding the babies, but they weren't lying uncomfortably on hard ground. They don't need to be held. They were as comfortable, happy, and fulfilled as any babies he had seen on Earth. They had simple clothing but didn't have diapers. They didn't have to be fed, burped, changed, or bathed. (Since eating is not required in heaven there is no elimination so bathrooms and diapers are not needed.) They were not resting on the grass at all because there was air beneath them, like they were on invisible air pillows, cradled in the perfect love of God. (Besteman, 128)

Miscarried and Aborted Babies

The angel took Mary K. Baxter to a hospital where a woman was having a miscarriage. The moment the miscarriage occurred the two angels that were with her caught the baby's spirit and put it in a basket and closed the lid. They lifted their hands in praise to God and then back through the gate into heaven with Mary and her angel following. They set the basket on the throne and bowed amid shouts of "Glory!" "Hallelujah!" and "Praise God!" The hand of God came out of the glory cloud around the throne and opened the basket, lifting the little baby out and laying it on the altar. He then worked it with His hands and perfect human form appeared that became a handsome young man. (Baxter, 83, 85)

Later God took her to see the place He prepared for children, children miscarried, children murdered in the womb, children born deformed, and others. They are all living souls from the moment they are conceived. Angels bring them all to God when they die and in heaven they are loved and become perfect beings. He makes their bodies whole and restores any parts that are missing so they have perfect bodies. They wore sandals and spotless white robes that were so bright they glistened. She saw children everywhere. They were engaged in many different kinds of activities. They were learning the Word of God and music. All

145

kinds of animals were coming up to the children and sitting beside them. (Baxter, 135)

Khalida Wukawitz also saw children under the age of six in heaven. Some of them were the results of their mothers getting an abortion, others died of sickness or murder. All of them were at Jesus' feet and were peaceful, healthy, and happy, not a single sad face. (Roth, 91, Malick, 83))

Children Playing

Rebecca Springer saw children laughing, playing, and running around with joy, catching bright-winged birds. (Springer, 11)

Willie Agnes Chennault saw children on a hillside playing. There were all raccs of children, but they were all wearing the same thing, blue jumpers, or overalls, with light blue flowers on them and white short sleeve shirts.

Richard Sigmund has a whole chapter on children and babies in heaven. I will share a few excerpts. Every child who dies goes to be with Jesus and enjoys his presence. Many times he saw the Lord draw little children to himself, hugging them and talking with them. Jesus seemed really to enjoy them being with Him.

One experience he had was seeing a little girl who looked about eight years old and had beautiful blond hair. She came up to him and knew him. He recognized her also and knew she had died of cancer. He got the impression she was an ambassador in heaven, who went from group to group and sang glorious songs.

She asked him if he wanted to see what she could do. Then she proceeded to mess up her beautiful hair, which she had lost because of the cancer. When she stopped shaking her head and messing up her hair, it immediately became perfect again. Apparently, there are not even bad-hair days in heaven. She then sang for him in a most beautiful, powerful, soprano voice.

He saw a young boy play a huge piano with a harp in the middle of it. He played beautiful music that was somewhat like Bach, Brahms, and Beethoven. The notes of the little boy's music were reverberating throughout heaven. People joined in singing the words, which Richard knew only while in heaven. Angels were at attention, some with arms raised in praise. Choirs joined in. It was glorious. An angel told Richard, the glorious music was all because he was there. In heaven even children can learn things that would be impossible to learn on Earth.

In another situation he saw a child that looked about five years old. He was sitting at an easel, painting a picture of the countryside. He merely had to tell the brush the color he wanted and the brush would turn to that color. He could even tell the paintbrush the hue he wanted, such as, "No, darker. The tree must be darker." The paintbrush would turn to the hue he wanted. Then he would just swipe the brush across the canvas one time and the tree he wanted would appear. (Sigmund, 30-32)

Many of the children he saw looked like newborns. In heaven, even the newborn babies had the power of speech and were completely responsive. They would know and understand what someone was saying to them and could reply. For Richard this capability of children in heaven was amazing. (Sigmund, 32-33)

He saw nurseries in heaven where angels or people cared for these babies. They didn't stay babies very long; however, in chapter 10, Meeting Family and Friends, we saw him telling of a World War II baby that stayed a baby until her aged mother arrived so she could have the joy of raising her baby. He saw both small and large groups of children. All the children were very happy. Their hair and clothing were perfect. Some were clothed in little playsuits while others wore robes.

He saw children who were old enough to walk and run and play, playing just like children do on Earth. It was like God intended for the children to play and have a good time and just be *children*. They were completely content just being children. They were experiencing a perfect childhood, which many adults here have missed. Everyone loves the children and the children love everyone also. Love permeates heaven. (Sigmund, 33) It makes me want to go there and enjoy the contentedness and joy of a heavenly childhood too.

In one of the games the children played, they would form a circle with just a few children or with many children. A child would be chosen, and he/she would float in the air, right in the middle of the circle. The other children would push him/her, giving the floating child a little shove. He/she would float back and forth. All the children, including the floating child, giggled with great glee and laughed. Richard thought it would have been a wonderful experience for him too.

In another game the children tried to see how far they could jump. Richard said they could jump a hundred or two hundred feet in the air and float down like butterflies. It was an amazing sight to him, wholly different from games on Earth.

He didn't see anyone play baseball. All the games he saw did not require equipment. In fact, they played games like we used to play on Earth before Xboxes, Nintendo, computers, and smart phones, such as hide and seek. He saw children climb tall trees and jump out of them. In this case, they floated down like little cotton balls. They were never injured when they came down. No one is ever hurt in heaven. Gravity can be such a bummer sometimes! It was great excitement for the children. Richard seemed to derive pleasure from seeing their activities also.

There were children playing on the shores of some of the many seas and lakes. They were never in any danger of drowning, because that never happens in heaven. They played in the water, on the water, and under the water, swimming or just sitting at the bottom of the lake. Many had a wonderful time playing with the rocks and building sand castles on the beach. Richard was again impressed with such a wonderful childhood. He said, "Oh, to have been raised in heaven!"

Jesus Himself came and hugged many children and told them cute little stories. There was lots of love between Jesus and the children. Richard said they were all 100 percent healthy children with rosy little cheeks, and they could run and play.

He saw children having foot races in one place. Richard was amazed that in heaven they can run faster than a horse on Earth can run. It was amazing. In another place, he saw them riding horses. The horses loved the children and loved giving the children rides. They had the power of thought and the power of speech, unlike horses on Earth. (Sigmund, 33-35) It seems like Richard had a wonderful experience seeing the children at play in heaven.

The children also attended school, but Richard Sigmund was not allowed to know what they were taught, except they would learn things geniuses on Earth could not possibly know or understand. Their intelligence in heaven is far above the highest level of intelligence here.

(Sigmund, 35)

The girl who came up to him and sang for him was the only child with whom he was allowed to talk.

He found all the children to be very friendly and loving. They called each other by their first names. They also called the angels by name, but Richard can't remember any of the names now.

In heaven everybody knows everybody, and each person is known by his/her name. Richard says heaven is a place you want to go, and the children are one of its most beautiful features. (Sigmund, 36) No wonder Jesus wants the people on Earth to know that he *really* loves the children!

In another chapter, Richard reports that a six-year-old boy ran up and hugged him. At the angel's prompting, Richard remembered that the boy had been crippled but after Richard's prayer had been able to walk. The boy said he had just gotten there; Jesus had come and taken him. He pointed out to Richard that he was no longer sick and ran off to play with the other children. (Sigmund, 80)

One day Matthew Payne was suddenly on the edge of a park in heaven where hundreds of children were playing. They were running and jumping and wrestling and playing on playground equipment like a carousel for example. No adults were watching because everything is safe in heaven. So the kids were free to run and play and take risks and be fully children. A girl about 14 sitting on a bench came up to him and greeted him by name. He asked how she knows him and she said she knows his son. She said she has talked with him and played with him in his dreams. She said she told his son how Matthew was doing since he had not seen his son for years. Her words gave Matthew tears. He said heaven is like that; it fills you with tears of joy. Hearing that his son dreams about her and plays with her in his dreams was very emotional for Matthew. She then took hold of his hand and led him to her favorite place, a meadow and grassland with a fence running up a hill. She showed him some buildings and a stable, a stable for horses. She comes here and rides the horses. She has even ridden with Michael, the archangel, who has a very special horse.

He said the whole park was full of children who had been aborted by their mothers. The park was a place for them to play and have fun.

Each one has foster parents and grandparents in heaven to care for them and mentor them. He said children who die before they are eight or ten are considered innocent and go directly to heaven. The children are hoping their mothers will accept and follow Christ so they we come to heaven and be with them.

They have a school in heaven. The children are taught the Bible. They are taught to read and write. They are taught arithmetic, philosophy, religion, and many other interesting subjects. Their life there is rich. (Payne, 18-22)

Heaven's Nursery

Jim Woodford saw a building with soft blue and pink light shining across it in alternating waves. The angel told him it is the nursery. It is for the maturing of the souls of aborted babies, miscarried babies, and children lost in their innocence. The light of God is in each one of them and longs to be back with God. Here they are raised to spiritual maturity to become what God intended for them to be. They mature much faster here than on Earth, but he said it is difficult to explain the passing of time to maturity in a timeless place. The angel said they are very much like children on Earth. (Woodford, 113-114)

Oden Hetrick said there is a room in the wall called the temple of instruction where children are taught. He said when children die this is where their angels take them. These are children who died in childbirth, in accidents, or in abortions. (I suppose sickness could be included also.) He said there are also rooms like a three-dimensional movie theater where they see things like the life of Christ as part of their education. They see Jesus hanging on the cross and that grieves them. But everyone going there must see this scene because Jesus' death on the cross is the very reason we are there in heaven and not somewhere else. (Doucette 2013-1)

Children's Names in the Nursery

Kat Kerr saw the nurseries in heaven and said they were very beautiful. Each baby had a bed that is like a seashell attached to the wall with his/her name above it. There were colorful ribbons for the girl babies and shields for the boy babies. The babies' names are those given by his/her parents. If you have had a miscarriage or an abortion and don't know whether it was a boy or girl, it is still important to give your child a name. You can give it both a girl's and a boy's name and in heaven the correct one will be associated with that baby. (Kerr 2007, 75-78 and Kerr 2010, 78)

When Colton met his miscarried sister, she did not have a name because the Burpos never named their miscarried child. (Burpo, 96) It is an awesome responsibility God has given parents that they are the ones to give their child the name it will have for eternity.

Angels give excellent care for each baby. The angels sing to them and rock them, and the breath of God sustains them. They are raised in God's perfect love and are filled with joy. (Kerr 2007, 76)

There were openings in the arched ceilings where birds would come in and sing to the babies. The babies do not need to sleep, but they do rest and play. They can think and communicate. When they reach toddler status they go through a ceremony in which they accept Jesus. The babies that were aborted know they were aborted and wonder why their parents didn't want them. Nevertheless they forgive their parents for ending their lives. Unfortunately this is one of the more populated areas of heaven because so many babies have been aborted in the last fifty years. Babies do not grow as fast in heaven in Earth years, (cf. Jim Woodford's comment in **Heaven's Nursery** above. He said "They mature much faster here than on Earth, but he said it is difficult to explain the passing of time to maturity in a timeless place.") So if you have lost a baby, maybe when you get to heaven it will still be an infant and you get to raise it there. (Kerr 2007, 75-79) I hope the mothers of aborted babies admit their sin, repent, and accept Jesus forgiveness, so they can be reunited with their child and his/her joy can be complete.

She also saw the places for older toddlers and children. As others have said, there they play and learn. They can play with animals and even slide down rainbows she said. It is fun and exciting to be a child in heaven, and there is never any illness, pain, sadness, loneliness, or rejection in heaven, only unconditional love, acceptance, and joy. (Kerr 2007, 81)

She visited the Babies Play Pond, created by God as a place to care for miscarried and aborted babies and give them much love and fun.

They can play on their own since heaven is perfectly safe, nothing can harm them, and they can do no harm. He made miniature daisy plants so the babies could pick pretty flowers with their little hands. He gave them bunnies, turtles, and butterflies that play with them, deer and kangaroos that give them rides, goldfish with which to swim, and dragonflies to tell them it is time to return to the nursery to be ready for a party with Jesus. They are never alone and many are staying with family members until the parents get there (assuming they do). Even though there is no marriage in heaven, families stay together and do things together while still being a part of God's one big family. They look in heaven like they did when they died, some so small they can be in the palm of an angel's hand, and there are no diaper changes or nighttime feedings. They talk, walk, play, and need only love, hugs, and lots of fun. (Kerr 2010, 76-78)

More on Aging in Heaven

Dean Braxton said the children do not age because there is no time in heaven. People ask him all the time if there are children in heaven. He tells them that there is no time in heaven, so there is no aging in heaven. He saw what we call children, or young people or old people, but there is no age in heaven. All are beings that can show themselves to you as they want you to see them. They can show themselves as they were when they were young, old, or as a child when they were on Earth. He says there are no children in heaven, as we know children here. He says there is no growing up in heaven because there is no time. He knew that children before the age of accountability will all go to heaven, so all aborted children are in heaven, but they will not be there as children. They are being everything that God created them to be, beings with pure joy and a big smile. (Braxton, 137-138)

This comment on aging in heaven differs from what others have said, reported above.

Children and Jesus

Dr. Gary Wood saw a little girl run and jump into Jesus' arms. He said most of the time he was there, he saw Jesus with children and teens. (Roth, 111) The girl that ran to him was a tiny little girl with long brown hair that had ringlets. She had a white robe that glistened and sandals.

Jesus reached down and caught her as she leaped into his arms. Other children of every race and color came running to see Jesus also wearing white robes and sandals. They sat at his feet and listened. Gary saw that their tiny faces glowed with rapture as they listened. (Wood, 30) He also saw some of the aborted babies. They were so young they were like small globs of flesh. Each one had an angel with him/her to help fashion the baby into the child it is destined to be. (Wood, 34)

Clearly, different people perceived the children in different ways. Even though there is no time in heaven, there still does seem to be a distinct childhood there. However, it is not clear how long it lasts and whether some people are eternally children. This raises another question for me. Since there is no marrying and giving in marriage in heaven (*"When the dead rise, they will neither marry nor be given in marriage; they will be like the angels in heaven."* [Mark 12:25, NIV], does that mean there will be no children born in heaven, and when this Earth passes away, that will be the end of children coming to heaven? Or will God have a way of adding children, or will some children not grow up, or will we all be like little children?

Animals

Mary K. Baxter saw many sorts of animals come up to the children or sit beside them when they were in school. (Baxter, 294)

Dr. Gary Wood saw many animals with the children who were around Jesus. There were all sorts of animals. He saw a lion frolicking with the children as if it were a kitten. Birds of elegant beauty sat on their shoulders and heads. (Wood, 30)

Akiane Kramarik painted the face of a male lion in heaven showing that since he no longer needs to kill to feed his family, he is gentle, strong, and has love in his eyes. (Kramarik, 49)

Richard Sigmund saw children riding horses. Both the children and the horses loved it. The horses loved the children and communicated thoughts with them. (Sigmund, 35) He also went to an area where he saw thousands of chariots and horses to pull them. All the horses were white with fiery red hooves. Some had wings. They never ate or left messes and had capabilities beyond horses on Earth. He said they were lots bigger than Earth horses and all muscular. He said he saw the Lord's chariot, bigger and nicer than the others, and a magnificent steed to pull it. (Sigmund, 93-94)

Mary K. Baxter saw beautiful regal pure white horses with large hooves. She said they looked like living marble statues. A smiling woman in a beautiful robe was having them bow their knees in praise to the Lord. She was reminded of Jesus' white horse and those of the riders with Him reported by John in Revelation 19:11-14. (Baxter 63)

Colton Burpo saw Jesus' horse. He called it a rainbow horse. (Burpo, 63) He also saw animals of every kind. (Burpo, 195)

Jim Woodford came to a large meadow that was bordered by a sight that thrilled him, horses. He has lived on a horse farm in New Brunswick, Canada, and feels that this part of heaven was made just for him. (Woodford, 85)

He later describes this in more detail or another scene like this one. They came to split rail fence and the angel told him to look. He looked across a lush green grass pasture and saw three horses trotting toward him. One was pure white and looked like Roy Rogers' Silver. That horse seemed interested in connecting with Jim. Another was a bay-colored horse. The third was a palomino. He said all three were the pinnacle of their breed and immaculately groomed. As the horses trotted across the pasture, the grass under them glistened. They came right up to the fence where Jim was standing, the white one first. Jim was thrilled. He has always been around horses and has found them more than pets or companions. He said he would be happy to take care of the horses when he gets back to heaven permanently. (Woodford, 95)

He also said he saw lots of dogs and cats and other animals besides the horses. They don't have cages or separate facilities, they like to run through heaven and are with the people they have loved and who have loved them. Any creature that had the capacity to love and return joy to you will be there in heaven to greet you and continue the love relationship. (Woodford, 114-115)

Michael McCormack said Jesus took him through lovely meadows where he saw rabbits, deer, foxes, and some other such animals. (Roth, 80)

Dale Black said the countryside was filled with "all types of animals." (Black 2018, 173)

Kat Kerr saw a park with miles of countryside in which there was every species of animals ever created, including dinosaurs. (Kerr 2007, 29) But since nothing is harmed in heaven and nothing dies, the dinosaurs are perfectly safe as are all other animals such as bears and lions. Kat Kerr thought they all ate grass. She also saw a lion with two cubs and saw and heard other safari type animals. (Kerr 2007, 66) At the Babies' Play Pond she saw babies playing with bunnies, turtles, and butterflies. Deer came to the pond and gave the babies rides. Kangaroos and turtles also gave the babies rides. Dragonflies announced to the babies when it was time to return to the nursery. (Kerr 2010, 76-77)

Dr. Gary Wood saw children petting lions like they were harmless over-sized kittens. (Roth, 111)

Rebecca Springer saw birds. She saw several graceful swans leisurely drifting about with the current on the lake. She also heard a delightful bird singing in the low branches overhead. (Springer, 11, 70-71)

Mary K. Baxter saw all kinds of birds, including some she had never seen before. They were beautiful. (Baxter, 86)

Khalida Wukawitz saw birds by Jesus' feet when she saw the babies there. (Roth, 92)

Richard Eby said there are no insect bites in heaven. (Roth, 173)

Steven Musick heard birds and "bugs," but didn't see them. Along with them were many other natural noises of the outdoors. (Musick, 38)

Eben Alexander saw dogs interacting with people. (Alexander, 39) He also saw many butterflies and was, in fact, riding on the wing of a butterfly. (Alexander, 40)

December 11, 1993, the Tulsa World ran an article by Carolyn Jenkins about a boy who visited heaven when he was three and reported that there are lots of puppies in heaven. When he opened his eyes, he told his mommy he wanted to go to heaven. He said he saw Jesus and the puppies, and he and Jesus played together with the puppies in heaven.

Revelation tells about animals in heaven that are unlike any counterpart on Earth. Richard Sigmund testifies about these, but gives no details except for one he saw that was a combination of a bull, a camel, and a horse. (Sigmund, 94) In his chapter on the Throne of God, he mentions winged creatures flying about it. (Sigmund, 110)

Pets

The dogs Eben Alexander saw seemed like pets. I assume based on the fact that all kinds of animals have been reported including dogs and horses, which are associated with humans, that there are pets there. Kat Kerr specifically says that if you had special pets on Earth, they will be there at your mansion. (Kerr 2007, 39)

Dr. Gary Wood saw pets in some of the mansions he saw. (Wood, 38)

Matthew Payne said all pets go to heaven and will be there with you. He expects to see there all the cats from his life, childhood and beyond. (Payne, 60)

Kat Kerr said that because God is so good and loves us so much, He lets our pets be with us in heaven. She has seen pets waiting for their owners, including her own dog. (Kerr 2010, 91)

She tells the story of an eight-year-old boy Bradford whose pet goldfish Chester had died. His family had a memorial service for Chester and his mother told him to say goodbye to Chester since he wouldn't see him again. He insisted that Chester would be in heaven when he got there. While they were talking, God took Kat to heaven momentarily and she saw the mansion God was preparing for Bradford. She saw orange and cheery Chester there in a waterway that went around the whole mansion. There were bowls off of the waterway in each room so Chester could be in any room with Bradford, and Chester could prop himself up to visit with Bradford, since all animals can communicate with people in heaven. There was a poolroom with a waterfall so Chester could slide down and swim with Bradford in the pool. When Kat told them this, Bradford got very excited and his mom was in shock since she had thought pets don't have souls and therefore don't go to heaven. Kat concludes that if God cares that much about Bradford and his goldfish, He must care just as much about everyone's loved pets. Bradford's mom later shared that one day Bradford had said he hoped he would have a pool in heaven where he could swim with Chester. Three years later Bradford is still thanking God that Chester is waiting for him in heaven. (Kerr 2010, 91-96)

Then Kat tells the story of her father's pet pig Sally. Sally started out weighing six pounds but eventually grew to 1100 pounds. Her father would talk to Sally about things of God and Sally would listen attentively. After she died and they buried her, he knew she would be in heaven. One of the times Kat was in heaven, she saw her father and a long line of former pets, of which her family had had many. They included Sally, her "brother Joey's duck Max, [her] brother RJ's alligator, Charlie, her cat, Little Bit, [her] brother Ray's iguana, Iggie," and many others. She affirms that the answer to the very commonly asked question about pets in heaven is definitely "yes." God's desire to please us and fulfill our wishes and dreams and loves is stronger than you can imagine and includes keeping the pets we have loved with us. (Kerr 2010, 97-99)

Kat then tells the story of her own dog, Molly. Molly was very smart and would wait by the front door at 11:00. When the postman dropped the mail in the mail slot, Molly would grab it and run all over the house with it. Fortunately she only tore up the junk mail. (How did she know? Does junk mail have a distinctive smell?) But Molly got old and died. Kat says her guardian angel took Molly to heaven because it is always one's guardian angel that takes one's pet. About two hours after Molly died, Kat was given a vision of heaven. She saw Molly running down a golden street with mail in her mouth. There is no mail in heaven, but an angel dressed like a postman was running in front of Molly occasionally dropping letters from a bag. Kat then saw another hundred or so dogs chasing the same "postman" angel. (Kerr 2010, 99-101)

How loving of God to provide even for our pets for their desire and joy. How much more can we expect Him to provide for us made in His image with our dreams and joys?

Summary

The children in heaven are healthy, happy, and fully little playful children. They have sharp minds and can learn things better than those of us on Earth. All miscarried and aborted babies are there and know their parents and look forward to seeing them. The aborted babies wonder why their parents did not want them, but they forgive their parents and hope to see them. Perhaps if more women really knew what happens to their babies, they would not have let them be murdered (aborted).

There are lots of animals in heaven. Each of these witnesses have seen animals but not all the same animals. One witness even saw extinct animals. No animals hurt any other animals or people. They do not eat each other. If they do eat, it must be vegetable matter or something else provided by God. Children have been seen petting a lion, playing with an alligator, things that would be dangerous here but are safe and normal in heaven.

There has been very little mention of pets, but those who have mentioned them assure us that our loved pets are there. And those pets are also having a wonderful life just like the humans. People and animals can communicate. Kids talk to horses and vice versa. A boy will be able to talk to his goldfish, etc.

In mansions of glory and endless delight,

I'll ever adore Thee in heaven so bright:

I'll sing with the glittering crown on my brow:

If ever I loved Thee, my Jesus, 'tis now.

William R. Featherstone, 1864

CHAPTER 14

Mansions In Heaven

Jesus said, "*In my Father's house are many rooms; if it were not so, I would have told you. I am going there to prepare a place for you. And if I go and prepare a place for you, I will come back and take you to be with me that you may also be where I am.*" (John 14:2, NIV).

Through the gate in the wall, Richard Sigmund saw many beautiful mansions along his golden pathway. They had verandas on all floors, even up to the fourth floor. He saw people stroll off their veranda and either float softly to the ground or just stay floating in the air. (Sigmund, 27)

On his way to the throne of God, Richard Sigmund saw an avenue just off the street he was walking on. On it there were mansions beyond comparison with any on Earth. He was told that they were for missionaries. Because they had given everything to the Lord, God rewarded them with everything they didn't receive here on Earth.

He didn't know the names of those missionaries who lived on that street, and he was not allowed to explore it. He knew some of them had been modern-day missionaries. Some who had just recently died were being met by large groups of people welcoming them at the veil. One was coming dressed in a beautiful robe made of spun gold. He beheld his clothes and saw how beautiful they were and how happy he was not to be in rags any more. Thousands of people were welcoming him. Richard noted that the rewards of missionaries are great; God loves mission-minded people.

The angel with him took him to one house on the street he was on. It was a mansion carved out of a single, giant pearl. According to Richard the house seemed to be two hundred fifty to three hundred feet across and one hundred feet tall. Angels had formed the furniture inside, including the chandelier, by carving the pearl into shape. The chandelier even glowed from within. This house was for a woman named Pearl, who had been a missionary known for giving to the poor, but she had died of starvation. This was her reward for a pure heart.

There were other houses on this street, and they were all different. There is no match for these houses on Earth. Can you imagine ever creating a whole house, including its furnishings, by carving it out of a single pearl?

Another house on a street corner appeared to be made of solid gold but with some wood. Hundreds of people were in this mansion, all people this missionary had led to the Lord. On Earth he had been a part of their families, and now they were part of his big family. Joy, peace, and tranquility were everywhere and unbelievable. Everyone is very friendly and waved and called to him, saying, "Hello, Richard. It is good to see you," or they would call from across the street, "Hello, Richard. How are you doing?" They knew his name, but he didn't know or remember any of them.

Besides the mansions, there were larger buildings on the street, but he never saw any locks, and the doors were always open. This included mansions, smaller homes, and apartment buildings. Everything in heaven will be just right for you, and some people will prefer an apartment or condominium. I don't know if you can expect an elaborate mansion if you haven't given of yourself as missionaries have, but your residence will be fabulous in any case. Some of the mansions had windows, but some did not. Since there are no storms or thieves in heaven, there is no need for locked or closed doors. Anyone is perfectly welcome to enter your house, whether you are there or not, but Richard doesn't believe anyone enters someone else's home when the resident is not there.

Sigmund then describes some of the architecture: pillars, porches, archways, brick, stone, and wood. He noticed that everything fits together so perfectly no nails or other fasteners are needed. He saw a veranda made of transparent onyx, inlaid with gold, silver, and precious stones. There was a home made of clear stone embedded with roses. The roses were alive and growing and gave off a beautiful aroma. He thought the architecture was extraordinary.

When he put his ear up to anything solid, he found that it hums beautiful songs. Some of the songs were ones we sing on Earth, but others were not. Everything in heaven gives praise and glory to the Lord. (Sigmund, 37-40) *"Some of the Pharisees in the crowd said to Jesus,*

'Teacher, rebuke your disciples!' 'I tell you,' he replied, *'if they keep quiet, the stones will cry out.'"* (Luke 19:39-40, NIV). In heaven they apparently do cry out; everything does!

On another occasion, he was taken to a home that was just off the main street on which he was walking. He said he was weeping with joy as he joined in the joy and happiness of everybody. This home was smaller than some of the others, but it was a fine home. He thought that on Earth, it would probably cost a trillion dollars, if it were even possible to build. It was larger than the White House. The angels had him stop there, saying, "Somebody wants to talk to you."

When he walked up to the house, he met his grandfather and grandmother sitting on the front porch. This house was their heavenly home! He fell down on his knees being amazed at the blessing of his grandpa. Then he noticed that his grandfather looked like he was only in his late twenties or early thirties, even though he was ninety-seven when he'd died. Now, he and Grandma were in perfect health. They hugged, and Richard didn't know what to say. After a moment, they told him he has an appointment with God, but that he will be back. They pointed just a little way beyond them and told him his home would be over there. They pointed down the street where there was an open lot for a home to be built. He never thought he had done anything to deserve all the goodness God was showing him, especially this. (Sigmund, 42-43)

Another time he was taken to an avenue named The Way of the Rose. Here there were some homes still being constructed. All the homes on this street were similar: three stories tall; similar front and back; beautiful, green grass; tall, flowering trees. They had spacious rooms nicely furnished with furniture that could have come from Buckingham Palace. The rooms were decorated with rose-colored woodwork. In the backyards were golden lawn chairs similar to wrought iron with cushions of spun gold. There was a large lake behind the homes. There were large, hand-carved scenes of heaven with figures that were animated and talked. They had libraries with books embossed with gold that were copies of books that had been written or were going to be written. (Sigmund, 59-60)

The houses Rebecca Springer approached and passed seemed wondrously beautiful and were built of the finest marbles with broad verandas encircling them. They had roofs or domes supported by different kinds of columns, some massive, some delicate.

There were winding steps that led down to pearl and golden walks. She had never seen any style of architecture like these. There were flowers and vines growing everywhere, and they were luxurious surpassing in beauty even those of her brightest dreams. She saw happy faces looking out from these houses, and happy voices rang out through the clear air.

Her brother-in-law, Frank, who was escorting her, turned onto a side path toward an exquisitely beautiful house with columns of light-gray marble covered by green overhanging trees. He told her it was to be her family's home. It had low steps leading to a broad veranda. It had a beautiful inlaid floor made of what appeared to be rare and costly marble. It had massive silver-gray columns, between which were vines covered with rich, glossy green leaves, intermingled with exquisitely colored flowers. It had the fragrance of a delicate perfume in the garlands. These broad verandas surrounded the house.

She explored a beautiful large reception hall, with an inlaid floor, marble columns, and a low broad stairway. In another room, there were gorgeous, long-stemmed roses of every variety and color strewn over the walls and floor. She attempted to take some of the roses and found they were firmly attached to either the floor or the wall. Frank explained that one day, when he was working on the house, a company of young people, boys and girls, came to the door and asked if they might do something to make the house beautiful for Mr. and Mrs. Springer, whom they used to know and love. The Springers were their friends and the friends of their parents. The girls began to toss the flowers that were in their arms onto the floor and the walls. When they hit the walls, they stuck there permanently. The boys had tools with which they were able to embed the roses in the marble floor. Since flowers never wither or fade in heaven, they will remain in the floor or on the walls always beautiful, always alive and growing. (Springer, 16-20)

Jesus showed Dawn Cypret numerous mansions on rolling hilltops. Some were big, some were not, but all were beautiful, different, and unique. They were each created for a specific person to reflect that person's taste, personality, and desire. She thought they were all spectacular, and Jesus replied that He will create only the best for each person. (May, 28)

Jeanne Enstad wandered a little farther from seeing her grandma and was awestruck at the beauty she saw with many mansions. There were beautiful pearl steps leading to elegant mansions. Each had unique architecture. They seemed to go on forever, and there was a crystal clear river lined with magnificent flowers going through the grounds of many of these mansions. Many kinds of trees bordered the sidewalks of pearl and gold that wound through these mansions. There were many sparkling foundations and everything was pure and perfect. There were many rooms in these mansions. She peeked in but was not allowed to enter any of the rooms; however, she was told when she comes back permanently she will be able to visit any she wants. (Enstad, 86)

Matthew Payne has seen his place in heaven over several visits there. He said our homes in heaven reflect what we value: simple house, forest house, tree house, farmhouse, mansion, etc. He never was interested in a large house, but his mansion in heaven does reflect all the things that had been his dreams and hopes. The entrance to his mansion is through two pillars through two open doors. To the right is a commercial kitchen. It has benches around the side and is full of equipment. Past the kitchen is what could be called a family room. Two of the walls have tapestries. One of them is a tapestry of Mary Magdalene washing Jesus' feet with her tears. He said when you get close to the tapestry it becomes a portal into Mary's house, which is located somewhere else in heaven. When you walk into the tapestry, you end up in Mary's house. On another wall is a tapestry of the Lion of the Tribe of Judah. It shows children around the lion, and when you walk up to the tapestry the lion comes alive, and it becomes a portal into the playground where aborted children are playing. All through the walls of his mansion there is a two-foot high aquarium with fish swimming in it that follow him from room to room when he is there. There is a long winding staircase leading to the second level where there is a 150-foot heated swimming pool. There is a 50-seat coffee shop past the pool and another kitchen behind the coffee shop. Outside is a balcony that overlooks the Crystal Sea, where there is a wharf and a yacht holding eight people is moored. Past the coffee shop is a fifty to seventy seat theater, showing both films made on Earth and films made in heaven. Past the movie theater is an office with staff, a television studio, computers, and a radio station, where he will lecture, write, and produce films and TV shows. Beyond that is a library with all the books he has ever read, wanted to read, or written. Each part of his mansion is made up of his secret desires. God pays attention to all our desires throughout our lives and fulfills them in heaven if we don't get them on Earth. God loves us far more than we can ever imagine. (Payne, 59-63)

Dr. Gary Wood got to see the mansion that was being prepared for him. There were three buckets of paints sitting in it. His friend John put a finger in one bucket and flung the paint against the wall. When the paint hit the walls, flowers appeared. So Gary took the bucket and flung the whole thing at the walls. Not only did a beautiful scene with flowers appear everywhere, but also the sweetest floral aromas he had ever smelled filled the room. (Roth, 108) Again some things are like Earth, in this case buckets of paint, but the paint there was radically different. It made recognizable patterns with flowers, which had natural fragrance in them.

It had great marble columns like a southern mansion. They (he and his friend John who was escorting him through heaven) entered what seemed to be a living room but there was no furniture yet. It needed painting and the paint was there in buckets, as described in the paragraph above. He saw other mansions, which had furniture and art on the walls. Some had pets. Anything you would want in a suburban home was there. No two mansions were alike; each is prepared specifically for the person who will live there. (Wood, 37-38)

Kat Kerr saw many different styles of mansions. Some were along the Crystal Sea or on an island in the sea. Some were located along cliffs in the Valley of Falls and looked like gemstones with many facets. These mansions turned slowly to give the inhabitants great views of the valley. She saw futuristic Sky Mansions each built high on a tall, transparent, cylindrical column. Someone would enter the column, announce his/her intended floor, and would immediately be zoomed up to that floor. Someone can step out on a deck more than one hundred feet up and see a spectacular view. And there may be a star cruiser parked outside on the landing pad. (Kerr 2010, 43-44)

164

She saw the mansion for a lady named Survilla, who would be arriving. It was a three-story Victorian mansion with a wrap-around porch. It was white with a blue roof and intricate detailing inside and flowers growing out of the walls. Her dining room on the top floor would seat sixty people and the table was set with gold and white china. The kitchen was big with many gadgets, equipment, and marble counters. Survilla loves to cook and serve people, so her mansion will enable her to do that far better than she ever could on Earth. All the appliances run on some unseen power (light she says in another location), and they never break down or wear out. She says usually when you sit down to eat, you order what you want and it just appears in front of you. When you are finished, it all disappears with no cleanup required. (Kerr 2010, 60-62)

She saw the mansion of a lady named Mrs. Mac, who loved to teach piano music. Her mansion has a grand piano and many other pianos. A little girl was also there, because Mrs. Mac had always wanted a child but had none. (Kerr 2010, 66-69)

Oden Hetrick saw his mansion. It has a rose arbor in front of it with a heart-shaped trellis and a row of flowers like Chrysanthemums. The mansion is on about ten acres. You enter into a large round vestibule about twenty feet in diameter. To the right is a door leading to the banquet hall and to the left is a door leading to the fellowship hall or living room. In front of you there is a spiral staircase leading up to the other floors. On the second floor is a balcony that overlooks the garden. There is also a music room with his favorite instrument, a guitar. He describes a banquet in the banquet hall, but I don't know if he saw one or he is just visualizing one with his friends and family and Jesus, with Jesus at the head of the table. With regard to Jesus being at his banquet while there are others going on also with Him present, Jesus can be many places at once. This is something we can't do; we are always in just one place. He said at the banquet, someone brings in a silver platter with things like bon-bons on it. They are like almond butter flavored with dried fruit. The tray is not piled high, just neatly arranged. When someone takes one, another appears in its place. There were little angels making music for the banquet also.

He also refers to his mansion as being a chamber in the wall. He heard music in his chamber but couldn't see from where the music was coming. He finally saw it was coming from water falling over rocks in a small brook making sounds like wind chimes. The front of the mansion has a big window that looks out over the place in front of God's throne. It is not a window with which we are familiar because someone can just step right through it. All chambers can look out at God. In the front room is something like a beanbag chair. When you fall into it, it takes your shape and fits you perfectly. There you can relax and see the face of God. The walls have beautiful blue, green, and wine-toned tints that can change shape like clouds in the sky. From the throne of God one can see rows of chamber mansions reaching two-thirds of the way around so God can look at all the people and the companions in each chamber mansion. He said there are 144,000 chambers in the row and 144,000 rows (for a total of twenty billion chambers, each with at least two companions.) He says the chambers are about twenty-five feet wide and fifteen feet high. (Doucette 2013-1)

This second description of the mansions as chambers seems to be different from his first description. Other witnesses describe the mansions quite differently.

Dale Black said between the central city and the city wall were numerous collections of homes he called townships. The townships had many brightly colored picture-perfect homes. They were not arranged in a symmetrical or uniform manner but were perfectly balanced. Each was unique; some were three or four stories high or higher. (Black 2010, 104-105)

All Mary K. Baxter said about the mansions was that on one trip to heaven she quickly saw beautiful houses and mansions. (Baxter, 114)

Jim Woodford said houses were not a major factor in the city of heaven. There is nothing there from which we need to take shelter. There is no rainy or stormy weather, no hot sun, no thieves, nor anything else from which we need protection like we do here on Earth. But they are quiet places where we can meet loved ones or go to meditate on the mysteries of God. He did see houses that flowed with the landscape of heaven. They were made with beautiful pastel colors and had rounded edges. They were rounded as in adobe style. (Woodford, 111)

When Richard Sigmund was looking at the fountains, he could not tell where the fountains drained. There were no pipes, no plumbing in heaven. There are no bathrooms so no plumbing is needed for them. (Sigmund, 75) Eating the fruit from the trees is optional and even if you do eat the fruit, it's delicious liquid will just flow down your throat. Then it just evaporates since there are no internal organs as Richard Eby observed. (Eby, 204) There is no esophagus, stomach, or intestines, and therefore no bodily elimination, so bathrooms are not needed in heaven. Baths are not necessary either, because no one ever gets dirty.

Also there are no bedrooms. Since heaven is lighted by God's glory, it is always light. There is no darkness or night. Also, people never get tired, so beds and bedrooms are not needed. None were ever mentioned by any of the authors.

There is no electricity in heaven. An internal light illuminates everything in heaven that is lighted. The glory of Jesus and his Father are the power for everything in heaven, including the chandeliers and lights.

Kat Kerr said the mansions in heaven are each perfect for the person who will dwell there. If you loved to paint and have an artist's gift, there will be a well-supplied painting studio in your mansion. If you liked horses, there will be horses at your mansion and they will require no care but will want to please you and your guests. Whatever gifts you have, your mansion will facilitate exercising those gifts in heaven as gifts of love to others there. Your mansion is perfect for you to continue the gifts you were given on Earth. (Kerr 2010, 34-35)

Willie Agnes Chennault saw mansions that had stones going all around the windows and doors. The stones "resembled amethyst, jasper, rubies, sapphires, diamonds, and crystals." (Chennault, 57)

Mary K. Baxter saw tables everywhere that she went. They were like Victorian or other style furniture with elaborate designs. They were more exquisite than any she had seen on Earth. Many had books on them and other things. (Baxter, 106-107)

Summary

The mansions where we will live in heaven are created especially for the person who will live there. They include details and splendor far beyond what we would expect as gifts of the Father's love. They will incorporate our deepest desires, even things we longed for but never had on Earth. They will be equipped to enable us to continue using the gifts God gave us and we used on Earth. The mansions of missionaries who gave up everything to serve the Lord are the most fabulous. Some will be for one person, some for couples, and some for whole families, including the spiritual families missionaries led to the Lord.

CHAPTER 15

The Throne Of God

Todd Burpo asked Colton if he had seen God's throne. He said he had seen it a bunch of times. He said, "It is *really, really* big, because God is the biggest one there is. And he really, really loves us, Dad. You can't *belieeeeve* how much he loves us!" He then went on to say that Jesus sits right beside his Dad. Todd asked him which side Jesus sits on, and then Colton indicated it was on God's right side, just as Scripture tells us: "A*nd sat down at the right hand of the throne of God*" (Heb 12:2b, NIV). Then Todd asked who sits on the other side of God, something Scripture never tells us. Colton immediately said that is where the angel Gabriel sits. He added that Gabriel is nice. (Burpo, 100-101)

At about ten-thirty one Saturday night in January of 1977, Roland Buck was meditating and praying at his desk, preparing his heart for the Sunday worship, when he was suddenly taken out of the room and into the Throne Room where the secrets of the universe are kept! God told him to relax. He relaxed even though it was so awesome. He didn't understand what was happening, but then God told him he wanted to give him an "overlay of truth." He went from Genesis to Revelation, showing God's plan for His people and discussing His character, saying He would do nothing in conflict with His nature or His character. God affirmed His plan is good and will be accomplished reminding Roland of His Word in Jeremiah, *"For I know the plans I have for you,' declares the LORD, 'plans to prosper you and not to harm you, plans to give you a hope and a future"* (Jer. 29:11, NIV]). God wanted him to see how He really felt about man; that He had man in mind before He made the ~~Earth, and He made Earth so m~~an would have a place on which to live.[4]

[4] I have notes on how science and mathematics show it is impossible for Earth supporting intelligent life to have happened by undirected natural means. *Reasons to Believe* (reasons.org) also has prepared documents attesting to this from evidence of science. See Hugh Ross, *Improbable Planet*, 2016, Grand Rapids: Baker Books.

He does not look on the evil when He looks at man, but at the very heart of man.

God truly gave him a glorious glimpse of the hidden secrets of the universe: of matter, energy, nature and space, all bearing the same beautiful imprint of God's design. As He gave this dazzling overlay of truth, Roland saw new beauty and unity to the entire Bible that he had not seen previously. Certain biblical truths were now perfectly clear, though before they had not been so clear. He could now see how all the pieces fit together in what God is doing![5] (Buck, 51-52)

Jesus took Michael McCormack to the throne room. He said, "It had sparkling lights and golden pillars and paintings like seen in old churches." There were two rows of angels with long golden trumpets with purple and golden banners on them. (Roth, 80)

There were three thrones joined together as one. They were golden and had lots of jewels of all colors on them. There were emeralds, rubies, blue sapphires, yellow stones, and purple stones. (Roth, 81)

Mary K. Baxter saw the throne of God several times. As Isaiah says, she saw it "high and lifted up" with the River of Life coming from underneath it. The glory of God overshadowed it with thunder and lightning and a rainbow of color all around it. In addition, there were many voices, those of the four beasts, the angels, twenty-four elders, and saints by the thousands. The rainbow was brilliant and glorious with many hues of colors. These colors mixed with light produced a dazzling display. The scene was awesome, nothing like anything she had ever seen before. (Baxter, 43-44, 99)

She said the four beasts or living creatures were large, had eyes front and back, and six wings. One had the face of a lion, another the face of a calf, the third the face of a man, and the fourth was like a flying eagle. They were constantly crying out, "Holy, holy, holy, Lord God Almighty." (Baxter, 100-101)

---

[5] Many of the results of recent scientific inquiry have confirmed this same message from God: that his creation is consistent with his Word and reveals the trademark of his handiwork, and that the Earth is so improbable that its existence too shows the trademark of God creating it as a special habitat for man.

Oden Hetrick called the throne "the Most Holy place," "the Father's presence," and the "Temple of Heaven." He said it is a large round building about 300 miles across and 800 miles high in the center of the city, the New Jerusalem. He said in front of the throne there is a large oval area about two hundred miles long and seventy-five miles wide. The area is filled with sapphire jewels making it blue and shiny. Hence it is called a "crystal sea" or "sea of glass" because of the sapphires. But it is solid, not liquid water. One time he saw the prophets gathered here and the martyrs saying, "How long o Lord, how long?" (or "How long, Sovereign Lord, holy and true, until you judge the inhabitants of the earth and avenge our blood?" from Revelation 6:10). This gave him the impression that Jesus is coming back very soon, something that has been echoed by many of the witnesses.

He also saw in this center thousands of saints with their garments of praise and jewels forming a sparkling cup of love for Jesus in return for his taking on the cup of suffering for us. Oden Hetrick sees this as the satisfaction Jesus received as predicted in Isaiah 53:11 *"After the suffering of his soul, he will see the light of life and be satisfied; by his knowledge my righteous servant will justify many, and he will bear their iniquities."* He has received the love of the saints He died to save. (Doucette 2013-1)

Richard Sigmund observed that everything in heaven moves toward the throne, no matter how one arrives in heaven. However you arrive there, all traffic moves toward the throne: from the veil, in the beautiful conveyances, and coming down from the sky. In whatever way God brings you into heaven, you move toward the throne.

He found that people there earnestly desire to get to the throne and to talk with Jesus. If they see Jesus on the street walking toward them, they look forward to talking with him. They excitedly exclaim, "He is coming! He is coming our way. We are going to get to talk with Him!" (Sigmund, 44)

In chapter 17 of his book, Richard Sigmund gives an extensive description of the throne and what happens there. It is lengthy, so I won't tell the whole thing. However, I hope the parts I share with you give you a good perspective on the throne of God from what Richard saw.

When he got to the throne, he understood that everything in heaven flows into and out of the throne. He said the throne pulsed like a dynamo, with everything being drawn to it or cycling around it.

The throne building was the biggest building in heaven. He thought it looked several hundred miles wide and at least fifty miles tall with a domed roof. There were flaming living statues, and he saw columns that appeared to be thirty to thirty-five feet across.

There were thousands of steps leading up to the throne where each step was significant and prophetic.

He saw hundreds of thousands or millions of people going into and coming out from the throne worshiping and praising God as he went up the stairway. He heard one person say that God is more than he ever thought. He heard someone say he really wants to go back to the throne.

The entry area to the throne had columns, and the number of them was also prophetic. Like everything else Richard saw there, the columns were huge. Some were tremendously tall and looked like they were a thousand feet across. He had no idea how many there were. The tallest ones were at the doorway leading to the throne.

After passing through the columns, he saw millions multiplied by millions of people prostrate on their faces toward the throne of God. It seemed like the throne faced every direction at the same time and was twenty-five miles tall. You can see the throne of God from any part of heaven. It was made of some heavenly material that was crystal clear. Yet it appeared to consist of gold and ivory and silver and precious gems and jewels, all sparkling. It looked like light rays came out of the material of which it was made. Great waves of glory, like liquid fire, swept through the material. The building itself gave off rays of glory.

He could tell there was a Being on the throne, but He was covered with a cloud of glory that radiated from Him. The glory of God was an all-consuming, enfolding fire in which He dwelt. It surrounded the Being on the throne.

He speculated that the fire of glory must have been the same thing Moses saw in the burning bush. He could tell that there was the throne in the fire and that there was a Being in the fire and that He was looking at him.

Around the throne he saw millions of people, some standing, worshipping God.

There were seven big pillars inside the throne Room, and there were nine pillars near to God. He believed they were the gifts of the Spirit.

There was an inner court surrounded by pillars and also a pavement area with millions of people lying prostrate. Some were on their backs, and all were facing the throne. The pavement was like the pavement Jesus had stood on, with what seemed like thousands of acres of inlaid jewels.

He knew the throne had a foundation, but was not allowed to know more about it.

He noticed an area with three levels of railings closer to the throne, beyond which humans are not allowed. The railings are made of gold and some other kind of material that radiates the glory of God. Angels stood at the railings.

Around the area surrounded by the railings were living stones shaped like potatoes that were on fire. They gave off blue and amber Shekinah glory. They looked like they were coals from the altar of God, and there was a name on each one of them. Richard's name was on one of these coals before the altar of God. Instantly, he was on his face before God, wanting for all eternity to give glory, honor, and praise to God. The feeling was multiplied millions of times over. He said he has the same feeling now, on Earth, when he is in deep prayer and seeking God. He doesn't want to come out from the joy of being in God's presence. (Sigmund, 103-109)

There is much more Richard Sigmund saw that I will not repeat here. Hopefully what I have shared from his account is enough to give you a sense of the magnitude and majesty of the throne of God.

Dean Braxton saw the Father God sitting on the throne. He was sitting on the throne and He is the throne. He had colors coming off Him, more colors than can be described, and they were alive. Everything that comes from God the Father is alive.

There were an uncountable number of heavenly creatures before the throne giving praise to God.

Regarding the throne of God, he saw that God was vast, as he said on a previous page, "God is large, huge, vast, infinite, enormous, immeasurable, unrestricted, unrestrained, never-ending, endless, without end, free, and at liberty to be God." and the throne was God, and God was the throne. He perceived that God was in the midst of the throne and connected to the throne. Where He was, the throne was. Dean says the throne and God are an integral whole and can never be separated. I don't think we have Earthly concepts sufficient to express what Dean Braxton saw.

The throne appeared as a cloud and was bright. The belief that God is sitting on a chair appears to be not the case. In reality the situation with God and the throne is far more complex.

When he talks about the throne, it has been hard for him to take in all he experienced regarding the throne of God. He is reminded of what God says in Isaiah, *"Heaven is my throne, and the Earth is my footstool"*[6] (Isaiah 66:1, NIV).

The main impression Dean has from looking at the throne is how much the Father loves us. He knew Jesus loved us so much, but to see the Father's love for us far exceeds that of Jesus! When he looked into His eyes, all he could think was His eyes were vaster than the universe itself. But what really stood out for him in all that he saw was the love that God the Father has for each and every one of us on Earth. (Braxton, 116-117)

As he was going to heaven and returning, he saw prayer flying past him like shooting stars. They were like balls of fire with fiery tails behind them. He said they went directly to the throne of God and even inside God. There were millions and millions of prayers going into Him becoming part of Him. The answers came directly from Him. (Roth, 32-33)

Based on the prayers, the Father gave Jesus the information in the prayers. Jesus then dispatched angels to carry out God's request in answer to the prayers. These were prayers of the heart, prayers of faith, knowing God's character and having faith in Him. (Roth, 34)

---

[6] Richard Sigmund said, "Again, I never saw God plainly. I was not allowed to see Him except for one of His feet. His foot seemed to be the size of the United States, and his toe looked the size of Tennessee. I don't understand how this could be, but this was my impression. These are just my words in an attempt to describe the indescribable" (Sigmund, 109).

As he looked at the throne, what stood out was how much the Father loves us, each and every one individually. Every time we breathe, that breath of air is God saying, "I love you!" In God's eyes, everyone is number one. (Roth, 36)

In a vision God took Matthew Payne to heaven and to the throne room. He entered the back of the throne room through double doors. Thousands of people were in the throne room. He went through them and arrived at an elevated spot in front of the throne. There were about 100 stair steps up to the throne. Jesus left him there, and the Father said, "Come up here, Matthew." He said, "Have a look at this." Then it seemed the roof of heaven blew off and he could see up into the galaxy. The stars and planets were very close, perhaps 1000 to 2000 miles away. Gravity would have caused them to crash into Earth, but they were hung in space and not affected by gravity. It was the best view he had ever seen. God told him He controls all of that and could send one of those stars into Earth and destroy it. Then He said, "Don't you think if I can control all of that, that I can control your life?" He had tears in his eyes because of the love and security God was showing him. He said he later read a book by an Indian apostle who had the same vision and heard the very same words from God. (Payne, 1-4)

He had listened to and sung, "I could sing of your love forever; I could sing of your love forever." Then at the throne Jesus sang it to him, He was deeply touched that Jesus would sing of His love for him even though he had a sin addiction that was continuing in his life. Jesus sang, "Over the mountains and the sea, your river runs with love for me, …" and then the chorus, "I could sing of your love forever." He was in tears that Jesus would sing this song about him even with his addiction still in place. (Later he was freed from this addiction, but not at the time he experienced this.) He then saw a progression of saints from the Bible who each waved at him. Jesus had given him a white robe but at this time it became a coat of many colors. He was wearing Joseph's coat. He saw God as a ball of light, while Jesus was God in the image of man. He didn't see the twenty-four elders or the four beasts described in Revelation. He didn't see a rainbow or lightning at the throne. (Payne, 6-12)

On another occasion Matthew was in church on his knees with his arms raised praising God (in obedience to Jesus) when Jesus appeared beside him also on his knees arms raised praising the Father. It was an amazing feeling to be praising God with Jesus beside him also praising the Father. After about twenty seconds they were no longer in the church but in the throne room at the base of the stairs praising God. They were on their knees in front of about 10,000 people standing and worshiping. He said it was an amazing jaw-dropping life-changing experience to see Jesus on his knees praising the Father. He recalled David's statement that one day in the courts of heaven is worth more than a thousand somewhere else. (Psalm 84:10, *"Better is one day in your courts of heaven than a thousand elsewhere; I would rather be a doorkeeper in the house of my God than dwell in the tents of the wicked."*) Whenever he recalls those two minutes at the throne, he said they were worth more than two thousand elsewhere. It was an awesome and mind-boggling experience he would not trade for anything. He saw that Jesus is not only obedient, subservient, and acknowledgment of His Father, but is under His Father's authority. (Payne, 30-32)

Kat Kerr said the throne is high and lifted up in the center of the throne room so people can gather all around it. There are four steps leading up to the throne so anyone there can go into God's presence anytime. There is a beautiful, full-circle rainbow from floor to ceiling totally engulfing the throne. She describes the colors as like our rainbows on Earth but with more colors: purple, sapphire blue, teal, emerald green, topaz gold, and glorious white. The twenty-four elders' thrones encircle God's throne with Jesus' throne right beside His. The Living Creatures of Revelation are there. When they sing out, "Holy, Holy, Holy," the room shakes with power, and fire and thunder come out from the throne. Worship in the throne room involves music and beings unlike anything on Earth. The seraphim with blue flames on their heads fly back and forth over the Father. Many people make flags and banners that fly as they run across the floor of the throne room participating in the worship. The images on the banners come to life, for example the roaring of a lion or the sounding of a shofar.

Our worship on Earth is presented in the throne room as incense. When you dance before the Lord in worship, the angels place a canvas under your feet, and your dancing paints a masterpiece of love that is presented in the throne room and then placed in your Praise Gallery, the place created just for you to display all things you create for worship. When you sing or play an instrument, ribbons of color stream from your mouth and are woven into a tapestry that is another masterpiece of your love. When you work on a painting, music notes come from the paintbrush and compose a symphony that is played in the throne room and placed in your Praise Gallery. When we worship, great love and power is created that not only brings glory to God in the throne room but also does serious damage to Satan's realm. (Kerr 2010, 70-75)

Marvin Besteman saw the throne from the gate. (In heaven we can see clearly much farther than here, perhaps as far away as we like.) He said the throne is dazzling with brilliant white light. There were huge white pillars and a very large throng of people around the throne, worshiping and dancing with arms raised in praise. (So why can't we dance and raise our arms in praise here when we worship. Some fellowships do, but too many don't experience heavenly worship in all its glorious joy in the way Marvin observed around the throne.) There were two Beings being worshiped at the throne. (Besteman, 185-186)

Dr. Gary Wood saw six-winged angels coming into God's presence at the throne with bowls containing the praises of God's people. There were others coming with bowls containing what looked like water. It was the tears of the saints still on Earth. Every time you shed a tear, God notices and keeps it on your behalf.

At the throne there were seven golden lamps having the fire of the Holy Spirit. There was a magnificent, crystal-clear body of water flowing from the throne. Around the throne were rainbows of more colors than the rainbows on Earth. There was also thunder and lightning, but it was not scary. (Roth, 105-106; Wood 27)

He saw the River of Life flowing from the throne, an awesome sight he said. He saw the twenty-four elders with their golden crowns around the throne. (Wood, 27) He saw angels carrying golden bowls of liquid, which were placed at the base of the throne. The angel told him these are the tears of the saints on Earth. He also saw angels carrying golden vials of a vapor-like substance. He was told these are the praises of the saints and are a sweet-smelling incense to God. (Wood, 31-32)

Robert Misst could barely discern the outline of the throne because of the brilliant, glowing light emanating from it. There was a circular rainbow around the throne with seven colors being painted by the sounds from seven musical instruments. He was told the throne is the mercy seat. The twenty-four elders with crowns on their heads were there, worshipping with holiness, love, and humility. He saw a large number of people in beautiful robes. The angel told him they were from every tribe, nation, and tongue, all worshipping together. Their body language expressed love, holiness, and passion for Jesus and the Father. There were myriads of angels above them with the cherubim higher up. The throne was a bright light in the center of all these people who had come to honor and worship their Lord. (Roth, 121-122)

David Taylor also saw the twenty-four elders as he went toward the throne. They were glorious and he understood they were like an executive counsel but operated differently from such a counsel on Earth. He gave no details. He was taken to a large room with glory all around him in the room. The power in the room was so overwhelming that he couldn't stand. He could not see clearly because of the intensity of the light. He was prostrate face down on the marble floor. He raised his head up enough to see the brilliant throne and God's arms and hands resting on the armrests of his throne, but could not see high enough to see God's face. He had no strength and was completely weak in God's presence. God was wearing a beautiful gold wedding band on his finger. He had no explanation at the time, but later Jesus told him that the wedding band represents that He is betrothed to each of us who have been redeemed by the Lamb. He cites several Scripture references to God being betrothed to us. (Taylor, 171-174)

Jim Woodford saw six contrails in the sky like those behind jets except these were going straight up. He asked the angel about these and the angel replied that these are prayers of your family and friends praying for your soul. They are coming up to God at the throne of heaven at this moment. The angel's words brought tears to his eyes. He found out later that at this time his wife, her three sisters, her brother-in-law, and her nephew were praying for him.

The angel told him that mankind is losing its will to pray. We have become so used to instantaneousness that we expect an answer from God quickly and are not patient to wait for God's timing. If we don't get the answer in our time frame, we assume God doesn't listen or doesn't care. The angel told him, however, that God hears every prayer and records it in his halls of knowledge. Other witnesses mention that God dispatches His angels with an answer to the prayer but that the completion of the answer may require other things to fall into place first. We are definitely heard and God definitely cares. (Woodford, 97-98)

Mary K. Baxter saw the things John described regarding the throne: the voice of many angels, the living creatures, the elders, ten thousands times ten thousands, the River of Life coming out from under the throne. Lightning, thunder, and voices, were all around the throne and coming from it. There was a rainbow above the throne. (Baxter, 45)

Then she saw a countless number of saints, clothed in the whitest, most gorgeous robes she had ever seen or imagined. There was the sound of trumpets that gave her a thrill she cannot describe. There were twelve angels, whose breastplates contained many jewels, ministering at the throne. Noting that the saints names were written in the Lamb's Book of Life, He placed a magnificent golden crown on each one's head. (Baxter, 58-60)

One day Matthew Payne was in worship, singing, dancing, and waving banners, all with freedom in the Spirit. He heard Jesus say to him, "I want you to waltz with me." He understood Jesus intended it to be right then. So there in the front of the church he held out his arms in a waltz position and started dancing. Suddenly Jesus was there in his arms waltzing with him, and he could feel him. After a minute they were at the base of the stairs to the throne room, waltzing in front of all the worshipers there. It was like a preview of the Wedding Supper of the Lamb, when we will all dance with Jesus. It was very exciting to be in the throne room. It is very anointed and full of energy. Matthew said it was glorious to be in the throne room dancing with Jesus. (Payne, 24-27)

Summary

The throne of God appears to be an awesome place, beyond earthly description, but nevertheless each author was able to find words to give us an impression of what they saw. Three things that stand out to me are:

1. Everyone is overcome with awe and praise in the presence of God. Typically they fall on their knees in worship. There are other beings

around the throne also praising God, the beasts that John described in Revelation, the twenty-four elders, and various angels.

2. Part of the awesomeness is the awareness of the unimaginable magnitude of God's love for every single person there. As Colton Burpo said, "You can't *belieeeeve* how much he loves us!" (Burpo, 100)

3. All prayers come to the throne room as they are prayed and become part of God, who gives them to Jesus who dispatches the angels in the prayer warrior's behalf. All prayers are effective and answered by God. If you don't see the answer it is only because God's timing is superior to yours, and you just need to hold on and continue the prayers. Ian McCormack's mother continued her prayers for her atheistic son and precipitated Ian's last minute redemption.

It is hard to comprehend the details of what the throne room is like with columns, steps, mist, hugeness, and the variety of descriptions of different witnesses. Whatever it is, we are going to stand in awe, humility, praise, and love before God at the throne of heaven.

CHAPTER 16
Archives Of Heaven, The Book Of Life

Archives

Richard Sigmund was taken to a very large building that had a huge archway. Inside were many rows of shelves with books. To him the shelves seemed to be miles long and miles high and the books about fifteen feet tall. He saw hundreds of angels taking care of the books. They were going in and out with a lot of activity. This large building contained the Archives of Heaven where God keeps records.

> *And I saw the dead, great and small, standing before the throne, and books were opened. Another book was opened, which is the book of life. The dead were judged according to what they had done as recorded in the books.* (Rev. 20:12, NIV)

The Archives of Heaven contain the books about our lives and are the books that are taken to God when the judgment time comes. The books contain the record of our works here on Earth. Every sin is recorded in one of the books.

Richard learned that when we repent, everything that we have done that was wrong or sinful in nature and was recorded in the books is erased for all eternity. Even God cannot find the record; it no longer exists anywhere. Would that human relationships were that way, and once we have repented of our sins, no one remembers them any more. No one would ever say, "I forgive you, but I can never forget what you did!"

He saw another very large building. In it there are books for every person on Earth about our lives. These books contain pictorial records showing every thought and every reaction. Everything is recorded in heaven.

He saw many different books for each person that were being taken care of by tall, slender angels. He said these angels appeared to be eight or nine feet tall.

He saw them pull out the books with their left hands and open their pages. In each page was something like a three-dimensional video screen. The images contained the history of that person's life. They were written, and the pictures were created, long before that person ever came to be. The tall angels wrote in the books holding one in his right hand while making the record with his left using a golden quill that was about five feet long and could write forever.

When I was woven together in the depths of the Earth, your eyes saw my unformed body. All the days ordained for me were written in your book before one of them came to be. (Psalm 139:15b-16, NIV)

Since God is outside of time because He invented and created it, He is able to go forward or backward in time. He is simultaneously in the past, present, and future. God sets up our tomorrows in response to our prayers and our seeking Him today. God knows and orders our tomorrows, but He orders them because we pray today. Richard saw that as we pray, the Holy Spirit speaks to our spirits and causes us to pray as God intends and enables us to seek God. He confirms His plans for us, and regarding things we ask, says "yes", "no'" or "not yet". Another perspective on this is that he was told all of our tomorrows are God's yesterdays. (Sigmund, 50-52)

In view of this, I believe God hears my prayers before in earth time they are prayed and takes them into consideration for the event about which I am praying. So I am free to pray for something that has already happened knowing God heard my prayer before the event happened and my prayer was effective for that event, even though in earth time the prayer was later.

Roland Buck gives a similar report from the time the angel took him to the throne room of God. One thought he had was whether or not God actually made individual plans for each and every life. Roland thought this gigantic task would be too big even for God!

God let him see the vastness of his heavenly archives! It was overwhelming! There was no way his finite mind could understand how God could keep track of this huge number of files. He said there must be billions of them! To help him understand, God took out a book to which Roland could relate: his own life book! He would not let Roland see the contents of it but did mention a few of the future items contained in it so he could use this as confirmation of his visit.

God allowed him to see the record books and His blueprints for many lives. He saw the book of the apostle Paul. In that book, it was revealed that he would be used to bring the gospel to rulers, kings, and men of authority, so God gave him a bigger brain capacity than normal. And He caused him to study under the greatest teachers of his day, finally being tutored by Gamaliel, the most outstanding teacher of that time. God had chosen Paul to write the epistles and His plan for the church and his body, so He prepared him for this task.

God allowed him to peek into Abraham's and Sarah's records. This was one of the most exciting things to him. As he glanced through them, he saw records of things with which he was totally unfamiliar. He saw records of Abraham's and Sarah's hospitality to strangers. He saw that they had a real regard for those less fortunate than they. They did things for their guests such as watered their camels, gave them a place to stay, and shared their food with them. God honored this, and it was written down, but he had never read this in Genesis!

He could not find the places where Abraham stumbled, such as when Abraham lied to the king of Egypt, saying his wife was his sister. It was not recorded there. Also another thing that was not recorded was the time his faith was weak, and he laughed because of unbelief in God's promise that a man of his age could become a father.

Roland then asked God where is the other book? God said He has no other book for believers. So Roland asked Him where he recorded the things just mentioned about Abraham. God emphasized He has no other book and stated, "*I do not record failures in heaven!*" (See Heb 10:17-18)

The files of heaven are not like man would make; they are more complete with everything being meticulously recorded. It is these records he will bring into focus when the books are opened at the time of judgment. The heavenly filing system is a totally different system than that of this world. It is far more complete, yet there is total expunging of things that have been erased through confession and repentance. It is an eternity of archives, some of which are active three-dimensional images. (Buck, 52-54)

Dr. Gary Wood was taken to the library containing volumes and volumes of books. These books contain all we have done in our lives. Everything we have done in our lives, both the good and the bad, is recorded there. He was allowed to see Earth and saw a man approach an altar and accept Jesus as his Lord and savior. When word of this came to heaven, an angel took the book with his name on it and completely erased all the transgressions he had committed so there was no record any more of his wrongdoings. Then the angel opened the Lamb's Book of Life and wrote his name in it. Then something I didn't see recorded in any of the other testimonies occurred. The angels went to his mother's mansion and sang to her a praise song telling her to rejoice because her son had been born again and received Jesus. (Roth, 102-103)

Apparently she died without knowing of her son's salvation. But her prayers for him were still effective and ultimately answered after she died. So don't give up on those you love, even after you die. God will ultimately honor your prayers.

He saw the sins of others erased from their books. He even saw his own book, and written in it were the words, "PAID IN FULL BY THE PRECIOUS BLOOD OF JESUS." He saw that the records contain all the events of our lives, our spiritual growth, how we grow in our relationship with the Lord, how we deal with various situations, and how we influenced others. We don't get to take anything with us except what is recorded in the books in heaven's archives, which is how we have positively affected others to bring them to Jesus. That is the only thing we take with us to heaven, our relationship and our impact on others. (Roth, 103; Wood, 27)

One set of books contains everything a person has thought, intended, or done from the day he/she was born. At the time of the great judgment the contents of these books will testify against those who have never asked to have their sins forgiven and accepted Jesus' gift of forgiveness for them. (Roth, 104)

David Taylor was taken to a large round room filled with huge white and gold books that had the lives of everyone who had ever lived or ever would. They contained all of God's plans for that person. The book of his own life was on a lectern in the middle of the room and a large angel beckoned him to come and look. It had all of the things he had done up to this time, age nineteen. Subsequent pages were blank, waiting to be filled in by the choices he would make in life. These would be recorded next to God's words about the plan He had for David. He was interested in a girl at the time and wondered if he should marry her. But he saw in the book that if he married her it would mess up the special ministry God had for him, which he knew nothing about at the time. (Taylor, 165)

Mary K. Baxter saw angels coming from Earth with reports of things done for the Lord including tithes given. These were taken to a specific room associated with the person for whom the report was made. The attendant in that room would ask the angel for confirmation, for example, "Did you see this happen?" When it was confirmed, the attendant logged it in that person's book in the archives, and eventually it was taken to the throne room. (Baxter, 107)

She also saw the expunging of the record of sins from the books when the subject of the book accepts Jesus and is forgiven all his/her sins. When the report of someone being born again came in, it was recorded that that person had given his/her life to Jesus. His/her name was written in the Lamb's Book of Life. Also angels with golden buckets went to each page of the record of that person's life and with a very beautiful red cloth that looked blood-stained and was mixed with "glory, light, and power," wiped each page of the record of that person's life removing all mention of any sins that person had committed. When they finished, there was no record of that person's sins in heaven any more. All that was recorded there was that he/she had just been born again. (Baxter, 109)

James Woodford described a building the angel called the hall of knowledge. It contains all the prayers and petitions that mankind sends to God and to the throne. It contains God's knowledge of heart and longings of all men. There were also the accounts of the good and evil deeds of all men. (Except others have testified that all the evil deeds of sin of those who have been forgiven and redeemed by Jesus' sacrificial blood have been expunged from the records.) This is where the books of our lives are kept. (Woodford, 110)

Jeanne Enstad was taken to a library with "thousands upon thousands of books." She saw one with her name on it but was not allowed to read it. The angel told her she was going back to Earth, her life is not finished yet. (Enstad, 87)

Book of Life

Richard Sigmund was shown the Lamb's Book of Life. He said it was a mile high and three quarters of a mile wide. Angels turned the pages, and he was lifted up so he could read what was written in three-inch golden letters outlined in crimson red on that page: "Richard of the Family of Sigmund: Servant of God". It was his entry in the Lamb's Book of Life. It had the date of his birth and that of his conversion. The letters of his name were in crimson red because the blood of Jesus covered him. (Sigmund, 26)

Dale Black saw the Book of Life on a pillar to the right of the gate in the wall. It was massive, with a cover made of pearl and gold lattice around the edges. The book was filled with living light that came out of the book like a vapor. Each page radiated this light. He knew that unless his name was written in the book, he could not now or ever pass through the gate into heaven. Nothing was more crucial or important than finding his name in the Book of Life. As he approached the book, it opened itself to the page where he could see his full name written. As he looked at his name, he vividly remembered the time as a youth that he gave his heart to God through Jesus Christ. There were other names there, but they were blurred, and he was prevented from reading them. There were numbers next to his name that he did not understand. The angel told him the first number was the day God created him, the day he was given life, the day he was conceived, not the day he was born. The second number was the date he gave his heart to the Lord, the day he was reborn. He was puzzled by the absence of a date for the day he died. It seemed clear to him that he had in fact died. The angel said he is not dead, he will never die, he is eternal. Then he realized that since he had left his body, he felt more alive than he ever had felt before. Then the angel had a big grin and stepped aside to let him enter the gate.

Marvin Besteman saw inside the gate a long shelf extending off into a mist beyond about twelve feet in both directions from where he was standing. On this shelf were piled three to four books all along the shelf in both directions. The books were thick like the telephone directory of a large city and bound in an antique black cowhide, worn but intact. These together were the Book of Life. Peter took one of the books that was maybe twelve inches wide and ten inches tall. Marvin couldn't see what language was written there or the font or size. He did note that once your name is written in the Book of Life, it is permanent and can never be erased. The Bible assures us that Satan can never steal us from God's hand once we have been redeemed by the blood of the Lamb. Marvin saw that this is true. (Besteman, 103-112) Marvin learned his name was not written in the book FOR THAT DAY. He was not supposed to go fully into heaven at that time. He argued with Peter, who disappeared saying he would talk to God. Marvin did not want to go back to Earth, as is true of everyone who gets that far, but God does not make mistakes.

There are no mistakes in heaven, none! Marvin would not be allowed any further into heaven and would have to return to this life. (Besteman, 115-118)

God seems to have chosen some of us to glimpse heaven and come back to tell us what God has prepared for our eternity, showing us His love far more deeply than we can imagine. As several have said, Jesus is coming back very, very soon. He wants His church to be ready. Also God wants all of us made in His image there with Him, but we have complete freewill. He will not force anyone who doesn't want Him in his or her life to be in His presence. He will be very sad when the time comes and He has to tell someone He has loved dearly, good-bye forever.

Summary

There are many, many books in heaven that record the lives of everyone on Earth, past, present, and future, in animated 3-D. These books will be consulted at the final judgment, and the recorded sins of those who have not been redeemed by the blood will prevent them from entering heaven. However, the sins of those redeemed by the blood of Jesus are not anywhere recorded in any of the books. In their case, the books will determine their heavenly rewards, but no one will have any lack, discomfort, or disappointment in heaven regardless of the record because of the infinite love of the Father and the Son.

In addition there is the Book of Life. This book is separate from the archives and contains the names of those whose have been redeemed from all their sins by receiving the forgiveness wrought by the blood of Jesus. This is in addition to having the record of all sins expunged from the archives when one accepts Jesus.

CHAPTER 17

Libraries, Education, And Other Buildings

Libraries

Betty Eadie was taken to large room similar to a library, which seemed to be a repository of knowledge, but she didn't see any books. Then she noticed ideas coming into her mind, filling it with knowledge on subjects she had not thought about for a long time, or, in some cases, not at all. It was at this point that she understood this was a library of the mind. By simply reflecting on a topic, all knowledge on that topic came to her. She could learn about anybody in history, or even in the spirit world, in full detail.

She was given any knowledge she desired there. She understood correctly every thought, every statement, and every particle of knowledge given to her. There was absolutely no misunderstanding. History was pure. Understanding was complete. She understood not only what people did but also why they did it and how it affected other people's perceptions of reality. She understood reality pertaining to that subject from every angle, from every possible perception. All of this knowledge brought wholeness to an event or person or principle that was not possible to comprehend on Earth.

But this was not just a mental process; she was able to *feel* what people felt when they did these actions. She understood their pains or joys or excitement because she was able to live them. Some of this knowledge was taken from her when she returned to Earth, but not all of it. She cherishes the knowledge granted her of certain events and people in our history, which were important for her to understand. (Eadie, 76-77)

Jim Woodford saw a building the angel called the hall of learning. It is a place where anyone can learn more about God and what He has done from the beginning of creation. It contains everything that has ever been written about God and Jesus. Here one can go deeper into the incalculable mysteries of God. (Woodford, 110)

Richard Sigmund was taken to the building containing the written library of God's knowledge. When you are there, your mind is automatically stimulated. He spoke with a man who said he had been there for two millennia and was only on page two. Millions of angels and people were coming and going at this library. When we pray for wisdom, the Holy Spirit and the angels come here to get God's knowledge that our prayers request. (Sigmund, 55)

Education

Richard saw great universities in heaven. People there were eagerly learning things from God's knowledge, and they never forget what they have learned. The universities are huge and can hold hundreds of thousands of people in huge auditoriums. He said all subjects are taught. You retain everything you learn and your education continues for eternity. There is always more to learn and your whole mind is engaged in the learning. Even so your capacity to learn keeps growing. He saw people praising God for all they were learning. (Sigmund, 56)

Kat Kerr saw a Word University where citizens of heaven are taught God's revealed word. Everyone needs to know God's revealed word, and so it is taught to everyone there far beyond anything taught here. Some of the classes are outside, some are inside, some have beanbag chairs, but all are very comfortable and conform to the student's body. Everyone remembers what he/she learns there.

Another university is the Royal University, where we are taught how to rule when Jesus establishes His kingdom on Earth. God's leaders in eternity will be filled with and operate in love, freedom, and grace, and the students will learn how to express God's love. Since there is no evil in heaven, there is no need to study defense. This building was like a castle with murals on the walls that come to life as you watch. There is a celebration at the end of the course.

One of her favorite places was the Creation Lab. This is a domed building in which are displayed in hologram form scenes from how God accomplished all of creation. This building has the unique feature that there are no entrances. You create an entrance by your faith, she said, but was not able to explain how that works. You will have to go there and see it for yourself. It took her a while to accomplish it. In the hologram she saw, God spoke and things began to form and spin in space. When Earth appeared He poured water out of His hand to form the oceans. Then He spoke and plants appeared, then atmosphere, then animals. She provides more details of what she saw in the hologram.

The Hall of Knowledge was a series of diamond-like towers that contained volumes on any subject. She took one, and a pedestal table suddenly appeared in front of her to hold the book. When she opened it a hologram appeared, and she "watched" the book instead of "reading" it. (Kerr 2010, 46-58)

Oden Hetrick said we will always be learning in heaven. We don't come there knowing everything or even getting all knowledge instantly. We learn from going to classes, observing, interacting with others, and having experiences. (Doucette 2013-1)

Marriage Supper of the Lamb

Jesus told the two angels accompanying Richard Sigmund to take him to His marriage feast, saying, "Let him see it. It is almost ready." The building was very tall with arched supports and columns fifty feet apart. The tables were gold inlaid with jewels. The tables were lined with chairs that looked like thrones. The tables and chairs were constructed beautifully. The building was a pavilion Richard estimated to be twenty miles long. There were three rows of tables arranged in a semicircle with a throne at the head. Each chair had a name engraved on the inside of the back that was engraved when that person's name was inscribed in the Lamb's Book of Life. Richard saw his own chair and wanted to sit in it. But Jesus would not allow him. That will happen when the Father says, "Sit at the marriage feast of My Son." At each place at the table there was a goblet filled with sweet nectar and a golden dish with heaven's best. Everything was perfect and was ready for the entrance of the Groom. The marriage feast had room for millions and millions of people. (Sigmund, 48-49)

Dawn Cypret also saw the location for the Marriage Supper of the Lamb. She said it is grand and majestic in design, like a castle or cathedral. It was long and tall, as Richard said. The building was made with jewels in the walls. She saw a long line of people outside as far as she could see waiting to enter the hall. Jesus took her to the head of the line and into a very elegant dining hall the size of several football fields. It is massive and the architecture is mind-blowing! Even the words "elegant" and "beautiful" don't do it justice. The ceiling is high above the shiny marble floor and tall stained glass windows line the walls. The long tables had pristine white tablecloths with the finest gold china and crystal stemware. There were beautiful floral centerpieces and gorgeous golden candelabras. Someone was lighting the candles, which is the last thing you do before the guests arrive. (May, 28-29)

Please note the significance of this. The original copyright on Richard's book is 2004, updated 2010. The copyright on Dawn's book is 2018. The candles were not being lighted in 2004 or 2010 but were being lighted in 2018. The implication to me is the time of Jesus return and His wedding supper feast is closer than you think! It could be very, very soon as Dawn and others have said.

One day Matthew Payne was in worship, singing, dancing, and waving banners, all with freedom in the Spirit. He heard Jesus say to him, "I want you to waltz with me." He understood Jesus intended it to be right then. So there in the front of the church he held out his arms in a waltz position and started dancing. Suddenly Jesus was there in his arms waltzing with him, and he could feel him. After a minute they were at the base of the stairs to the throne room, waltzing in front of all the worshipers there. It was like a preview of the Wedding Supper of the Lamb, when we will all dance with Jesus. It was very exciting to be in the throne room. It is very anointed and full of energy. Matthew said it was glorious to be in the throne room dancing with Jesus. (Payne, 24-27)

Auditorium

After Dr. Gary Wood left the archives building he went to an auditorium. Suddenly he was aware of being in a glowing robe, which he was not in before. (Apparently we change clothes to whatever is appropriate for where we are and what we are doing without any action on our part.) He saw a beautiful staircase winding up into the heights of the atmosphere, but does not say anything more about it. There was also a beautiful crystal clear river, which I describe in chapter 6 on the waters of heaven. (Wood, 27)

Other Buildings

There are many other buildings in heaven. They each have some special function. Richard Sigmund reports on some of these, including a huge castle in which are stored all the hopes and dreams of God's people that He wants to fulfill in our lives. (Sigmund, 91-92, 103-104)

Richard's accompanying angel told him of the rewards building, but he was not taken there. In this building are all the rewards we do not receive on Earth. What we give on Earth is in this building and will be given back to us in heaven.

He was taken to a large building with many beautiful rooms inside. Even though he said he was not taken to the rewards building, this building sounds like it is part of the rewards department. He saw a chair like a recliner that folded itself around the man sitting in it making it extremely comfortable. It seemed that each room was where preparations are being made for someone on Earth for when that person comes to heaven. Someone read from a book of the desires of a Christian man on Earth and preparations were being made to fulfill those desires. They were planning his heavenly home and the heavenly events in store for him. As he saw a group making plans for someone, one person said, "Let's do this," and he waved his hand in the air. As he did so, sparks flew off, sparkling like fireworks. The rooms were huge and had chandeliers that glowed different colors from within. Richard said that from this one building, he saw that God wants to bless us far more than we desire to be blessed. (Sigmund 70-72)

He saw numerable memorials that commemorated great events or people wherein He was glorified or many people saved or blessed. (Sigmund, 57-58)

Oden Hetrick reported that we are rewarded for the things we do on Earth; there are no rewards for what we do in heaven where there is no battle against the temptations of sin. So now is when we need to be doing things in response to God and to His glory. We cannot make up for our lack when we get to heaven. But there everyone is happy with what he/she gets. There is a lot of laughter and happy fellowship there. (Doucette 2013-1)

Richard Sigmund was taken to an amphitheater, like a movie theater, but where the stage would be was a huge window, floor to ceiling, wall to wall, that looked out on all of heaven. No one was allowed to speak there, just to behold the beauty of heaven and praise God. He said this is the meeting place where people first encounter the cleansing power of heaven's glory. They leave with all the cares of Earth cleansed away. He felt a peace and quietness that made all previous cares and problems melt away. (Sigmund, 81)

Jim Woodford saw a hall of healing. This is not for the healing of injuries or diseases as they have all been already healed by arrival in heaven. This hall is for the healing of the soul for people who have had difficult lives and need a time of recovery. They may have been involved in drugs or trauma of various kinds. They may have turned to Jesus at the last moment as Jim did. God's love is there to heal them from all these wounds of the spirit so there is no more crying or pain of any kind. (Woodford, 110-111)

Others report this healing and cleansing from the cares of the Earth by contact with the water of the River of Life. See the chapter on the waters of heaven.

The angel showed Mary K. Baxter a long hall with rooms that were labeled "Storehouse." The angel said these rooms are where God has stored up blessings for His people. They are waiting in heaven for the future recipient to claim them and receive them now on Earth. Jesus was there and told her these rooms contain healings that will make His people whole. That is his desire for them. But the people just have to believe that He is the Christ and is able to perform the miracles and healing to receive these gifts of healing. (Baxter, 45-48)

The angel also showed her the room of tears that glowed with holiness and power. It had a grand entryway with no doors. The inside walls were lined with crystal shelves that radiated light. On the shelves were bottles that looked like glass. Some were in clusters of three, and there was a plaque under each bottle or cluster with a name on it. Inside the room she saw a glorified man in a beautiful purple velvet robe. There was an elegant table that glowed with majestic splendor. On it were beautiful books sewn with a silk-like material and embedded with diamonds, pearls, green and purple stones, and lace. The books were absolutely stunning.

The man in the beautiful robe told her to come and see. A large beautiful and majestic angel came in the entranceway with a small golden bowl in his hands. It was filled with a liquid. The man said the angel had just brought him a bowl of tears from the Earth and said he would show her what he does with them. There was also a note inscribed with the name of the person from whom the tears came. The man read the note and then went to the bottle labeled with the same name. He then took the nearly full bottle over to the bowl and poured the liquid from the bowl into the bottle. He said he would show her what they do in heaven with the bottle of tears from the saints of God. He said, " Tell the people on Earth about this." He took the bottle to one of the books whose pages were blank. He poured one drop from the bottle onto the first page and beautiful handwritten words began immediately to fill the page. He continued to pour one drop on each page and each page filled with words. He said the most perfect prayers are those bathed with tears.

Then the angel took her to the Throne Room. There she saw a huge cloud or mist with a Being in it. Before the throne was a large altar and on it was a book like she had just seen into which the tears had dropped. Something that looked like a man's hand came out of the cloud and opened the book. Smoke that had the smell of the most beautiful perfume came out of the book and filled the air. The angel told her the book contains the prayers of the saints. As God opened the book, pages flew out to angels on horses as God's voice thundered out to take the answers to those who had prayed. (Baxter, 33-36)

Besides buildings there are memorials to how we have unselfishly served others. Kat Kerr saw a memorial to a Christian woman who cared for and helped orphans and the abandoned of this world, in spite of being maligned by both the secular world and some Christian leaders. Her memorial was made from mother of pearl and shone brightly with beautiful waterfalls and a large fountain. The lower wall of the fountain had children's happy faces and the upper wall had very real engraved butterflies.

Another one that she saw also had a large fountain. It had a transparent bridge that went over the fountain. Looking down one saw not his/her own reflection but the faces of those people whom the person of this memorial had helped. It had roses and baby's breath around the fountain and up the huge columns that were part of the memorial. There were platforms on which symphonies of heaven came and performed. There were areas for sitting and fellowshipping, which this individual liked to do. It had an area for the entertainment of children. One feature was a structure with a dome at the top, out of which a bubble would come and encase the child there. He/she would then float around in the bubble and bump into friends' bubbles. When he/she tired of this activity, he/she could simply pop his/her bubble and float to the ground. (Kerr 2007, 103)

These memorials are made regardless of whether or not the honoree ever accepts Jesus and comes to heaven to see the memorial. An example of this is in Acts chapter 10 which records God's honoring the Centurion Cornelius for his acts of kindness and gifts to the poor before Peter came and he received Christ. (Kerr 2007, 103-104)

Kat also described the Hall of Superheroes. This is an amazing place where God honors those who stand in the gap for others praying for them. It glows with the Glory of God. There are long corridors with the faces engraved on the walls of the prayer warriors now living in heaven. She said as you gaze at one, light forms around it and you are pulled back into the time on Earth of that prayer warrior. You hear him/her crying out in prayer on behalf of others and see the Throne of God right there in front of him/her as he/she prays. As he/she prays, his/her words are formed into a sword, which the angel of the Lord takes and uses to fight the enemy. Her conclusion is that your prayers do make a difference. (Kerr 2010, 125, 126)

Dr. Gary Wood was taken to a long storage building. In it were lots of body parts. He saw the prayers of saints for someone for whom the doctor said something was bad and needed to be removed. The prayers shot up to the throne room of God, who then dispatched angels to come to this room and get the healing miracle and take it to Earth to the one for whom the saints were praying. He also saw angels with the answered miracle from God being harassed by principalities and power stopped by doubt and unbelief from the mouth of the petitioner. The person would say something like, "It's not God's will that I be healed." He said there is never a place in Scripture where Jesus says, "It is not my will that you be healed." (However God chose not to heal Paul of his "thorn in the flesh," but God made it clear to Paul and did not leave it up to his imagination.)

The angel would turn around and bring the miracle back to a room for unclaimed miracles. (Wood, 35-36)

Oden Hetrick saw a Temple of Instruction where children are taught in a room inside the wall of the city. There were other rooms like theaters except the TV-like or movie-like pictures are three-dimensional. One of the scenes there was the life of Christ. The children watch this as part of their instruction. Everyone who goes to heaven is required to see this scene since the story of Christ's life and death for us is basic to why we are in heaven. There is also a videotape of each person's life. This is in addition to the books that record every event of our lives. Since all record of our sins is wiped from God's records when we accept Jesus and those sins are forgiven, the videotape of our lives does not contain a portrayal of any of our sins. (Doucette 2013-1) (It could be a very short video in that case!)

Summary

There are libraries separate from the archives. These contain all of knowledge and one can go there and learn anything. It seems that you don't read in these libraries, the knowledge just enters your spiritual mind. In these cases the knowledge is communicated directly from God's mind to our mind, but there is also written knowledge available.

There are universities in heaven where our education will continue for eternity without any memory loss. We will have access to all of God's knowledge. There is a university for studying the Word of God, a university where we learn how to rule when Jesus establishes His kingdom on Earth and a lab learning all about how God did creation.

There are cinema-like rooms where we can see a video of Jesus' life or our own lives.

The building for the marriage supper of the Lamb is massive and elegant and ready for all the guests. Between the two witnesses we can see the progress toward being ready for the great feast to begin. It could be any day now.

There are many types of buildings there with special functions. There is a castle in which all our hopes and dreams that God wants to fulfill are stored. There is a rewards building that contains the rewards God wants to give us for our work on Earth. There are memorials for great spiritual events. There are also memorials in heaven for everyone who has given of him/herself for others, whether or not they come to heaven. There is a Hall of Superheroes for those who have been faithful and diligent warriors in prayer.

It looks like our lives are going to be very full there, but it will all be very joyful and never onerous. It also appears there is much we are missing here that God would love us to have but doubt and lack of prayer is holding back the blessing.

CHAPTER 18

Life In Heaven

Happiness, contentment, joy, love

The universal experience of everyone being in heaven or being in the presence of Jesus in a dream or vision is of overwhelming love and peace and acceptance. Richard Sigmund said he experienced peace and tranquility there greater than any human has ever known on Earth. (Sigmund, 77)

Dawn Cypret said one thing that is constant in heaven but rarely found on Earth is a constant peaceful happy feeling that caused her spirit to rejoice and know she was home. (May, 21)

Richard Eby said in Heaven there is total love, confidence, and peace, and everything is perfect, blissful; there is no fear, just total joy and peace. (Roth, 169) He further said God's love is so far beyond our experience here that our minds cannot fathom it. We are infused with that love the moment we enter heaven. He is in us and we are in him in wonderful ways beyond anything we can know here, but we still have our unique identity. He does not take that away when he enters us. (Roth, 172)

He said experiencing the full dose of God's love and peace seems perfectly normal there and magnificently limitless. Heaven is all about God. (Roth, 173)

Steven Musick said heaven feels like "being inside pure joy." We have no words to describe it; we have no context in which to understand it. Heaven defies depiction. (Musick, 39). Heaven is beyond imagining!

Dale Black said as he was standing in the gate immersed in music, light, and love, vibrant life permeated everything. It was not just around him, it was in him. It was the most wonderful thing he has ever experienced. It felt like he belonged there; it was what he had been searching for all his life. He didn't want to leave. (Black 2010, 107) He said there is no pride, pretense, or selfishness in heaven. Heaven is not about what we get; it is all about God. (Black 2018, 12)

Eben Alexander received the message, "You are loved and cherished; You have nothing to fear; and You can do nothing wrong," which all boiled down to the knowledge that love in its purest most powerful form is the basis of everything. (Alexander, 71)

That sense of overwhelming love and peace is a feeling that seems to be what life is really all about. It is a love that the person has never known before—stronger, purer, and more real than any that person has known. Heaven is a connected community where everyone is giving glory where glory is due, to God alone. That creates joy and gratefulness among all those in heaven. (Black 2018, 13)

Kat Kerr adds that you are loved and accepted by everyone there, even including any who may have been enemies on Earth. (Kerr 2010, 34)

The people who have been there and experienced this love come away longing to stay with Jesus. People who have had the chance to see what heaven is like don't want to leave or do look forward to coming back.

Heaven defies earthly description

There is no disobedience in heaven but Oden Hetrick said the Spirit of God is very patient with us. (Doucette 2013-3)

Marietta Davis said there are no words that can accurately describe what she saw and experienced in heaven, the beauty, the perfection, the purity of thought. (Davis, 9)

Steven Musick said heaven has paradoxes. One is that he felt absolutely held but at the same time absolutely free. Once you have felt being held in the arms of the Father, there is nothing else that you would want. It is an overwhelming wonderful sensation, being held tight but still completely free and secure. Another is that it is a place of explosive peace that pursues you, moves toward you, and explodes in you. It is not passive, it is actively seeking you. It is not just a lack of conflict as we might think of peace here, it is something at a deep level that reassures us that all is well, everything is all right. (Musick, 39)

There he felt relationship as a child belonging to Someone higher. It is a sense of a true home, total acceptance and belonging. His heart leaped as this was that for which his spirit always longed. It was right and natural. (Musick, 40)

In heaven there is no thought of the past and thoughts of the future have no meaning. All Steven wanted to do was stay right there in the present, he was so captivated by the sense of "now." It is not that he had no sense of the past, but just that he was "totally present, totally joyful, totally here." He had no thoughts of ever seeing his wife or parents again; he was totally occupied with the glorious present of the heavenly now. (Musick, 40)

Mary K. Baxter said everything in heaven is perfect. There are no flaws or faults in anything, unlike here on Earth. Satan and fallen angels and any who have rebelled against God are not allowed to be there and spoil the perfection. She said the beauty and wonders are beyond human description, (hence the title of this book). The splendor and beauty of heaven is indescribable and wondrous to behold. (Baxter, 27) No human qualifies for the perfection required of heaven. Any humans that are there are only there because they have allowed Jesus to replace their imperfection with His perfection.

You will be unbelievably happy there. Memories of home on Earth will be far away. She affirmed Scripture, Rev 21:4, "*He will wipe every tear from their eyes. There will be no more death or mourning or crying or pain, for the old order of things has passed away,*" saying there is no sadness there, no sorrow or grief. (Baxter, 76)

Besides experiencing first hand the love of Jesus and the Father, the experience of heaven is literally beyond this world. There we have more than five senses, and they are all more refined than here. All the human emotions are present in heaven but are much deeper. At one point, Eben Alexander was not allowed back in the central part of heaven and experienced a sadness unlike any he had ever known before. But in his sadness he became aware of all those who were praying for him. These prayers gave him energy in contrast to the sadness he had felt and gave him a confidence that everything was going to be all right. He knew he was on his way back but not alone, never alone because God would ALWAYS be with him, directly and through his angels. (Alexander, 102-104)

Being in God's/Jesus' presence the best

Jeanne Enstad said life in heaven is glorious being in the presence of Jesus all the time. It is one great brotherhood, the head of which is

Christ and the cornerstone is love. Everyone loves everyone else. (Enstad, 32) She was enraptured by the beautiful golden streets, the amazing illuminating light of God everywhere, and the peace and love. But what she treasured most was the presence of our Lord. His love and grace are more than you can imagine, and He is always present. She also remembers heaven as a perfect place. There are no wars, no pain, no bad economy, no anger or jealousy. Everyone loves everyone else and praises God in all things. There is no evil at all. Wherever she went there were people talking and laughing, enjoying each other, and being kind to each other. It was a kind of love she had never found on Earth.

There is no sadness in heaven, so people were always freely joyful and having fun together. There was no arguing and wherever she went she was greeted in love. The children were playing everywhere with merry shouts of laughter. They were playing simple fun games without computers, smart phones, and video games. (Enstad, 88)

There was no darkness, everything was breathtaking, everything was loving and peaceful. The best part of heaven is the loving presence of God Himself. It is like the description of the Garden of Eden in Genesis. She observed in heaven, there is "no more death, no more crying, no more pain, fear, sin, or sorrow. We will be free to become all God created us to be. Never again will we have to experience the consequences of our fallen nature." (Enstad, 87)

Jim Woodford observed that all the people seemed to be in their early thirties. His angel explained that God so loved Jesus and his sacrifice for us that he decreed that everyone in heaven would be the age Jesus died. Exceptions are some of the patriarchs and prophets of the Bible. Whenever they pass by everyone else steps back in deference to them. Their robes have a pastel quality to them. The other exception is children who are any age less that thirty down to preborn infants.

The people were from every tongue and tribe, some walking arm in arm, some in family groups. Their faces showed the love and the joy of life in heaven. They all exhibited restful purpose, but it was not the worldly purposes of this life, like trudging off to work. The purpose they had showed up as joy and anticipation of delight. Some carried books, others musical instruments. All were wearing clothes of shimmering light. (Woodford, 112-113)

In spite of the beauty of the landscape, the parks, the streams, the city, the light, the music, and the love and joy that permeates everything, the greatest joy to him was being face to face with Jesus. (Woodford, 115)

Oden Hetrick said heaven is all about relationships and companionships, especially our relationship with Jesus. The relationships are perfect. We will enjoy fellowship with constant companions and the presence of Jesus. We will have companionship with relatives, loved ones and even those we haven't met yet. (Doucette 2013-1)

Everything better than Earth

The colors are richer and the sounds more melodious. The trees are bigger, the grass is greener, and the flowers are more beautiful. In addition, there is no death in heaven, no death of anything—leaves never fade and die, flowers never wither and die, even picked flowers continue to grow when dropped, the grass never turns brown, no animals die, and there is no death or sickness or pain or suffering. Nothing can ever harm you; you can't drown, you can't fall, you can't even get a cold. No animal ever bites anyone or any being. I assume there are no ticks or mosquitoes there, or if there are, they do not bite. (They bite us here to get our blood, but our heavenly bodies have no blood.) Richard Eby said there are no insect bites in heaven. (Roth, 173)

Everyone is friendly and glad to see you coming. There is great joy in meeting loved ones and friends who have gone before. You can have long conversations, you can go places together; you can enjoy many things there including the forests, the meadows, the River of Life, the lakes, the seas, the choral music, the voices of people and angels singing praises, the beautiful architecture. Each home there is made especially for the person who is to live there and is better than any home on Earth ever could be.

Since children can jump and run and play, I assume anyone can without limitation. There is no arthritis, no bad knees, no fatigue, no hindrance. Maybe I will be able to run even better than when I was in college. Everyone sings better than he/she ever did on Earth with higher highs and lower lows.

Gravity does not bind us in heaven. While the children could float down like cotton balls or stay hovered above a ring of children, people can stroll through the sky as well as on the ground. Richard Sigmund reported rising up and seeing more and more distant villages. (Sigmund, 83-84) He also said distances are not limiting, one can easily stroll to locations seemingly far away, and one can even just appear at a place when conceiving of being there. (Sigmund, 41)

We don't have to eat in heaven, but if we choose to eat, the fruit on the trees along the River of Life and elsewhere is fantastic. When touched to your lips, it melts into a liquid that is like pear juice, peach juice, and honey that runs over your hand and face and down your throat for an incredible, delicious taste. Then whatever is left over, including that on your face and hands, just evaporates. Any fruit that is not used just evaporates. New fruit immediately grows to replace one picked.

A friend of mine said once that he is looking forward to grilling a wonderful steak in heaven. I asked him if that means a cow must die. He didn't have an answer. Unless God provides something else for grilling, I assume that is one of the activities we enjoy here that we will not have and not miss in heaven. He very well could provide non-animal-based steaks made out of some other wonderful substance in heaven superior to beef. I think there are many activities we have here that have no place in heaven, but we will not miss them. The activities God has prepared for us there will be far more satisfying than the ones we have here. On the other hand, some of the wholesome activities we enjoy here will be there also. God desires to make our lives in His kingdom absolutely wonderful.

Similarly to the fruit juice on your face evaporating completely, being in the water does not make you or your clothing wet. Everything stays dry. You can play under the water and never drown. This is a result of nothing in heaven can harm you in any way.

Also bathrooms are not needed at all, due to not having to eat and never getting soiled. Richard Sigmund observed this and said none of the houses he saw had bathrooms. You don't have to eat there, but if you do it turns into delicious liquid and then just evaporates. Also you never need to take a bath because you never get dirty. (Sigmund, 75)

We will each have work to do there. Those who were just visiting weren't assigned any work other than to tell the world when they return about Jesus and the Father and how great is their love for us and that they don't want anyone to miss heaven. But some of the residents reported having work to do.

Whatever illness or incapacity we have when we enter heaven is completely healed, and we are restored to what we would be in our prime. Several people who just visited came back healed. Betty Malz was completely healed from her ruptured appendix. Richard Sigmund was suddenly well when he returned after being dead eight hours. Don Piper, George Ritchie, and Samaa Habib miraculously returned to life, but still had a long recovery healing to go through.

Rebecca Springer (Springer, 70) and Richard Sigmund (Sigmund, 87) both witnessed other communities in heaven, including some of other Earthly cultures. But no matter what village one was in, the same joy, praise, peace, and enjoyment was there for each one. All communities in heaven are just part of one holy community, united in God's and Jesus' love for them and the great mercy they have shown us. Richard Sigmund told us that the throne of God is central to heaven. Everything flows into and out of the throne, and it is visible from every place in heaven.

Betty Eadie said that many of our inventions and technological advances were first developed in the spirit world and then given as inspiration to mortals. She said that spirit prodigies in heaven first created many of our important inventions and even technological developments in the spirit. Then individuals on Earth received the inspiration from the Holy Spirit to create the inventions here. (Eadie, 48)

When he was with Jesus in 1943, George Ritchie was shown the plan for a nuclear submarine engine test facility although, at the time, he didn't know what it was. Then nine years later, he saw an architect's drawing of the same thing in a *Life* magazine article. It was exactly like he had seen nine years before, before scientists had even conceived of it here. (Ritchie, 71, 119-121) We will be creative and inventive in heaven as we are here.

CHAPTER 19
Life Here After Heaven Visit

Everyone who has been to heaven and seen the perfection, the joy, the peace, the love, the beauty, and the relationships is profoundly affected upon their return. Life is not the same for them as it was before. They have a new sense of what is important and what this life is all about.

Matthew Payne said the strong presence of God felt there gives one a feeling of bliss. Since heaven is such a beautiful place and it is so enjoyable there and being in the presence of God is so wonderful, coming back to Earth is really a jolt. (Payne, 44)

Betty Malz

When Betty Malz was returning to her body in the hospital after being dead for half an hour, she saw all the church steeples of Terre Haute and was suddenly aware of God's love for all His churches. Her prejudices were resolved, and she loved all His people. When she was back in her body, she sat up and looked out the window and noticed the beautiful green grass, which she had been too busy for years to notice. I think the beautiful green grass on the hill she climbed in heaven gave her a new sense of God's grass even on Earth. She also saw a black man carrying a case of soft drinks into the hospital. She had never cared for black people, but now she was feeling a great love for the man. (Malz, 89-90) She used to have a fear of high places. Since her visit to heaven and her healing, she has no more apprehension of high places. In addition to healing and cleansing her body from the appendicitis poisons, God cleansed her of lifelong prejudices toward minority groups and a distaste for certain personalities. She had a new love and respect for her mother-in-law she never had before (although it still needed some work!) (Malz, 98)

Her mother-in-law had complained about how they lived beyond their means and were always in debt. Now she understood and appreciated her mother-in-law's perspective. She cared much less about things and cared more about being a good wife and mother. She was going to point out some verses of Scripture that her mother-in-law needed to read. As she was about to call her mother-in-law and read the first verse from Proverbs, her eyes landed on Psalms 141:3, which she read from the KJV, "Set a watch, O Lord, before my mouth; keep the door of my lips." What God told her was not to call to correct her mother-in-law but instead to meet with her and ask her to forgive Betty's years of unfriendly words, thoughts, and actions against her. (Malz, 100-101)

Her caring less about things now was abundantly confirmed a few years later when the new house they had built was hit by a tornado and totally demolished. Nearly everything they owned was gone or destroyed. But she was surprised at her calmness at the loss or destruction of all her prized possessions. Things did not matter to her since her time in heaven, and she recalled the verses of a hymn:

A tent or a cottage, why should I care?
They're building a palace for me over there;
Though exiled from my home, yet, still I may sing;
All glory to God, I'm a child of the King.
(from Harriet E. Buell, "A Child of the King") (Malz, 104)

A few years later, her husband John's health had deteriorated. He sensed death was approaching, and he feared it. He also did not want to leave all the things and people he enjoyed here. So he asked Betty to tell him again about what she experienced in heaven. She told him again with a clarity of memory that others have described about their heavenly journey. While memories of things here diminish, it seems ones memory of heaven does not diminish. She described the feelings of joy and lightness, the beautiful colors, the wall and jewels, the glorious music, the warmth of Jesus. John thought, since many of those things are here, why leave to be there? She said the person and presence of Jesus was the most glorious thing about her visit there. She could learn anything she wanted from Him, He knew her better than anyone, yet He loved her unconditionally in spite of her faults. It was that love that most impressed her in wanting to stay there. Her words helped him become relaxed about his future, and he said he was beginning to feel some of the intense love of Jesus she had felt. (Malz, 106-107) It was not long after that that John did indeed go to heaven.

What he saw there went far beyond what Betty had told him, because she just had a glimpse of heaven from the green grassy hill, the gate in the wall, and the city beyond the gate. After reading this book and the testimonies of so many witnesses, you know more to anticipate than did her husband John.

Steven Musick

Steven Musick had a transformative experience with Jesus when Jesus knew everything about him for his whole life, all the hurts and joys, and had worked all of it for his good. As a consequence of that, healing and reconciliation occurred with all of his family. When Jesus showed him what people who had hurt him felt and why they were the way they were he had an understanding he never had before. He had understanding and sympathy and was able to forgive and be reconciled to every one of them. He loved his mother and father in ways he never had before. He forgave his brother for the hurt his brother had caused before anyone knew his brother had been diagnosed with bipolar disorder. Even his good relationship with his wife was positively affected. (Musick, 45-46)

As he recovered in the hospital, he kept having memories of his walk with Jesus and the extreme love and understanding that came through Jesus. He longed to return there. This world seemed bland compared to the presence of heaven and all the rich sensations there. (Musick, 53-54)

He struggled in the years following his experience with Jesus in heaven trying to understand it and what to do with it. But never once did he have any doubt that it was as real or more real than this life, not a dream, not a hallucination. The hyper-reality of it, the vividness and strange otherness, the clarity and details, and its spiritual and emotional effects all testified to its reality. (Musick, 68-69)

He became an avid student of the Bible, trying to understand the nature of the God he had met, the experience he had had with Jesus, and how to live this life in light of that experience. He bought a study Bible and read it through several times. This was one of the profound effects of his time in heaven, one of the ways he was dramatically changed. (Musick, 72-73)

Four years after his temporary death and experience walking with Jesus in heaven, he started having what he called bubbles of heaven. Occasionally, some of what he experienced in heaven would impound on Earth. In one example he suddenly had the inspiration, wisdom, and spirit power to confront a father abusing his son at a restaurant with the result that the father broke down in tears and in asking his son for forgiveness broke a cycle of abuse from his own childhood.[7] He had

---

[7] A father reached across the table at a restaurant and slapped his six-year-old son so hard he fell out of the booth onto the floor. Steven got up and went over, picked up the boy, put him back in his seat and sat down beside him.

"Sir, you need to ask your son to forgive you for what you just did."

"Who are you to tell me what to do?"

"I'm just a guy who doesn't allow the things I just saw go unchecked. Now I need you to ask your son to forgive you."

"And what if I don't?"

To the cashier, "Call 911. Tell them to send over a police car, an ambulance, and someone from Social Services for the boy."

To the father, "If you don't apologize to your son right now, I am going to do to you what you just did to him."

"What gives you the right to stick your nose in my business?"

"What gives you the right to smack your son around? I know this is not the first time."

"It's the way my father raised me. Get outta here!"

"When you were your son's age, how did it feel to get smacked
210

others where there was a supernatural result akin to what he had experienced in heaven. (Musick, 81-96)

After about ten years after his time in heaven, he was touched with a supernatural healing of the physical problems left from his sickness when an associate pastor at his church placed a hand on his chest. He went to the floor unconscious and lay there for twenty minutes, during which time he was in heaven again, in the very same place he had been before. This time Jesus said, "Things will be different now." When he woke up on the floor his permanent lung disability was totally healed as confirmed by his doctor. Then he began seeing more heavenly occurrences in his life. (Musick, 102-105)

After his supernatural total healing from an incurable scarring of his lungs, he felt he had to repay God for this gift. So he made monetary donations, volunteered his time, and led small groups. He was under the assumption we have to earn God's gifts. But his experience in heaven made it clear to him that God's gifts are freely given out of His amazing, abundant, and overwhelming love for us. We don't have to beg for them nor earn them nor pay Him back. They are free, totally free, and given completely out of His love by His authority and will. He writes, "He is a father. He loves to give good things to His kids. Things we need. Things that make us joyful. Things that are good." (Musick, 112-113)

From then on he started seeing healings and other miraculous events that each reminded him of heaven in such a way as he was seeing the heaven he had experienced played out on Earth. Heaven is not just for after we die, heaven is all around us. We can begin our journey to

---

around?"

Tears filled the man's eyes.

To the cashier, "Tell the dispatcher it was a mistake. Everything's going to be okay."

To the man, "Break this cycle of violence in your life. Right here. Right now. Ask your son to forgive you."

He did.

heaven, our experience of it, here in the physical life. (Musick, 113-117)

Dale Black

Dale Black said he was "dramatically changed by the experience." (Black 2018, 4) For a long time he did not share this experience with anyone because he didn't want anyone to be impressed with the sensational aspect of his story. It was all about God and what He had created, not about Dale. He now had a deeper sense of what was really important in this life, and that was to honor and serve the God who made everything and who has such profound love for us. "What I experienced was so real to me that my entire life, the way I lived it, changed completely and permanently." (Black 2018, 6)

When he first came out of his coma, there was a nurse standing next to him. Even though one eye was bandaged shut, he could see her perfectly in 3-D with two eyes. Something had happened to his eyes to enable him to see things differently from before. He thought, "Does she know Jesus?" Then he thought, "What if she has an accident and dies? What then? Will she go to heaven?" He had never had thoughts like this before. He felt a love for her that was not a human love. It was something he had never experienced before. It was totally unlike the thoughts he had about girls in college.

The drugs lulled him back to sleep, and when he awoke again the doctor was standing there and asked how he was doing? He gave Dale a quick update on the accident and how they were helping him recover. Again Dale felt a love for him he had never had before. He felt like he knew the doctor, his demeanor, his hair, his hands, but couldn't think how that was possible. He had feelings and concern for the doctor more like a doctor for his patient than a patient for his doctor. He felt tenderness for him, not sympathy but compassion and deep inexplicable love. He knew it was beyond him and beyond human. He couldn't remember anything. It was as if his mind had been taken away, but he had been given a new heart, a real one that works the way a heart was meant to work.

He was seeing the heart of strangers and feeling enormous love and compassion for them. It was supernatural. At this point he had no memory of what had happened during his coma, but he had had a major transformation in the way he saw people and felt about them. He had no explanation for it. He was afraid this new way of thinking and feeling would wear off as he was weaned off the morphine and painkillers. But as the painkillers wore off, his new way of seeing and feeling did not diminish; it only became stronger. Before the crash he was the center of his life focus. Now God and His way of thinking was the center of his focus. But he still didn't know how that happened. Now he had God's heart for people, all people even complete strangers. It wasn't a shift in his thinking or theology; it was deeply and profoundly personal. The feelings were real and they were permanent.

One day his parents brought him the Bible they had given him when he graduated from high school. He had hardly read it since, but now he eagerly studied it. This, too, was a radical change from before the accident.

When he learned that his mentor and friend, Chuck Burns, had died in the crash, he felt a deep remorse. This depth of feeling surprised him. (Black 2010, 38-41) From his hospital room he looked out on the Ventura Freeway. When he saw all the cars zooming by he paid no attention to the type of car but instead focused on the drivers and passengers. He thought they need to know God. He said, the thought was not some "vague, warm and fuzzy, feel-good concept of God," but "the one true God. Those people may think they know where they are going today, but the truth is that most of them are lost. They need to know Jesus Christ, need to know how much He loves them, what He did for them to pave the way to eternity. They can't get there by any road, no matter how smooth it is or how attractive the scenery is along the way. He is the way, the only way. They need Him." His thoughts surprised him and his feelings surprised him even more. He had no idea what caused all of this because of his head injuries that caused him not to remember his trip to heaven. He thought the three days he spent in a coma from which he had no memory must be the key to this transformation. (Black 2010, 52) Apparently when someone comes face to face with God, his/her mind and spirit are transformed whether he/she realizes it or not. Another change was that he coveted a relationship with God, which he had never thought of before. He said, "God wasn't theoretical any more. He was personal. And now my relationship with

Him was personal." (Black 2010, 70)

Another change that came with his renewed love of God and relationship with Him was a greater sense of urgency to tell people about God's love and Jesus sacrifice for them. He had to go back for surgery on his shoulder. He was placed in a room with Joel Green, a seventy-seven year old man who was very cranky and angry. At first Dale thought it would be difficult to share the room with him, but then he felt God's love for Joel. He talked with him, learned his story and how he had spent his life running from God. Dale eventually was able to help Joel accept God's love and be redeemed. He prayed with Dale and received Jesus and His forgiveness in his heart. The next morning during Dale's surgery, Joel died, but Dale knew he was now in heaven and that is the reason God arranged his surgery at that time and had him in the room with Joel. (Black 2010, 89-92)

Nine months later his memory started coming back. In a dream he experienced again exactly what he experienced in the crash. He re-experienced the ambulance ride and being out of his body. He began remembering heaven and all that he saw and felt and heard. (Black 2010, 93-96)

He said when he saw his body on the emergency room table, he knew it was his, and he was attached to it, but he didn't need it to be his real self. His body was simply the physical structure in which his spirit and soul dwelt. He saw that he is eternal, much greater than the physical part of himself. He no longer had any fear of death, as it would be just a passing of his spirit from one realm to another more beautiful and real one. (Black 2018, 141)

After his experience, he had an eternal perspective, and worldly matters, countries, governments, politics, whether man set foot on the moon, or whether he even would fly planes again did not have the importance that they once had. (Black 2018, 142)

His senses were more pronounced and he had a new awareness of spiritual discernment. Now he daily thinks about eternity and the spiritual condition of every living person in the entire human population. (Black 2018, 146, 151)

His perspective on all nature has changed, as he now sees every plant as a descendent of God's original perfect creation. Every plant and animal is infused with God's creative love. (Black 2018, 177)

Peter Baldwin Panagore, Marissa Valbona, Dale Reppert

Peter Baldwin Panagore understood that "time and life on [Earth] were not real in the way God is Real. Only God is Real; all else is both real and an illusion." (Panagore, 95) He recognized that our lifetime here is just a blink compared to eternity. Eternity is what really matters rather than all that we experience here. So he was focused on the "Love-Hope-Joy-Beauty-Truth-Charity-Kindness-Compassion-Love-Patience-Beauty-Love" (Panagore, 96) that he came to understand that as God's presence.

He feels like he is always on two paths at once, one heading one way, and the other heading a different way, giving him two experiences of life. The path through life here is always changing, but the path leading to There never changes. It has a deep truth and a centering inexplicable love, always there but just out of reach. He longs for that love he felt in God's kingdom; he belongs to God. (Panagore, 177)

Marisa Vallbona died after being struck by a car while she was running. Her experience is described in Chapter 21 Non-Heaven Experiences. After she recovered from the accident, meeting God and learning that He is very real, she was changed very dramatically. She became less judgmental and more focused on seeing the good in people. Serving God in everything she does has become paramount, and she now has no fear of death. She has never again questioned her faith; she knows with certainty that God is real and that we are accountable to Him. She says it would be crazy not to believe in God and have a relationship with Him. One can die at any moment, and the time to get your faith in order is *right now*. Now is the only time you have for that. (Garlow, 64)

Dale Reppert treasures his experience as something most people do not get to have. He knows he was in heaven, and because of that his life is forever changed. He has a peace he never had before and now has no fear of death, knowing he will return to heaven when it is his time. (Reppert, 56)

He said he now recognizes each day as a gift. He enjoys the beauty of things he previously overlooked, such as birds and sunsets. He enjoys leisurely strolls with his wife. He has been catching up with old friends, laughing and recounting memories. He is enjoying his grandchildren and their curious minds. He now enjoys the joys of a simple life rather than the meaningless pursuit of wealth or status. His self-worth now centers on kindness and generosity. He is happier and more fulfilled than he ever was before. He knows that the way we use our time, which is a nonrenewable resource, is what dictates our happiness. He now knows that money, status, or fame don't really matter eternally. He said the wealthiest at death are those with the fondest memories. (Reppert, 155-157)

Mary Neal

Mary Neal wrote that after her accident, she "felt as though she didn't belong to the world," and, "That like so many others who have experienced death, I no longer felt the pull of Earthly concerns." (Neal 2012, 143, 144)

She also said, "I had been given the many experiences of my life, my death, and my return so that I could use my experiences and observations to help others stop doubting and just believe—believe that: The spiritual life is more important than our physical one; God is present and at work in our lives and our world; and we are each a part of an intricate tapestry of creation. There is no such thing as 'coincidence'." (Neal 2012, 165)

She said her experience changed her in spiritual ways. She now knows God's promises in the Bible are true and that our spiritual life is eternal. She knows God has a plan for each of us. She does not fear death and has changed the way she experiences the deaths of others, even her own son. She knows every day matters, and we must be about God's business. She knows now personally that God loves all people deeply and unconditionally. (Neal 2012, 218-219)

She has written a second book telling more fully how her life has been impacted: "*Seven Things I Learned in Heaven.*" In it she tells of her life review and that not only did she see scenes from her life, she saw how she felt, her emotions, and everything about the others in those scenes. It gave her an understanding, compassion, and forgiveness for those who had hurt her since she saw their hurts as well. She also saw Jesus' love and grace through all the scenes, not just for her but also for all the others in the scene, as she understood all their backgrounds as well. This was the first lesson from heaven: that what really matters is love and grace. Knowing God's love and grace enables us to offer that same love and grace to those around us. A consequence of this is that now whenever someone cheats her, cuts her off, or otherwise is unjust toward her, she recognizes in that person all his/her hurts and emotions past and present and feels grace and compassion toward that person she never would have had before. (Neal 2017, 24-27)

Marvin Besteman, Mary K. Baxter

Marvin Besteman didn't want to tell anyone about his experience in heaven because of fear he would receive negative reactions. Yet God sent him back because he had work to do and that work turned out to be telling people what he had seen. He finally told his wife and then his children, but that was to be the end until God made it clear that was not enough and provided him a doctor for whom his story was a needed healing. But all this time his mind kept considering how wonderful heaven had been, so much better than anything here. He frequently hears some of the heavenly music, usually when he is lying in bed. He and his wife have become much more aware of God in their lives and are closer to Him. He has spoken in many places as have many of the others, and these meetings are usually accompanied by healings of the heart and spirit, a renewal of a relationship with God, and a hope and peace about their future.

Mary K. Baxter said we need to focus our hopes and desires in this life on the eternity we are going to spend with the Lord. (Baxter, 31) Many of the things that occupy our desires here do not have eternal value. Jesus said we are to love our God with our whole heart and love our neighbor as ourselves. That is what is going to matter in eternity. Our house, our car, our fame, our fortune, our golf game, are not going to contribute anything to the eternity that awaits us. What we have done to love God and others is what really matters.

Jeff Olsen

Jeff Olsen was in a terrible roll-over auto accident at 75 mph. His car veered off the freeway and he overcorrected sending the SUV rolling over seven or eight times down the middle of the freeway. He was trapped on the floorboard under the steering wheel. He heard his son Spencer crying in the back seat. He didn't hear his wife Tamara and youngest son, Griffin; they died in the crash. He struggled but was trapped in the vehicle in searing pain. Eventually he heard voices and sirens and then went unconscious. He was in a different place, a place of joy and light, and his senses were magnified to a much greater degree. The place felt real and he didn't hurt. It felt like his real home. He saw and felt Tamara right beside him. She was alive and more powerfully present than just her physical presence. She was crying and upset, but Jeff could not figure out what happened since he felt alive and not dead. Where were the boys? Then Tamara said, "You can't stay here. You have to go back. You can't be here." Crying she said, "You can't come. You cannot stay." He still couldn't figure out what was happening, but he knew he did not want to leave this place of joy in the presence of his dear wife. She continued insisting he had to go back for their eldest son, who had not died. He told her he loved her and realized the truth of what Tamara was saying and returned to this life. (Olsen, 29-34)

But his brief experience in heaven gave him a new spiritual perception. When he returned he was following his body in the hospital, and he could see in the spirit everything about the people he saw in the hospital before he returned to his body, hence the title of his book, *I knew their hearts*. He could see their joys, sorrows, love, hate, pain, secrets, and more. He then gives several examples of what he saw in the people attending him. Through all this he felt compassion and love for them. That is one of the changes being in heaven, even for just a moment, does for people. (Olsen, 35-36)

His recovery was long and painful. At times he wanted to die. But with the help of others, his brothers, the Holy Spirit, and the memory of Spencer for whom he came back, he accepted his role here. One especially encouraging moment came a couple years later when the original emergency room physician and his attending nurse visited him in a different hospital. The nurse, with tears in her eyes, told him that when they attended him she was aware of his wife Tamara standing there beside him. She saw her surrounded in a light in the shape of a woman. The doctor then said he didn't see her but felt her presence and love. She communicated to him why he had to save you. As he worked on Jeff, he felt her behind him and her say to him, "Thank you." Their report brought tears to his eyes and renewed his hope and courage. (Olsen, 65-66)

When he had recovered enough that plans were made for him to return home, he had a dream. It was not a normal dream but a real and vivid dream. He was in heaven again where he had last seen Tamara. It was like walking through the doors of a childhood memory. He had no pain and he danced and ran. He moved rapidly down a long corridor where there was a baby crib at the end. Griffin was in the crib. He was alive and well and slept peacefully. Jeff picked him up and held him close, feeling his warmth and softness. Jeff felt him spiritually also; every cell of his body was full of light and life. The presence of God came up behind him, someone who was so eternal, so powerful, so personal. He felt the overwhelming love of the Father behind him. He spoke to him things he is not able to repeat and even if he tried he could not give justice to what he learned. He was given the opportunity to give Griffin to God rather than have him "taken" from him. He had peace and a new sense of awe. He realized he could exercise his will in everything and turn it to good and not evil. He was able to let go of all that had happened and not blame God or himself, but be content that all was in God's hands and is very good. God gave him the grace to understand and accept all of this. Remembering that he was created by God in His image, he was able to accept himself fully as he was, surrender everything that had happened to God, and actually walk with God, empowered by what he had learned. (Olsen, 84-88)

God's Spirit Enables Us to Cope

Another consequence of any time we experience a painful crisis or a horrible loss is that we find God's Spirit within us to enable us to cope and to have hope, maybe even a miraculous healing. This is what I experienced when my first wife was murdered. People told me, "I could not have done what you did," (forgive the guy who did it), but my answer was that it was not me; it was the spirit of grace God gave me at the time of my deepest need. And He is prepared to do that for everyone who trusts Him. After enduring such an experience, we are able to reach out to someone else who is experiencing a similar pain or loss and help them have assurance and hope.

Don Piper

Don Piper had this experience when he took some youth to a church conference. He saw a boy in a wheelchair and was led to go see him, even though walking was stressful. When he got to him he saw he was wearing an Ilizarov frame, the same thing Don had had to wear for eleven months to help his leg grow new bone to extend his leg to its normal length. It is very painful as frequently they turn the screws that break the bone apart so it can grow back together a little longer. He was able to understand exactly what the boy was going through and how he felt. Don was a big help to the boy, who wrote to him a few times afterwards. (Piper 2004, 160-162)

In another instance he was able to help someone with an Ilizarov frame recognize an infection that, left untreated, could have been very bad, even possibly causing death. He could do this because of his own painful experience with the Ilizarov frame. (Piper 2004, 163-165)

While this is not an effect of heaven on Don's life, it is related, because most of the time someone experiences heaven there was some tragedy that caused the temporary death. Then when one shares his/her experience in heaven, dealing with the complications of the cause of death is always there.

Although I didn't find Don saying this directly, here is what the wife of one of those he helped because of his experience in heaven said with regard to him, "[Her husband] said listening to [Don's] experience and seeing the positive glow in [Don's] life made the difference." (Piper 2004, 172)

People who have experienced heaven first-hand do come back with a positive glow in their lives, and an assurance and an eager expectation about what happens after death. They also have a new purpose in this life. They would much rather be back in heaven, but believe they are here for a purpose and this is the new focus of their lives. Don Piper said, "When God is ready to take me He'll release me. In the meantime I try to offer as much comfort to others as is possible," and "I still long to return to heaven, but for now, this is where I belong. I am serving my purpose here on Earth." (Piper 2004, 191)

One change in people's lives is that as they have opportunities to tell their stories, people are eager to hear and are affected. They find that they have new ways of helping people just by sharing their experiences in heaven. Don Piper wrote that one woman came up to him and said God had made her come because her mother died the previous week and she needed to hear his story for assurance about her mother. He said he has heard this response hundreds of times. He said it amazes him that he can be a blessing to so many just by sharing his experience. I have had the same response from people who have read previous editions of this book even though I have never been to heaven. Just sharing in detail what heaven is like from people who have been there has been very helpful and a blessing to many people. Don Piper says, "For those who already believe, my testimony has been reassuring; for skeptics, is has opened them up to think more seriously about God." (Piper 2004, 158) It is my hope that this book achieves the same result.

Crystal McVea

Crystal McVea now knew that God loves her and has always loved her regardless of all the problems and sin in her life. The old thought that God couldn't love her after all she had done was just a lie of Satan. It was now replaced with a deep knowledge of God's love that permeated her with a new motivation. She said His love is greater and more powerful than any other kind of love. More than understanding it she felt it, heard it, saw it, and tasted it. (McVea, 176) She said she felt liberated from all the old baggage she had carried around. She started asking others of her family to forgive her for things she had done and not done. She no longer cared for material things like she had before. She came to realize her fortune was the family, friends and God's love, and the rest didn't matter. (McVea, 180) She saw that all those people who had hurt her had been hurt too, and God loved them as little children just as she had experienced His love for her. She didn't want anyone in the world, including her enemies to stand outside God's radiance and share in His glory. (McVea, 181) Her doctor and her husband were moved to tears when she first returned and said, "I am in the most beautiful light," and told about being with God. (McVea, 181-182) In her fleshly mind she could not remember most of what she saw and learned in heaven, but

221

what she did remember was enough to change her life and enable her to share important parts of her experience with others and affect them positively also. This included knowing that God has a perfect plan and work for us here, even though we may not know that perfect plan now. (McVea, 188-189)

She describes an event that the reading of which brought tears to my eyes and I think it would yours too if I were to quote the whole thing. Her life before her nine minutes in heaven was fraught with sexual abuse, emotional abuse, failed marriages, abortion, and many other things to the point she was sure God could not love her. But in heaven she was filled with more love than she had ever known. God's love, acceptance, and forgiveness filled her soul. She then understood God has always loved her no matter what she did. All her past was washed away, and she came back with a new life. But God wanted her to tell "everything".

She was invited to share her testimony with a group of four women. She didn't want to but sensed that is what God wanted, so she accepted. She especially did not want to "share everything". However, she prayed for a sign that she wouldn't have to follow through with her talk up until the last minute before she was asked to come to the podium to share her message. The four women had turned into thirty some women. She knew if she shared all the problems of her life, she would be judged, rejected, and thought to be crazy or a liar.

She started by sharing about the little three-year-old girl she saw in heaven dancing and singing and picking up beautiful things for her basket. God had told her that little girl was her the way God has always seen her. It was his sign of His full acceptance of her. Then she started sharing all the things in her life for which God had given forgiveness and healing. But she covered her face with her hands and wept as she spoke. She could not look at them and see their faces of judgment and rejection. But she told everything just as God had told her. When she finished, she hurried to the back of the church to leave before she had to face their rejection.

But her way was blocked by a woman, who thanked her for coming and then approached her and gave her a warm hug. As the lady was holding her, she saw a long line of women waiting for their hugs. There was no judgment and rejection in that church meeting. Instead there was joy, thanks, and a kind of electricity. One lady said the light next to Crystal (which had been God's presence) was beautiful. God had not left her alone. One woman broke into tears in her hug and finally said she had had an abortion and knew God could never forgive her. But Crystal's testimony of God's forgiveness assured her that she too could be forgiven by God. At that point Crystal began crying too. A sudden wave of love and insight washed over her as she realized something significant had taken place in that meeting. She suddenly realized that woman was the reason God had her come back to Earth and share her painful testimony! She understood finally that God did not make her do this to punish her for her past misdeeds, but He knew her testimony would help others with their healing.

Finally there was a seventy-five year-old woman at the altar crying and praying. Crystal went up to her. She said when she was five her grandfather started molesting her and she could not get her mother or anyone to do anything to stop it. She figured that God didn't help her because He didn't love her. Tears were streaming down her face and at that point they were streaming down Crystal's face also. She said through her tears that now because of Crystal's testimony of God's love for her, she now knows that God loves her and that He always has. At that point she gave her life to Jesus and was changed. As Crystal walked out of the church into the sunlight, all she could say was, "Oh God!" (McVea, 194-199)

Jeanne Enstad, Laurie Ditto, B. W. Melvin

Jeanne Enstad got the message from God that "it is all about love. He says love always believes the best about people, covers a multitude of sin, never says anything unkind, is a decision each of us must make, treats everyone the same, never controls anyone, is an action, and does not magnify sin. ... If you love someone you need to set [that person] free, and if [he/she] comes back, you know it is love. When I was dating, I was definitely not at the level of my Christian walk that I am now. I did not realize until after dating the one gentleman that ended our relationship how much I really tried to control him by wanting him to spend more time with me. That is not love. It was a tough lesson learned." Now she would want to love someone more like God loves us. (Enstad, 91)

While these other stories are about how the experience of heaven changed the authors' lives, Laurie Ditto's life was transformed significantly after her visit to hell. She went to heaven in the spirit several times but the book I read, *The Hell Conspiracy*, was all about the time in a vision she had a terrible experience in hell. Laurie Ditto was in a prayer service at Kansas City Evangelists' Fellowship when suddenly the back of the church opened up with hell in view. Hell and the prayer room were both together in plain view to her but no one else saw the image of hell. The gates of hell swung open and a fingerless arm came out and grabbed her with a strong suction and pulled her into hell with the gates closing behind her. She screamed in terror. (Ditto, 26-27) She realized she was there because she had refused to obey God and forgive those who had hurt her. The last 60% of the book tells how her life was changed afterwards. For the first 30 months she lived with the memories of the terror, pain, and torture of hell, and feared that she would be going back to hell. She did try to forgive all the people she had refused to forgive before, which was the reason she was in hell in the first place. The main takeaway from her experience is that hell is very real and very terrible, more terrible than we can possibly imagine, more terrible than we have words to describe, and we must take seriously Jesus teaching about hell. She saw that after receiving Jesus forgiveness that was bought for us at a huge price, we must recognize we are in debt to Him and change to obey and serve Him in all we do. Willful disobedience could nullify the forgiveness wrought by the cross. But after the thirty months she did come to understand that God allowed her the vision of her being in hell because He loves her and He never forsook her even though she felt forsaken. It did have the effect of causing her to be more aware of her sin of unforgiveness and make the necessary changes to be obedient to Jesus. She said, "After seeing the fires of hell, I have a renewed awe to live my life holy and for Jesus! My attitude is great but I desire that it would increase every day. ... I live my life very differently since I experienced the burning in hell. I take all sin very seriously." (Ditto, 100, 101) Jesus allowed her the experience in hell for her own freedom from the entanglement of sin and also so she could tell the rest of us about it for our warning and freedom also, which she does regularly now.

B. W. Melvin had an extensive visit in hell because he died temporarily as an atheist. His story is told later in the chapter "The Bad News." But his experience in hell was also life-transformative. He went from being an atheist to being an Evangelical Christian. Before he reached for all the gusto he could get without any thought about how it would affect other people or make life ugly for those around him. But afterwards, he recognized that life is temporary and he enters each day looking for how he can make life shine and be alive for those around him. (Melvin, 197-200)

Conclusion

It appears that God has been giving many people an introduction to heaven because He wants those people to share what they have experienced with others to prepare His Church for what is coming. I believe He has given me the inspiration for this book to bring the essence of all these testimonies together for an even more complete telling of how much He loves us and the wonderful eternity He has prepared for those who been redeemed by the blood of the Lamb. But we should also take note of the seriousness of ignoring or disobeying the One who made us in His image for a love relationship with Himself. The consequences of such ignoring or disobedience are real and to be avoided at all costs. We have to choose between the most wonderful and perfect eternity we could possibly imagine with love, peace, joy, wholeness, and relationships far beyond anything we could imagine or eternity originally reserved for Satan and his followers that is the very opposite, filled with no love, no peace, no joy, brokenness and pain, and no companionship at all. (See the Appendix on the Bad News for more on this last alternative.) The changed lives of the people who have had these experiences is a powerful testimony to the truth and importance of what they have told us about heaven, the loving nature of God, the source of all love, and being in His presence.

CHAPTER 20

Physics Of Heaven

Heaven, in many ways, appears like Earth but radically different. It is made of some substance different from this world. Here, substance is made of atoms and molecules, but it appears that there are no atoms and molecules there. When Jesus was resurrected, he had a body that looked like his Earthly body but had the capability of appearing and disappearing without regard to walls. His Earthly body of atoms and molecules had been transformed into his heavenly body of heavenly substance. When he ate the fish with his disciples, that fish got immediately transformed into heavenly substance because it didn't smack against the wall when Jesus left. When he ascended into heaven, he rose through the clouds without gravity affecting him. These are not qualities of atoms and molecules. People in heaven can hover or float in the air without any gravity tying them to the ground, although they can walk on the ground as if there were gravity. Sid Roth quotes Dean Braxton as saying there is no substance on Earth to compare with the substance God used to make everything in heaven. (Roth, 30) Richard Eby also said the physics of heaven is totally different from the physics of Earth. There is no weight or gravity in heaven. Walking on the ground or flying through the air are equally possible. (Roth, 171-172)

There is no time in heaven. Richard Sigmund said there is no yesterday or tomorrow; it is always *now*. (Sigmund, 86) Crystal McVea said she has to report everything in sequence, but in heaven, it all happened at once but not rushed. It didn't even happen; it is just that her awareness of everything was instantaneous. In heaven there are not minutes, hours, or days. There is no such thing as time. (McVea, 11)

Studies in physics, including Einstein's General Theory of Relativity, have also confirmed that time is a function, dimension, of this creation. The testimonies of heaven confirm that time is part of this life and not that of heaven. People who have long ago died do not experience time passing before greeting loved ones coming through the veil. Yet even in this, there is a perceived sequence: the loved one is not there, is then on the way, arrives, and starts enjoying heaven and the relationships. It sounds like time is passing, so the timelessness of heaven is something that we have trouble comprehending as long as we are bound by the time dimension of this universe we are in. We inevitably relate the experiences of heaven to our own experience with time. An eternal *now* is beyond our understanding. In another article I have described *now* as a thin membrane slowly moving along, transforming the future into the past. As an application of this, that God is outside of the time dimension of this universe, I freely pray for something that is past if I don't know how it came out. I believe that God knew my prayer at the time it was needed and considered it in His answer, even though it was rendered after the time of need in Earth time.

Jim Woodford said heaven is not a globe or sphere but a continuous panorama extending infinitely in all directions. There is no disappearing horizon. The terms we use for time, relative size, distances, and colors are not useful in describing the infinite nature of heaven. (Woodford, 80)

This fits in with others who have said they don't have the words to describe what they have seen and experienced in heaven.

Mary Neal said the moment she left her body time stopped and she was in another dimension where the past, present, and future as we know it are all together as "now", a vast web of time and space. It is more like a space in which you dwell than a line over which you walk. Time is enjoyed in the current moment and questions about what will happen in the future or thoughts about what happened in the past are irrelevant. (Neal 2017, 21-22)

Also there is no space in heaven in the sense that two objects can occupy the same "space" at the same "time." Some people reported walking on the grass and having the blades of grass coming through their feet. Others would hug a friend and their arms passed through each other. But nevertheless our heavenly bodies seem to have edges. Kat Kerr saw a door suspended in the air and going through the door she found herself in another part of heaven. (Kerr 2010, 37)

Scientists have determined from their mathematical simulations of the earliest universe that originally ten dimensions were created, but as the universe expanded, only four of these expanded and the other six remain dormant. Eben Alexander reported that he saw countless higher dimensions that cannot be known or understood from within our four-dimensional space. He said our world is intricately involved in these other worlds of higher dimension and is not completely apart from them. But in those other worlds one could access any place and time in this world. This is just as angels from heaven can access any place and time in our world, making heaven one of these worlds of higher dimension. (Alexander, 48-49)

There is water in heaven that looks like water on Earth, but it doesn't make anything wet, and people can breathe under water as well as out of water. I am not even sure there is breathing in heaven, although Rebecca Springer talked about breathing under water (Springer, 13). Richard Sigmund also referred to this. He said he saw people there approach the water of the lake without fear. He saw what looked like millions of people down in the water, walking hand in hand or even swimming. They could apparently breathe under the crystal-clear water. (Sigmund, 28)

Dr. Richard Eby, observed his heavenly body and saw that it was translucent, he could see right through it to flowers on the other side. He saw no internal organs, no bones, no heart, no lungs, no alimentary canal. (Eby, 203) So without lungs, do we really breathe there in the way we do here?

Richard Sigmund said that the people who went down into the water were instantly dry when they came out of the water. (Sigmund, 28) This is the same as Rebecca Springer experienced. Richard also said the water had texture to it, and it caressed his hand. (Sigmund, 28) This doesn't sound like water as we know it, but a liquid that is a superior form of water.

The flowers are like those on Earth; some even look like Earth species. But they tend to be larger, are always fresh, never fade, and never die. They give off melodies as well as fragrance. That is not like Earth flowers. The trees are like Earth trees but are bigger, and some bear many different kinds of fruit. The fruits are delicious and any part left over immediately evaporates, leaving only a sweet fragrance behind. And their leaves and branches never die.

People communicate by thought more than speech. People can sing beautifully even if they couldn't on Earth, can sing higher and lower notes, and can hear notes well outside the audible range on Earth. People can travel quickly by just thinking of being somewhere. They can rise in the air and look around. They can walk on water. Children have been seen to jump higher and run faster than on Earth. And their intelligence surpassed any intelligence on Earth.

It appears that heaven is made of something other than atoms and molecules. It appears the laws of physics as we know them don't apply. If there is gravity, it behaves differently. There is no entropy and second law of thermodynamics. There is no decay or running down. Heaven is the same forever. Biology seems to be different also. It is amazing how God made atoms and molecules with the properties that when combined into an organism of complex biochemical molecules make such a good imitation of what we see in heaven. Here trees, flowers, animals, and people made in His image are all made of biochemical molecules composed of elementary atoms. The fact that all of these resemble their counterpart in heaven is another cause for giving God praise for His creative genius.

After a presentation I made on how the universe shows the glory of God, one person asked where in the universe is heaven. I said heaven does not appear to be made of the stuff the universe is made of, and it does not follow the same laws of physics. So heaven cannot be a part of this universe. God created heaven separate from this universe. They are connected in some way, because we can go there when we die (and come back as all these people did) and angels go back and forth between the two creations.

In thinking about heaven being like Earth but different and in every way better, I don't think it is true that heaven is like Earth. I think the truth is Earth is like heaven but is just an excellent but inferior imitation. It appears God made heaven and then made Earth as a model of heaven—to be like it in many ways but fundamentally different and inferior—but He still put enough creativity into the design of His model that it works perfectly for what it does and does give a picture of the heavenly reality. As much as we enjoy this world with its limitations, how much more will we enjoy the real one in heaven?

Consider water. It is made of two hydrogen atoms and one oxygen atom. When you get in water the H_2O molecules get all over your skin, in your hair, and throughout your clothes. When you get out, you use a

230

towel to transfer as many of those molecules as you can to the towel. The rest on your skin vaporize into the air in a few minutes. You use a hair dryer to speed up the transfer of the molecules in your hair into the air. The towel is hung up in the sun to vaporize all the molecules in it to transfer them into the air. But none of that happens with the waters in heaven. It is not even correct to call them waters, because without atoms there can be no H_2O molecules. The liquids in heaven are not water but something that resembles water on Earth. The vision God gave Ezekiel (Ezek 47:1-12) about the waters flowing from the throne and becoming a wide river and John's vision in Revelation (Rev 22:1-2), which repeats Ezekiel's vision, both call the liquid flowing from the throne "water". But I think the liquid is called "water" because that is the only way it could have been described so the hearers would comprehend.

However, unlike water (H_2O), no pieces of the liquid are separated and remain on you. In the chapter on the River of Life I mentioned that Dean Braxton saw two different and distinct liquids under the throne that never intermingled. So whatever is in the River of Life and the lakes and seas, God has made it to resemble our water but with different and better properties. Or more correctly, God made water on Earth to resemble the liquids in Heaven. From a different perspective, if water is an imitation of the liquids in heaven, it is amazing how God was able to create H_2O molecules to model the liquids in heaven and to have the properties that make life possible.

Consider air also. It is composed of N_2, O_2, CO_2, and other gases, which are either atoms or molecules. With no atoms, what comprises the air in heaven? If we don't have our Earthly bodies with lungs and the necessity of biochemical processes, do we really breathe in heaven? So I think air, as we know it on Earth, is also just a model of whatever the atmosphere of heaven is.

Consider also our vision. In the radio spectrum of the electromagnetic radiation, there is no special meaning to any particular frequency. A radio or TV station can change the frequency on which it broadcasts, and it is all the same to us. However, with visible light, our vision processing center in the brain assigns colors to different wavelengths, so there is distinctive meaning attached to each wavelength, unlike the radio band. There is no physical reason why we should see color. Just because the cones in our eyes can register different frequencies does not automatically mean we should see color any more than different radio frequencies are perceived differently by a radio receiver. I think we perceive color from the different frequencies of visible light because God made our brains with this capacity to give us a glimpse of heaven where there are many more colors and more vivid colors than our eyes (brains) perceive here.

I think the purpose in creating the model was to have a laboratory in which He could create beings that can relate to Him but have free will. They can freely choose to appreciate and accept Him, or they can follow the self-seeking rebellious ways of the demons cast out of heaven. Thereby He can have beings that freely choose to love and accept Him to populate His real world, heaven, where there is no self-seeking and no rebellion.

Betty Eadie said she learned that everything was created of spirit matter before it was created physically. The solar systems, suns, moons, stars, planets, life upon the planets, mountains, rivers, seas, etc. were all preceded by some spiritual counterpart. She saw all this process, and then to further understand it, the Lord gave her a comparison. He told her that the spirit creation would be like a sharp, brilliant print and the Earth would be like its dark negative. This Earth is only a shadow of the beauty and glory of heaven but is what we needed for our growth. She also reported Jesus told her he created other worlds and planets with life. (Eadie, 47-48)

Eben Alexander said God told him through the angel with him that He created many universes and that love is at the center of all of them. He said trace amounts of evil are in all of them. Evil is necessary for free will to operate which is needed for our growth into becoming what God longs for us to be. In the long run love will overcome evil. He said he saw that some of these other universes have intelligence far advanced beyond what human beings have. (Alexander, 48)

Since the odds of there being a planet capable of supporting intelligent life are so small, even the existence of one such planet in the whole universe is beyond being a mathematical possibility. Yet if there are other worlds, God had to have made them just as He did this one for His purposes. I doubt, though, that SETI, the Search for Extraterrestrial

Intelligence, has the capability of discovering any other worlds God may have made.

Earth being only a shadow of heaven is consistent with the theory that the universe and Earth is a limited model of heaven, that heaven is the true reality. Betty Eadie said Earth is not our natural home, heaven is the true home for which we were created, and Earth is only a temporary place for our schooling. Sin is not our true nature, just a deception of Satan. This is consistent with heaven being the true reality, and Earth only a foretaste of heaven for the unique purpose of preparing a bride for the Lord.

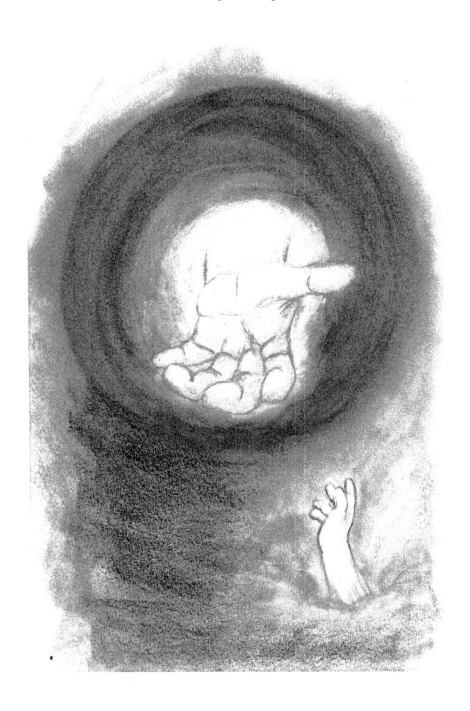

CHAPTER 21
Non-Heaven Experiences

We can learn some things from people who die temporarily but don't quite make it to heaven. Some of these are mentioned in this chapter.

Peter Panagore

Peter Baldwin Panagore died at age 21, trapped on a ledge on a mountain in Alberta while ice climbing. His rope was stuck and he couldn't get it loose. He fell off a ledge when he was exhausted and hypothermic and swung, dangling on his rope, hitting the rock wall, which led to his death. Fortunately he came back to life. God gave him the choice of staying or coming back. Although he wanted to stay in that world of perfect love, he chose to come back to spare his parents and others of pain and loss. After he came back, he pulled hard on the rope, and it came free so he and his climbing partner could continue their descent and get off the mountain. While he was gone he did not see heaven, even though his book is entitled, *Heaven Is Beautiful*. But he did discover that the real "he" was the soul or spirit that indwelled his physical body. Also because he remembered things that he learned while his brain was not functioning, he knew memory was more than brain cells. He communicated with God and learned the depth of His love and forgiveness, more than anyone can imagine here. He learned sin is when we hurt others, either directly or indirectly. The only thing that matters is how we love others. But sin is at the basis of this universe. Everyone sins and needs God's forgiveness. Along with this he saw that the spirit world of God is what is real, this world is merely a poor reflection of that spirit world. God is perfect, and His world is perfect. This world, this universe, is not. This experience changed his life and the way he views the world. Death is not an unknown to be feared any more. It will be a releasing of his spirit from this inferior world of sin to reach its full potential in a world of perfect love.

Marisa Valbona

Marisa Vallbona had been raised a Catholic but became impressed with the Protestant view of a personal relationship with God. Through Young Life during high school, her relationship with God continued to grow. But after enrolling in a liberal university, she began to question whether or not God was real. One day she was running along a street and was struck from behind by a large car. As soon as she died, she was filled with a deep peace and well-being and an awareness of the presence of God. He was *very* present, and she felt *very* good. Communication was different in this realm. She only had to think of a question and the answer formed in her. As many other witnesses have said, she was unable to find the right words to describe her experience. She was aware of others around her on a spiritual plane, all made of beautiful, radiant, white light. She had a sensation of moving upward, although she had no sense of to where she was rising. She had a conversation with God and expressed she was too young to die, and could she go back and make a difference with her life. God said He would send her back and enable her to make a difference now that she knows He is real. Then she was back over the scene of the accident and suddenly was back in her body with excruciating pain. She hadn't seen heaven, but she experienced some of what heaven is like. (Garlow, 61-64)

George Ritchie

George Ritchie died of double pneumonia in 1943 at U. S. Army Camp Barkeley hospital in west Texas following an exercise on the field as a strong cold front came. When he died, he left his body but didn't know he was dead. Looking for his clothes, he was surprised to notice someone else was already in his bed! Since he had been released to go to Virginia Medical School to become an army doctor and was in danger of missing his train, he couldn't be bothered with the anomaly, but strange things began happening. An orderly walking down the hall ignored him and almost ran into him. When he saw the door at the end of the hall, he thought the Jeep might be outside waiting to take him to the train station, and suddenly, he was outside. He started flying over the mesquite bushes and then the trees and then towns. He didn't know how he could be doing this. When he crossed a large river, he stopped at the town on the other side, intending to find out where he was and if he was on the right way to Virginia. A man ignored him and when George put his hand on the man's shoulder it went right through. He tried to lean against the guy-wire of a pole but fell through that too. He thought he must have lost his solid part and realized he couldn't go to medical school without it. So he flew back to Camp Barkeley. When he found his solid part, it was the first time death occurred to his thinking. As he mulled over this problem, Jesus appeared and led him on a heavenly journey, though never actually in heaven. He was shown the states of people who die and don't go to heaven. This will be covered in the Appendix.

Jesus showed him scenes from his life, living scenes all around him in 3-D, and asked him what he wanted to show him. Everything George pointed out, the answer that came back was "that served you." Along with the Eagle Scout award, he saw his own selfish pride; along with his desire to be a doctor and serve others, he saw the yacht, limousine, big house, and all the other things he would get from his large income. He finally realized the question was, "What have you done with your life that unselfishly served others?" He said it was like coming to the final exam and only then learning what the course was all about. However, even though he judged himself, he didn't receive any judgment from Jesus, only love and acceptance. In fact, being with Jesus the whole time he was gone, he experienced the most incredible love of his life and didn't want to leave, but Jesus told him he had to go back and tell others.

After George came back, his heart miraculously started beating and continued. He had a long recovery, but it was continuous. He eventually went to Europe in the D-Day invasion as a medical orderly. All the horrific things he witnessed there just made him long to be back with Jesus. Why had He made him come back to this? He was assigned to a soldier who had been driving a Jeep that drove over a land mine. This man had a good spirit, and George enjoyed taking care of him, but it seemed like George knew him from before. They compared notes, and there was never a time their paths had crossed. Finally, George realized it was Jesus in this man that he recognized. That turned the corner for him, and he started looking for Jesus in others.

One day, George was looking at a *Life* magazine and saw an artist's rendering of a test facility for nuclear submarine engine. It was a round pool with a dome-shaped structure in the middle. George recognized this picture. He had seen it nine years earlier when he was with Jesus, before man had even thought of the idea. That is when he knew he had to write his story.

Jim Woodford

Jim Woodford contracted Guillain-Barré disease and subsequently became wracked with excruciating pain. He was on potent pain medication and was becoming addicted to it. But he was willing to accept anything that would relieve the pain. He drove his truck out to a job site and saw a beautiful sunset. While watching the sunset he took several more of his opiod pills. But instead of getting relief, the bottom of his feet began to burn. The burning crept up his legs and into his torso. He knew something was wrong; something was catastrophically bad. He raised his arms and said, "God forgive me." This was the first time he had recognized God or someone else's help. His body was shutting down; he was dying. Then he slumped over and hit his head on the steering wheel. After an indeterminate amount of time he leaned back and sat up straight. The burning was gone, he could see, he felt good, terrific actually. He thought, "Wow, that medication really worked!" He was rejuvenated, got out of the truck, and walked about fifteen feet. It felt like a heavy garment had been taken off, leaving him light and alive. He felt more alive than he had felt for along time. Shortly he saw a person in his truck leaning on the steering wheel, who, he soon discovered, was himself. He was outside his physical body and he could look through his shoes and see the ground underneath. He could see and feel and had all of his physical senses but no pain. He wondered how this could be, but at that point, he came to grips with the fact that he was dead. (Woodford, 42, 52) While this is not an experience of heaven, it does illustrate what others have said about their experience, namely that they feel more alive than they ever were before they died. In that sense it is a part of everyone's heaven experience.

Colton Burpo, before he visited heaven, left his body and saw his dad in a room by himself praying and his mom in another room talking on the phone and praying. Sometimes this is all that a person sees before being resuscitated. Other times it is a precursor, as it was in Colton's case, to a bigger adventure. Since our goal here is learn what we can about heaven, we will ignore these other out-of-body experiences that don't bear on our goal.

CHAPTER 22

Conclusion

Here is the earliest testimony of heaven, John's testimony given in the book of Revelation:

Revelation 21:1-22:6

> Then I saw a new heaven and a new Earth, for the first heaven and the first Earth had passed away, and there was no longer any sea. I saw the Holy City, the New Jerusalem, coming down out of heaven from God, prepared as a bride beautifully dressed for her husband. And I heard a loud voice from the throne saying, "Now the dwelling of God is with men, and he will live with them. They will be his people, and God himself will be with them and be their God. He will wipe every tear from their eyes. There will be no more death or mourning or crying or pain, for the old order of things has passed away."
>
> He who was seated on the throne said, "I am making everything new!" Then he said, "Write this down, for these words are trustworthy and true."
>
> He said to me: "It is done. I am the Alpha and the Omega, the Beginning and the End. To him who is thirsty I will give to drink without cost from the spring of the water of life. He who overcomes will inherit all this, and I will be his God and he will be my son. But the cowardly, the unbelieving, the vile, the murderers, the sexually immoral, those who practice magic arts, the idolaters and all liars — their place will be in the fiery lake of burning sulfur. This is the second death."
>
> One of the angels who had the seven bowls full of the seven last plagues came and said to me, "Come, I will show you the bride, the wife of the Lamb." And he

carried me away in the Spirit to a mountain great and high, and showed me the Holy City, Jerusalem, coming down out of heaven from God. It shone with the glory of God, and its brilliance was like that of a very precious jewel, like a jasper, clear as crystal. It had a great high wall with twelve gates and with twelve angels at the gates. On the gates were written the names of the twelve tribes of Israel. There were three gates on the east, three on the north, three on the south and three on the west. The wall of the city had twelve foundations, and on them were the names of the twelve apostles of the Lamb.

The angel who talked with me had a measuring rod of gold to measure the city, its gates and its walls. The city was laid out like a square, as long as it was wide. He measured the city with the rod and found it to be 12,000 stadia [1,400 miles] in length, and as wide and high as it is long. He measured its wall and it was 144 cubits [200 feet] thick, by man's measurement, which the angel was using. The wall was made of jasper, and the city of pure gold, as pure as glass. The foundations of the city walls were decorated with all kinds of precious stone. The first foundation was jasper, the second sapphire, the third chalcedony, the fourth emerald, the fifth sardonyx, the sixth carnelian, the seventh chrysolite, the eight beryl, the ninth topaz, the tenth chrysoprase, the eleventh jacinth, and the twelfth amethyst. The twelve gates were twelve pearls, each gate made of a single pearl. The great street of the city was of pure gold, like transparent glass.

I did not see a temple in the city, because the Lord God Almighty and the Lamb are its temple. The city does not need the sun or moon to shine on it, for the glory of God gives it light, and the Lamb is its lamp. The nations will walk by its light, and the kings of the Earth will bring their splendor into it. On no day will its gates ever be shut, for there will be no night there. The glory and honor of the nations will be brought into it. Nothing impure will ever enter it, nor will anyone who does what is shameful or deceitful, but only those whose names are written in the Lamb's book of life.

Then the angel showed me the river of the water of life, as clear as crystal, flowing from the throne of God and of the Lamb down the middle of the great street of the city. On each side of the river stood the tree of life, bearing twelve crops of fruit, yielding its fruit every month. And the leaves of the tree are for the healing of the nations. No longer will there be any curse. The throne of God and of the Lamb will be in the city, and the servants will serve him. They will see his face, and his name will be on their foreheads. They will not need the light of a lamp or the light of the sun, for the Lord God will give them light. And they will reign forever and ever. (Revelation, 21:1 – 22:6, NIV)

Confirmation of Scripture

Believers in recent times have seen many of these things John saw when he was on the Island of Patmos in the first century. We have been given their testimony about God dwelling with his people, and there being no tears or death or crying or mourning or pain in heaven. All these witnesses have seen heaven lighted by the glory of God and the Son, more brilliantly than any light shining on Earth. Some have seen the Holy City, the high wall, the city of gold, pure as glass, the gates, and the foundation with twelve layers of precious stones, matching John's description. The size of the city has not been measured but in general terms seems to match or exceed the magnitude John described. Some have seen the throne of God, the archives, and the Lamb's Book of Life, Jesus' horse. The water, clear as crystal flowing from the throne, has been seen, as well as the trees bearing fruit.

Richard Sigmund noted that the Bible is not the sum total of all God is and has done. He limited Himself when He gave us the Word, partially because on this Earth we cannot comprehend all that the infinite God is and can do. In heaven we have minds that can comprehend more than we can here on Earth. So, as a result, many other attributes of heaven not described by John have been given to us by those fortunate enough to have been there. Typically when they have returned to this life, much of what they knew there has been lost. (Sigmund, 85) I say "fortunate" regarding those who have been privileged to see and experience heaven because, in most cases, it took a painful dying experience to open the doorway to heaven and a miraculous recovery to come back, usually attended by prayers of others.

Some of the other things we know are how delicious are the fruits growing on the trees, the intense color and vibrancy of the grass and flowers, which never die. In fact, nothing in heaven ever dies, even a blade of grass. There is no decay in heaven. Fruit that is not eaten just evaporates. Clothes are never soiled; nothing needs washing. The colors are more numerous and intense. The air is fragrant, like citrus and lilac. No one drowns in water, and the water has healing qualities Earthly water does not have. People there have a joy, happiness, peace, and wholeness that Earthly words cannot fully describe. Jesus is everywhere at once. Time, as we know it, does not exist in heaven. Gravity and other physical laws of this universe do not apply there. One can travel in the air; one can even get someplace just by thinking of being in that place, faster than the speed of light. Communication is largely by thought and voices are mostly used for singing and praise.

By all accounts, heaven is a wonderful place and the fulfillment of everything missing from life here. If you haven't obtained your ticket yet, I encourage you to do so, and as soon as possible. You do not want to miss this eternal event. God has lavished His creativity and love in abundance beyond anything you can imagine to prepare heaven as a wonderful dwelling of God with man.

Some people will dismiss these stories as hallucinations. But hallucinations occur in someone's mind. It is not possible for two or more people over and over to have the same hallucination. Yet there is consistency in all these stories, even among things not described in Revelation. That precludes them being merely hallucinations. It is also not a made-up story to which they have all agreed because the stories are not exactly alike, and they come from people of many ages, many locations, many times, both genders, precluding the possibility of any collaboration to deceive us. The differences reflect individual experiences of heaven. So the consistency of these stories and their differences all contribute to their veracity and to the veracity of the Biblical accounts of heaven.

Conclusions

From all of these encounters I have drawn some conclusions. First, relationships are what really matter. Our heavenly experience will be primarily profound relationships with family, friends, and everyone across the globe of heaven. All those in heaven are part of one big family, God's family. Our relationship with the Father and the Son will dominate everything. The things that we value above relationships here pale in comparison with what God has prepared for us in heaven. It then behooves us to focus this life on relationships and not things. The relationships we will take with us; things we will not.

Second, heaven is love—deeper, purer love than you can ever know here. Richard Sigmund said he was engulfed in a flood of the greatest love and acceptance he had ever known. (Sigmund, 120)

Third, there is joy and happiness in heaven. Anticipating our joyful future, we should focus on the good around us and be content. Don't stress about things, but instead be forgiving, considerate, compassionate, and whatever else can contribute to a peaceful joyful life.

Fourth, heaven is full of beauty. The colors, fragrances, tastes, views, and plants, are all superior to their copies here on Earth. It would seem then that we should enjoy all the beauty of heaven God has given us in this world. It is all an anticipation of what God has prepared for our future. Don't just take a beautiful flower, a rainbow, a landscape, a view, or anything else here as something to abuse or ignore. It is a treasure to enjoy and prepare us for our eternity.

Fifth, those in rebellion against God will not be there, and where they will go, no one should go. God does not want anyone made in His image not to be where He is. So with gentleness and respect we should encourage those we know that are rebelling to get right with God. But we do it with humility, because we have done nothing to deserve what God has prepared. We are the beneficiaries of an incredible gift. Jesus loves them and so should we.

For all of these witnesses, being in the presence of Jesus and the Father in the eternal kingdom they have prepared has changed their lives. They have a deeper appreciation of Jesus' and the Father's love. They have a more focused purpose in their lives. They are more aware of God's presence with them every day. Most of my readers and I myself do not get to have this direct experience with heaven. However, I hope for you, as you have read all that these people have seen and experienced, to have vicariously some measure of the same life-changing experience. I know putting this book together has had that effect for me, and it is my prayer that that would be the case for you, too. Jesus is coming back very, very soon. We are encouraged to get our houses in order. And we are encouraged to help as many who are willing to be prepared also.

Further Reading

Of all the books I read, Richard Sigmund's *My Time in Heaven: A True Story of Dying and Coming Back* is the most extensive heaven experience. Kat Kerr's *Revealing Heaven* series adds many things the others did not experience. While there are some new things in the others, there is more in Richard's book than I could put in this book. You could learn more about heaven from his testimony. I recommend his book as a continuation of what I have presented here. Kat Kerr's *Revealing Heaven* series and Rebecca Springer's *Within Heaven's Gates* are perhaps the second most extensive and Don Piper's *90 Minutes in Heaven* tells more about the music of heaven and relationships.

John Burke's *Revealing Heaven* is a lot like this book but from a different perspective. While I have shared extensive eyewitness testimonies allowing the readers to form their own impression of heaven, John Burke has given his descriptions of heaven he has derived from his sources, many the same ones I have used, augmented by some quoted sections of the books he has used. There are also books about heaven from the point of view of what Scripture tells us. Randy Alcorn's *Heaven* is probably the best of these.

Final Summarizing Story

I will conclude with one last story that seems to pull all of this together. It is from Dr. Reggie Anderson's book, *Appointments with*

Heaven, Chapter 25.

Dr. Anderson became an atheist after he could not understand how God, if He really existed, could have allowed all six members of his closest family friends and coworkers, the Aldays, to be gruesomely murdered. But he became attracted to a Christian girl, Karen. She put him off because they were not spiritually compatible and couldn't be together. He volunteered to help her memorize Scripture for a Bible study she was leading. One day, he went off camping in the wilderness in Tennessee. Karen had given him a copy of *Mere Christianity*, by C. S. Lewis, with the message, "I don't want you to hate God. When you deny him, you're just denying the truth because of the pain you've been through. C. S. Lewis struggled with the same pain and many of the same questions you struggle with. I hope reading this will help you not to hate God." Then she encouraged him to pray, "God, if you're real, make yourself known to me." He took that book with him and the Bible his mom had given him. On that camping trip, he had a vision of heaven. In that vision, all the members of that murdered family came to him, and he saw their joy and happiness and wholeness, more than they ever had in life on Earth. God also told him he would marry Karen, have four children, and become a country doctor in rural Tennessee.

Seeing the joy of the Alday family resolved his issues with their murder and freed him to turn to God. He finally understood that God had taken care of them, just not in the way he wanted. All that God had foretold eventually came to pass, and his practice in Ashland City, Tennessee, eventually grew to include a clinic, then an ER, and then a hospital. After many wonderful years there, he began to question whether he was still needed there. Perhaps they should move to be closer to their parents, but the whole family had developed very close relationships with another family there, and it would be hard to leave.

He said that he and Karen were committed to following God's leading wherever that might take them, whether staying in Appleton City or moving to be nearer parents.

One day, he was in the local hospital having a routine visit with one of his elderly patients. Then the nurse told him he needed to come immediately and look at the EKG machine that was hooked up to his patient for a routine test. When he looked at the EKG machine, he was stunned by what he saw; his patient was having a heart attack!

His patient, Eunice, was in her late sixties. She was diabetic and had high blood pressure, complications that had affected the circulation in her legs. She had to use a walker or a wheelchair. Eunice asked what is wrong and tried to sit up to see the EKG machine, but the leads prevented her.

He told her it appeared she was having a heart attack. So he called an ambulance to take her to the hospital in Nashville, and then called the hospital and advised them that she was on her way. He talked to Dr. Wong, the cardiologist on call.

Dr. Wong said they would see her in the cath lab, and Dr. Anderson asked that they take good care of her, one of his first patients. Dr. Wong assured him that they would.

About five hours later, Dr. Wong called Dr. Anderson about Eunice. Dr. Anderson assumed he would say, as had been the case many times before, that they found a small blockage and cleared it. Dr. Wong reported that they did indeed find a blockage, almost 99 percent in one of the cardiac arteries, and everything was going well. He said "We opened the vessel with the balloon and then," at which point he paused. This caused Dr. Anderson to wonder if something else was wrong.

He asked Dr. Wong to go ahead. Dr. Wong then surprised him by saying her heart stopped, and she died, right there on the table after the procedure to open her blocked artery. He started CPR and continued for an hour. He gave up but his intern wanted to continue for the practice. Dr. Anderson had a hard time believing that Eunice actually died. He asked what time was her death as in his mind he tried to figure out how to tell her family. Dr. Wong explained that after the second hour of the intern doing the CPR, her heart started beating on its own again. It was incredible that she was back alive after being dead for two hours. She was put in ICU in a coma, and Dr. Wong had doubts about her condition after two hours of CPR. Dr. Anderson was stunned but also grateful.

Three days later, Dr. Anderson got a call from the hospital saying his patient wanted to see him. She had awakened from her coma, was fine both mentally and physically, and had something important to tell him. He was surprised to hear that she was awake, so he and his wife left their dinner and went to the hospital. When he announced his presence, he was immediately escorted to Eunice's room, with the nurse emphasizing that Eunice had been asking for him.

When he got to Eunice's room, he was surprised at how good she looked after a heart attack and being dead for two hours just three days earlier. Her voice had strength and enthusiasm, and she looked better than she had in years, like a young woman again. She had him sit down for the story she had to tell.

She remembered seeing people working on her and saying she had died, but then she was gone somewhere else where she said she was more alive than she had ever been, and unlike here, it was peaceful and calm—the exact opposite to what was going on in the hospital. It was like she was floating, and she had no more pain, none from her arthritis and neuropathy, no burning in her legs any more. She said she was walking beside a cool stream and felt its icy water blowing onto her face. She drank from the stream, and the water was cold, fresh, and sweet. It tasted like honey. She saw an astounding array of colors, more colorful than anything she had ever seen or imagined. She walked around a bend in the path and came upon an open field with the greenest grass she had ever seen, a green that was new to her. In the middle of the meadow, she saw a horse-drawn carriage and remembered that her father had loved horses.

But suddenly, a crowd of people blocked her view of the horse and carriage. Then she saw in the crowd her father, sweet mother, and dear brother, who had all died years before. She saw others she recognized in the crowd. She said they said they were all doing great, and they specifically asked her to tell Dr. Anderson, "What you are doing here in Cheatham County needs to continue." They wanted to encourage him.

Her welcoming committee had prepared a picnic for her, so she sat down with them in the grassy meadow. She was in heaven, in a manner of speaking, because she could eat anything she wanted; there was no diabetic food!

She said it was so peaceful and content, it was like being snuggled in a velvet robe; she wanted to stay there, but Jesus came and asked her if she could come back here for a while so she could encourage others. She would be able to come back there soon. One reason Jesus wanted her to come back was to encourage Dr. Anderson. He told her to tell him, "that you are doing his will and that you should stay the course." She didn't know what that meant, but Dr. Anderson did. Jesus was answering his prayer about moving by telling him to stay in Appleton City. It brought tears to his eyes.

The second reason was to tell her family and friends that Jesus and heaven are *real*; she had seen both and can testify to their truth. She stayed around for seven more years before returning to heaven. During that time, she told everyone she could every day about her experience and the reality and peace of heaven. She also told Dr. Anderson every time she saw him to "Keep doing what you are doing." (Anderson, 223-230)

Conclusion

What we have seen through these pages is that heaven is grander, more loving, and more fulfilling than we can possibly imagine. It is perfect. No one who goes there wants to leave, but all these witnesses had to return (or we would never have had their stories!), but they eagerly await the time they can return permanently. The lesson for us who haven't had that experience is to learn from them and anticipate our being there also. Hopefully, that also implies we will begin living this life with heavenly priorities: building relationships, loving others, forgiving those who have hurt us and seeking forgiveness for the ways we have hurt others, loving and trusting God, and leaving behind lust for wealth, power, fame, and fortune, things that go away when we leave this life.

But since we are not perfect, "for all have sinned and fall short of the glory of God," (Rom 3:23), we cannot be allowed in heaven because our imperfection would spoil the perfection of heaven. We must be healed of our sin and rebellion against God and Jesus. God loves us too much to deprive us of the glory He has prepared for us, but He cannot accept our sinfulness and cannot allow us into His Kingdom until we are healed and made perfect. Jesus gave His life to take our sin upon Himself to free us from our guilt and rose from the dead to guarantee our place with Him in heaven. We must humble ourselves and accept His gift of love. If you haven't done this, I hope you will soon so you, too, can enjoy the world I have described here, the one eyewitnesses experienced.

23 for all have sinned and fall short of the glory of God,

24 and are justified freely by his grace through the redemption that came by Christ Jesus.

25 God presented him as a sacrifice of atonement, through faith in his blood. He did this to demonstrate his justice, because in his forbearance he had left the sins committed beforehand unpunished—

26 he did it to demonstrate his justice at the present time, so as to be just and the one who justifies those who have faith in Jesus. (Romans 3:24-26)

14 Just as Moses lifted up the snake in the desert, so the Son of Man must be lifted up,

15 ...that everyone who believes in him may have eternal life.

16 For God so loved the world that he gave his one and only Son, that whoever believes in him shall not perish but have eternal life.

17 For God did not send his Son into the world to condemn the world, but to save the world through him.

18 Whoever believes in him is not condemned, but whoever does not believe stands condemned already because he has not believed in the name of God's one and only Son. (John 3:14-18)

Just pray to God, admit your sin and your inability to save yourself, and accept Jesus gift of perfect eternal life in place of your imperfect life, agreeing to honor and serve Him the rest of your days. And then I will look forward to seeing you in God's perfect Kingdom someday witnessing first hand all I have described in this book that fifty eyewitnesses saw.

APPENDIX

The Bad News

The common view of heaven is that good people go to heaven when they die and bad people go to hell. But the definition of "good" is what we think good is and has little to do with God. Very few people would put themselves in the bad category. So most people think that when anyone dies, he/she goes to heaven and there enjoys a continuation of this life without all its hassles, sicknesses, infirmities, maybe even without the squabbles with others. He/she enjoys all the same things he/she did here. So if the person enjoyed golf, there are golf courses there and golf equipment to use. We know he/she can't take his/her clubs with him/her so some must already be present there. Someone once suggested that since everything is perfect in heaven, every hole would be a hole-in-one, and there would be no challenge! I heard of someone who had departed that it was said he was on the great fishing trip in the sky. Someone else I know was looking forward to some superb grilling of steaks when he gets to heaven. It was said of someone else that he is probably enjoying meeting Carrie Fisher (Princess Leia) who died about the same time he did. No matter what someone's favorite activity or passion, the belief is that he/she is enjoying it to the full in heaven.

The bad news is that the popular myth is not true. First, heaven is not a continuation of our physical life in a different location. Rather it is totally what God has wanted for our lives, and it is far more satisfying and rewarding and fun than anything we have here. It may include some of the activities we have enjoyed here, but they will be much superior. Second, not everyone will be going to heaven. Most people think that would be a person such as Hitler or Stalin or a serial killer or anyone who has been evil. But the problem is, as we have seen in the testimonies, everything in heaven is perfect; God is perfect, and He created heaven to reflect this perfection without all the imperfections of this world caused by sin and rebellion. Jesus stated in the Sermon on the Mount, *"Be perfect, therefore, as your heavenly Father is perfect"* (Matt 5:48, NIV). Are you or anyone you know able to say you have been perfect and have perfectly kept all God requires? Have there been times you have hated someone? Maybe you took something that didn't belong to you. Maybe you took advantage of someone. Maybe you ignored someone in need. We have all been selfish at some point. So where do we draw the line that separates those going to heaven from those who aren't, somewhere between Mother Theresa and Hitler, but always below me?

Here are some testimonies of people who died temporarily (fortunately for their sakes it was temporary) and went in the direction of hell or actually went to hell rather than heaven. Some followers of Jesus were taken to hell when they were in heaven. They could see what hell is really like and were able to come back and communicate back to us that hell is real and far more terrible than anyone would like to admit. It is the destiny that awaits someone who dies with his burden of sins committed weighing down him/her, rendering him/her imperfect. Hell was prepared for Satan and his followers since after their rebellion they could no longer be in heaven, God's Kingdom, in which they would be totally in His presence. What follows are these testimonies of people who experienced the bad news after they died, but were fortunate enough to come back and have a second chance.

Glimpses of Hell by Passersby

When Mickey Robinson died and appeared in heaven and was approaching the portal of pure white light, he became aware on his right side of a blackest black abyss of emptiness, blacker than anything he had every known. He was aware that anyone in this abyss would be conscious and have desires, but with no sight or touch be unable to fulfill them. It would be a lifeless state of unending hopeless remorse, state devoid of all life. That person would have dreams and desires that would never be fulfilled, instead replaced with "conscious nightmares of dark despair." It would be final and never-ending. He felt the terror of it, an eternal solitary confinement. He did not mention an awareness of anyone there but felt the terror of it anyway. (Robinson, 103-104)

Just Missed Experiences of Hell

A woman upon whom Maurice Rawlings, M.D. reports, whom he

254

calls Mrs. S., was struck by lightning on a camping trip and found herself with the answer to a question she had always had, is there a God? The totality and reality of His presence exploded in her in ways she cannot fully describe. She said every atom of her body was filled with His glory. But then she was horrified to see that she was going away from Him, not toward Him. She panicked and begged Him to spare her life. She did recover, but the rest of the story was not given. (Rawlings, 64)

Bill Weiss tells of Donald Whitaker, Ph.D., a research science specialist, who was an atheist. He was very successful and didn't need God. He had a Christian friend, Ron, who tried to tell him about being saved, but whom he ignored. Then he developed an acute hemorrhagic necrotic pancreatitis, a fatal condition. As he faced death, he decided he needed to listen to Ron, but Ron couldn't be reached. Dr. Whitaker started losing consciousness, he faded away into a total darkness that invaded his soul like no darkness he had ever experienced. He saw no light or felt any warmth or love. Instead he felt untold terror. He frantically tried to keep from going any further because he knew that if he let himself go any further he would never get back from this deep terrible darkness. He had to hold on until his friend Ron could get there. He held on through the night until Ron could get to him in the morning and help him pray a prayer of repentance and be saved from that terrible darkness. Dr. Whitaker was a staunch atheist until he faced death for real and experienced temporarily the eternal consequences of atheism. Weiss 2013, 43-44)

Second Chance Experiences of Hell

Maurice Rawlings, M.D., writes in his introduction that as a cardiologist exposed to critically ill patients in the coronary care units of several hospitals, he has had many opportunities to resuscitate people who have clinically died. He has found that interviews immediately after the patients have revived reveals as many bad experiences as good ones. (Rawlings, xi)

The first experience Dr. Rawlings reports is of a patient who had been experiencing chest pains. Dr. Rawlings attached an EKG machine to him and had him slowly increase activity on a treadmill while Dr. Rawlings monitored changes in the man's heart. The change that occurred was his heart stopped, and he fell over on the floor dead. Dr. Rawlings began CPR while nurses took care of his breathing and obtained other equipment. When he would start coming to, the doctor would reach for something, interrupting the CPR and he would die again. Each time he regained heartbeat and respiration, the patient screamed, "I'm in hell!" He was terrified and pleaded with Dr. Rawlings to help him. This episode literally scared the hell out of Dr. Rawlings! It terrified him enough to write his book.

He then noticed a genuinely alarmed look on the man's face that Dr. Rawlings described as being worse than the expression seen in death! The patient had a grotesque grimace expressing sheer horror! His pupils were dilated, and he was perspiring and trembling. He looked as if his hair was on end.

The patient said, "Don't you understand? I am in hell. Each time you stop I go back to hell! Don't let me go back to hell!"

After several death episodes, he finally asked, how does one stay out of hell? Dr. Rawlings told him that he guessed Jesus Christ would be the one whom you would ask to save you.

The patient asked Dr. Rawlings to pray for him and repeated it, so Dr. Rawlings, who didn't have much experience praying and in fact was not active in a relationship with the Lord, had him pray, "Lord Jesus, I ask you to keep me out of hell. Forgive my sins. I turn my life over to you. If I die I want to go to heaven. If I live, I'll be 'on the hook' forever."

The patient's condition stabilized, and he went to a hospital. He had two more episodes of dying, but these times he had a good experience, and not the horrors of hell. Later, after he was recovering in the ICU, Dr. Rawlings asked him what he had seen that was so terrifying, and he could not remember anything about his terrifying visits to hell. They were apparently too terrible for his mind to contain them. (Rawlings, 3-5)

Dr. Rawlings has found subsequently in his practice that most of the bad experiences are soon suppressed deeply into the patient's subliminal or subconscious mind. The patient will usually remember only the pleasant details. (Rawlings, 47)

Vortices to Hell and Cells in Hell

Another atheist Bill Weiss met was B. W. Melvin. He was working outside Tucson on a very hot day and took a long drink of contaminated water from which he contracted Vibrio Cholerae and became deathly sick. Ultimately he left his body and traveled down an extremely dark tunnel toward an astounding light, which turned out to be a man in a white robe, and he was told it is Jesus. Rays of brightness came from Jesus' hand, and he knew his fate appeared to be sealed. He was without excuse. He saw unspeakable horror, smelled an extremely putrid stench and felt intense heat. He heard intense screams and saw people being tortured in cages. He was terrified and felt an eternal hopelessness until Jesus came and took him out of there. Suddenly he came back to physical life and was taken to the hospital and recovered. He abandoned his atheistic beliefs and became a follower of Jesus after his experience in hell. (Weiss 2013, 47-48)

In his experience of hell, he saw tornado-like vortices bringing people who were deposited in 10 by 10 foot cubes, demons would enter these cubes and morph into images of people the victim knew or stage props to make the person feel like they were in a good place. They could walk as if going somewhere and the deceptive image would change to accommodate the illusion. Eventually the person begins to figure that he/she is being deceived and in fact is alone. Many of them were being treated by demons the way they had treated others in life. He saw some of the most evil people the world had known and they were being tormented the worst of all. One former German SS officer who had enjoyed tormenting and killing all the "undesirables" was now being tortured over and over as those victims of his were. He felt himself being raped, being shot with a baby in his arms, being buried alive. He felt the heat of the fires that burned homes and felt the loss of the children he orphaned. All this went on continuously in his cell with no letup, no relief. (Melvin, 170-171)

"Good" is Not Good Enough

There were people who thought they were good people but they missed what life is all about. Their "goodness" was hypocritical. The phrase "God chose us to choose Him but will we?" shows up many times regarding "good" people who never chose God, but chose instead to live the life they wanted. People who did good things, but for wrong selfish motives, were there. He said a "uniquely arrogant, condescending, asserting-your-rights-no-matter-the-cost attitude" is what brought many people there. He said many used this attitude to justify administering "justice" to those they considered wrong "according to their own twisted opinions," seeking to destroy careers, marriages, hopes, and dreams of those they opposed. (Melvin, 155) His experience is very lengthy, taking up most of his book, and includes many examples from many eras from Roman times until now. A voice speaks to him throughout his journey telling the way of God and the answers to the questions and arguments he had always posed as an atheist. He repeats a Name and a Title (Jesus Christ) over and over throughout his journey to ward off the taunting demons all around him. He is eventually shown his cube and told to go in. He refuses saying the Name and Title over and over with increasingly loud taunting by the demons that want him. But at that moment Jesus comes and takes him out and lets him go back to life. He glimpses heaven from a far distance before returning to Earth. (Melvin, 65-182)

Other Testimonies of the Horrors of Hell

Bill Weiss then goes on to tell of similar testimonies of a dark tunnel, an open pit that smells of sulfur and other putrid odors, cries of pain and terror, people being dropped into the pit of fire, people in iron cages, and evil demons. Besides the pain and suffering there is absolute aloneness. Some report recognizing some of the people there. One had been shot and bled to death; another died of drug overdose; another went to church but didn't take it seriously. In one case, the person there told the guest, "Don't come to this place. If you come here, there is no escape. There's no way out." Many of these stories came from Maurice Rawlings' book.[8] (Weiss 2013, 49-56)

He tells of meeting Lori Haider, *Saved from Hell*, who said she had a very painful brain aneurism and left her body. She saw a reptilian creature with its claws in her head. She saw a prison cell in hell that was

---

[8] Rawlings, Maurice, 1993. *To Hell and Back.* Nashville, TN: Thomas Nelson, Inc., Publishers.

for her, but fire was closing in on it. She was going to be burned alive, but dying is not an option any more there, so she would repeat the burning alive experience over and over forever. She saw ten sinister looking demons around her cell that were ready and eager to torture her. They had instruments with which they could torture her inflicting unimaginable pain. When her pastor prayed for her, the demon that had its claws in her head was ripped away and her spirit went back into her body. After she recovered she repented of her sins and Satan left her for good. (Weiss 2013, 75-78)

Ron DeVera died during quadruple bypass surgery. He had gone to church regularly as a child, but now he attended only occasionally. Religion and salvation were not matters of importance to him. Even waiting in the hospital for his surgery, he only considered matters of insurance and taking care of his family, not what might occur to him after he died. He was basically a good person and thought that was enough. But when he died during the surgery, he had a rude awakening. He awoke with horror and dread. He was in a dark forest of dead, barren trees and an ashen sky. Sticky, black gook hung from the tree branches, and he knew it would harm him if he touched it. All around him among the trees were hundreds of demons, some with horns and claws, other like misshapen humans. One of the human-like demons sat down next to him and tortured him by pushing a claw into his hand to have joy seeing Ron's pain. He knew he was going to be tortured like this forever if he didn't get out. He thought, "I don't belong here. I am a good person." He started praying earnestly to God, pleading for help. As he prayed, the demons started to leave, the little horned ones first. The larger human-like ones required more intense prayer. But as some were driven away, others would take their place. He prayed so continuously and intently that he got tired and fell asleep. When he awoke he was in a small dark cave with the walls and ceiling pressing in on him. In spite of being so cramped in his situation, there were five or six demons pressing down on him. They were translucent and ghostly white. They had hideous, bright red eyes. They were doing disgusting things to each other and Ron knew they were intending to do those same things to him. But Ron didn't give up his belief that he didn't belong there and continued to pray to God for help. Suddenly a bright light came into the darkened cave, and he heard human voices. He had been delivered from that hell back into his body. When he came to, he immediately wanted to get baptized, but had to wait until he was out of the hospital. Needless to say, he made drastic changes in his life and made God a priority and became a faithful follower of Jesus, the only one that can save anyone from that hell. He now knows just being good is not enough. (Garlow, 54-56)

Experiences of Hell by Some Not Going There

When Mary K. Baxter returned from her divine revelation of hell, her soul was in severe shock and she was so afraid of going back that she would scream in hysterical fear. The torment she endured there was so awful it made her sick enough to make her frantic enough to plead with everyone, "Please repent of your sins before it is too late!" (Baxter, 133) The details of her testimony of hell are given below in **A Divine Revelation of Hell**.

Ian McCormack to Hell First, then Heaven

Ian McCormack was an atheist and for ten years denied God's existence. During that time his mother kept praying for him. He was an experienced night diver, but one night off the coast of Mauritius, he got too close to a box jellyfish, aka sea wasp, whose sting is more deadly than sharks. He was stung, and before he got to shore, another stung him. He knew he only had minutes before he would be dead. Emergency was contacted and the ambulance hurried to the hospital to get him antitoxin. In the ambulance, his life flashed before his eyes, and he knew he was going to die. His mother's face appeared before him and said, "Ian, no matter how far from God you are, if you cry out to God from your heart, God will hear you, and God will forgive you." He didn't know how to pray and to which god to pray, so he thought his mother's God. At the same time, God had shown her Ian's face and told her, "Your son is nearly dead. Start now, and pray for him."

Now he thanks God for his praying mother who did not give up on her stubborn, rebellious son. He remembered his mother prayed the Lord's Prayer, but he couldn't remember the words. He prayed, "God, if you are real and this prayer is real, help me remember the prayer my mother taught me. If there is anything soft or good left in my heart,

260

please help me remember the Lord's Prayer." Then pieces started coming to him. First, "forgive us our sins." So he begged God to forgive him. Then "Forgive those who have sinned against you." Verses kept coming to him and with each one he responded in his heart. He came to "Thy will be done on Earth as it is in heaven." He thought about how he had always been doing his own thing for twenty-four years and promised God he would follow God's will for him the rest of his life if he came through this. Death kept getting closer and he knew it. He tried to keep his eyes open, but soon he couldn't and closed them with a sigh of relief. At that point he died and was clinically dead.

But as soon as he closed his eyes, he was awake again standing beside what he thought was his bed, but it was total darkness so he could not see anything, even his hand in front of his face. He tried to touch his face, but where it should be, he felt nothing. It was as if his hand passed through without touching it. He found he could not touch any of his body; it was like he was a complete human being but without any flesh or bones. He didn't know where he was, but he could feel intense evil around him. He sensed a total evil presence approaching him and looking at him even though he could see nothing. A voice said, "Shut up!" as if it could hear his thoughts. He backed away, but another from the other side said, "You deserve to be here." He put his hands in front of his face to protect himself and said, "Where am I?" A third voice said, "You are in hell, now shut up." He realized hell is not the party that atheists think it will be, and it put the fear of God in him for the rest of his life. When the darkness was the deepest a brilliant light drew him out. He could see the darkness fading on each side as he approached a circle of light. Later God told him if he hadn't prayed the deathbed prayer in the ambulance, he would have stayed in hell. God's mercy extends to the very last second of life. But Ian now doesn't recommend waiting that long!

As he traveled in the tunnel toward the light, parts of the light broke off and headed toward him, giving him waves of warmth and comfort, the most incredible soothing feeling he had ever experienced, and then total peace, a peace he could never find in all his worldly pursuits. Here he could see his hand and all of himself, and he was all a spirit form, full of radiant, white light. The third wave gave him joy and excitement. (Roth, 63-69, Sharkey, 23-27)

Howard Storm: Dying in Paris

When Howard Storm died in a Paris hospital, he stood up between two beds, his and Monsieur Fleurin's. He could not get the attention of either Monsieur Fleurin or his wife Beverly who was in a chair beside his bed. He felt fine; none of the pain in his abdomen was there, only the memory of it. He touched himself everywhere and he was alive, more alive than he had ever been in his life. All of his senses were heightened and alert, as if he had just been born. He then saw a form in his bed, which he recognized as himself. He didn't know how he could be standing by his bed looking at the physical form of his body. The thing in the bed could not be him, just something irrelevant to his being. Somehow he had been split into two parts, but he was more alert and conscious than he had ever been when his two parts were together. (Storm, 10-12)

Then outside he heard voices calling him, "Howard, Howard, Come out here. Let's go, hurry up. We have been waiting for you for a long time." [9] He replied that he couldn't come; he is sick and waiting for surgery. But the voices continued to pressure him, "We can get you fixed up, if you hurry up. Don't you want to get better? Don't you want help?" He was concerned about to whom the voices belonged. They were young and old, male and female. But they would not answer his questions about who they were. When he moved toward them they moved away so he could never see them. He thought they must be there to take him to surgery so he started with them. While he could not see them clearly he could tell they were pale and their clothes were gray. They were going deeper into a fog. But the farther he went with them the more suspicious he became. The number of people seemed to be increasing and they became more demanding and taunting. The more miserable he became the happier they seemed to be. He decided they were deceiving him, but when he looked up to go back all was dark. When he told them he could go no further, they began pushing and shoving in a wild frenzy of taunting, screaming, and hitting. They were biting and scratching him

---

[9] At the time he was an avowed atheist, not believing in God or heaven or hell.

and causing great torment. He did not want to recall any more of the torture they inflicted because the memory is too terrible. (Storm, 13-18)

As he was lying on the ground in torment he heard a voice like his saying, "Pray to God." He thought that to be a ridiculous thought so he ignored it. But it repeated, "Pray to God," but he did not know how. After the third time it said, "Pray to God," he tried piecing together all the prayer like things that mention God he could think of: "Yay, though I walk through the valley of the shadow of death, I will fear no evil for thou art with me. For purple mountain majesty, mine eye have see the glory of the coming of the Lord. Deliver us from evil. One nation under God. God bless America." To his amazement every time he mentioned God, the voices became more hateful and backed further way. He kept it up and eventually they were all gone. (Storm, 19-20)

Then he remembered as a child singing "Jesus loves me." He thought someone out there in that vast darkness must love him. He saw a pinpoint of light in the far distance and it was coming toward him at an incredible speed. He said the light was more intense and more beautiful than any he had ever seen. Soon it was on him and he recognized it was the King of Kings, the Lord of Lords, Christ Jesus the Savior. He thought Jesus must love him. Jesus held him close and they rose upward at an incredible speed, like a rocket they shot out of that dark hell toward an area of light far, far away. Inside the center was a very large concentration of light. Outside this were spheres of light moving in and out. (Storm, 24-27)

Terance Hopkins: Heaven then Hell

Dr. Gary Wood shared a testimony he received from Terance Hopkins, who was brought back from the dead by Dr. Wood's prayers when the doctors had given up hope. As a child Terance believed Jesus died for his sins and was baptized. But when he was older he forgot Jesus and was living for the temptations of the world ("wine, women, and song"). Then his vehicle was struck by a train he didn't see, which tore it in two. Terance's head was crushed and he died instantly. At first he saw heaven with all of its beauty, peace, and joy. He stood on a hill looking over a sparkling gold city. He experienced a wonderful sweet feeling. Then he saw Jesus and fell at his feet. Jesus told him He has work for him to do and he showed him the place he will go if he doesn't do that work but continues the way he has been living. As far as he could see, there were pits of fire with high walls. He saw thousands of people in these pits, some trying fruitlessly to climb out only to be knocked back into the fire which continuously burned them but didn't consume them. The demons that knocked them back into the fire also struck them with clubs with long spikes in the end. He heard mournful cries and scream upon scream from the pain. He was gripped with fear and shook uncontrollably. The demons tormented him saying, "You could have had Jesus. You could have had heaven." He sobbed and pleaded with Jesus to take him away. His moment in hell gave him an awareness of grief, sorrow, and eternal death more than he had ever had before. He never imagined hell could be so horrible, a place of unbelievable sorrow. (Wood, 49-51)

James Woodford Stood on the Brink Hell

When Jim Woodford arrived at the end of the tunnel of light, he landed on a verdant landscape of grass brilliant with light. There was a median line to the right of which a brilliant soft light filtered through a mist, but to the left the ground sloped downward into a deep dark crevasse. The walls were black, glistening, and coal-like. From the crevasse came screeching sounds that filled him with soul-shuddering terror. The slope disappeared into a roiling black mass of clouds rolling rapidly up the slope as if to overtake him. Also there was an awful stench of sickness, death, and hopelessness. The massive black cloud was filled with a clammy murkiness and a damp chill devoid of life and warmth. Then a gruesome creature crawled out and Jim knew it was coming for him. Its eyes focused on him like burning coals. Its hideous mouth had saliva dripping from its fangs. Voices started coming from this dark fog. At first they were indistinct but then he heard them saying his name, "Jim! Jim! Come this way. Come with us." The more he turned away from the pit the louder and more insistent they became, "Jim, come with us. We are here for you. This is where you belong." He felt a sharp scraping of a claw or talon on the back of his shoulder. The voices expressed a gleeful anticipation of excitement, presumably at Jim's expense. The more he turned toward the light, the more the darkness tried to draw him in. He felt evil was about to get him when he cried out, "God help me!" an acknowledgement he had not made before, acknowledging that he was not in control and was willing to submit to God. At that moment as if they had been waiting for him to call out to God and surrender his need to control, three points of light came from his right, the side away from the abyss. They approached from different directions at a very rapid rate. They got bigger and brighter as they approached. Their light flooded over him and struck the creature from the darkness, causing it to shriek and roar in pain and forcing it back into the darkness. The creature and its stench recoiled violently and scrambled back into the darkness of the crevasse. Woodford says in retrospect, "Darkness and evil cannot exist in the light of *God*!" Jim had been rescued from evil, rescued from his self-sufficient complacency by the mercy of God and the salvation gained by Christ. (Woodford, 55-59)

Laurie Ditto: Hell Is Too Terrible for Words

Laurie Ditto was in a prayer service at Kansas City Evangelists' Fellowship when suddenly the back of the church opened up with hell in view. Hell and the prayer room were both together in plain view to her but no one else saw the image of hell. The gates of hell swung open and a fingerless arm came out and grabbed her with a strong suction and pulled her into hell with the gates closing behind her. She screamed in terror. (Ditto, 26-27)

She said there are not the words to tell how terrible hell is. Words and emotions are needed that are only for hell where God is absent. They do not apply in the presence of God. . Limited vocabulary is an issue and also her memories of the indescribable torture make her speechless. This made it hard for Laurie to describe her experience in hell. (Ditto, 28)

She understood hell is a relational issue. It was created for Lucifer and the angels who rebelled against God. God never intended hell for the beings He created in His image. One sin doesn't send us there. We have all sinned, but hell is not a sin issue. A person goes to hell not because of sin but because of disobeying and disrespecting God. Hell is about refusing to love God and have a relationship with Him. Such a relationship must be based on His terms, acceptance of the sacrificial gift of His Son. She saw that she was in hell because, even though she had accepted Jesus and received forgiveness for her sins, it was her unwillingness to love God and forgive others. Everyone is in hell because they will not love and obey God. She wouldn't receive God's love and let that love change her. She wouldn't obey His command to forgive others as she had been forgiven. (Ditto, 34-37)

In hell there is no taking a break, no time out, no shutdown; the fear and torment and pain are continuous. In hell she had an identity of zero value. There she had a never-ending onslaught of crushing regrets: regret for her sins, regret for her unforgiveness, which she knew was a sin but did it anyway, regrets for the opportunities with God she passed up. (Ditto, 38-40)

She was suspended over something black and bubbly that was very hot. She was trapped in a teardrop-shaped flame cell and isolated in the darkness and fear. She could hear other souls but could not reach them nor they her. In hell one is utterly isolated, the very opposite of the fellowship and loving companionship of heaven. The atmosphere was layers of utter darkness. As she felt her bones drying up, she longed for water but here was none. She tried to find relief from the pain of the flames, but no change of position offered any relief. Her bones were grinding against each other and the marrow turned from yellow to black. The flames began to burn her but one can't get relief by dying, because in hell one is already dead. The pain and suffering just continue and get more intense. The pain was unbearable. It was like getting her hand burned cooking bacon, but in hell there was no ice or anything to cool the burn, only the heat and flames to make it more intense. The pain was unbearable and terrible. There was no way for her to get relief, no rest, no sleep. It caused her body to contort in unnatural ways as she tried to find a position of relief. The flames were not a normal fire; they embodied a wickedness that seemed to plan more ways to torture its victims. Hell is filled with darkness and untranslatable fear that never ends, but only grows with each passing second, fueled by hatred of God. (Ditto, 40-43)

She said death is everywhere in hell, but it is not the end of suffering when everything stops. Death is the increase of pain and suffering with no relief ever forever. One can't appeal to God or Jesus or the Holy Spirit because they are not there. (Ditto, 47)

Hell is darkness, blackness, and it is devoid of color in a way she can't describe. The flames were not red, orange, and yellow; they were just blackness, hell-type evil blackness that has a sound that strikes fear into every thought.

She found that hell is not just physical pain. Her mind, will, emotions, physical body, and spirit all hurt. The pain was worse than anything she had experienced in life. (Ditto, 48-49)

In hell she knew the people she cared about were forgetting her. This just added to her pain. She began to wish they would be in hell, too, something she would never normally wish for anyone. This was an indication that in hell we become more and more like Satan himself, even hating God. (Ditto, 52)

When she tried to breathe, she found the air of hell is designed to poison and cause more pain, fear, and torture. She said there is no breath of life in hell. Attempting to breathe through her nose was worse because of the terrible stench of hell. Everything reeked of a very bad smell she had never smelled before, perhaps like a mixture of sulfur, ammonia, bleach, and toxic chemicals. It made her nauseous and sick with a headache. (Ditto, 53)

She said hell has more people than heaven and is constantly expanding to take in more that are coming. Many are people who did not love God on Earth but there are others who, like her, knew Jesus was who He said He was and believed what He said, but not enough to change. They were unforgiving and proud as she was. Jesus told us to forgive others and humbly enter his Kingdom as an innocent child, unforgiveness and pride do not qualify. (Ditto, 56-57)

She said there were little demons that were in complete opposition to God and were filled with hatred for God. They would pass through her and change whatever part they passed through into hatred for God also. Everyone in hell becomes self-hating, others-hating evil beings like those for whom hell was made. Hell is many times worse than all the evil people do to one another here. (Ditto, 58)

All her sins that resulted from her unforgiveness were there in hell to haunt and hurt her and accentuate her suffering. She realized her being in hell was just and right because she had disobeyed God. She said, "Sin is evil! Sin has a weight and it hurts now and it hurts there. ... (I Thess.

5:22). We are to flee from sin. Flee from the devil. ... I thought I could handle it. ... I had no idea before going to hell how much sin God saved me from." (Ditto, 62-63)

She says that since her experience in hell she has had an overwhelming need to be able to point people to our great and loving Father to know the way He has prepared for us to be with Him where He is. We were not made for the fires of hell; we were made in God's image for an eternal beautiful love-filled life with Him. Everyone needs to be told about Jesus and what He has done for us. (Ditto, 102)

Kat Kerr Saw People in Hell

Kat Kerr was taken to hell one evening when she was praying. Fortunately she didn't have to experience the horrors of hell, she only was a witness to what people there were experiencing, and that was scary enough. First of all, the demons assigned to hell hate God and everything having to do with him. That means they hate humans that are made in God's image; in fact they hate humans vehemently. Their greatest pleasure is causing humans as much terror, pain, torture, and suffering as they can. The screams she heard there were terrifying and unbearable. There is no mercy there; fear rules. Even if the physical torture stops momentarily the mental torture never does. She said if two friends happen to arrive together, they are separated and one has to watch helplessly as the friend is dragged away and torn to shreds screaming for help.

Sometimes people are in fiery pits, and small animals bite continuously causing endless pain over and over. The heat is unquenchable and causes blisters over the whole body. The stench of scorched flesh is pervasive.

Another torture is a stone tomb too small to do anything except stand and that just barely. It is absolutely black and spider demons crawl all over the person screaming blasphemies. The sounds pierce the person's head until he/she thinks he/she is going to go insane. When the person becomes exhausted, there is no way to lie down. If he/she attempts to slouch, the sharp stones in the walls cut into the person's legs.

There is also suffering starvation as there is never anything to eat and dehydration because there is no water anywhere. Kat makes the point that some people state they can't believe a merciful, loving, forgiving God would send anyone to a place like this. That is true; He doesn't send anyone there. He banned all the rebelling angels there, and people only come there when they choose of their own free will not to follow God but in effect follow Satan, the only other choice, is the result of his rebellion against God. (Kerr 2007, 107-111)

Dale Black saw Demons Coming to take Chuck to Hell

Dale Black, his instructor, Chuck Burns, who was a mentor and friend, and another man were killed in a crash soon after take off in a small, twin-engine plane on a commercial flight. Dale and Chuck were loaded into an ambulance and rushed to the nearest hospital as the medics gave him CPR. Dale in the spirit flew along with the ambulance. In the emergency ward, Dale would occasionally go back into his body and then die again. His spirit always stayed near his body, supposedly so he could go back into it because it wasn't time to complete death yet. He became aware of something terrible going on in the adjacent room. Something catastrophic was taking place with the person in the next room. He saw demons going into the room, and he had the most awful feeling of dread he had ever had. He said wave after wave of heartbreaking anguish crashed over him. Dale said the light seemed to be sucked out of the room. Someone's eternal destiny was in the balance, and the awful outcome had already been determined. He sensed all this because it was happening in the realm he was in, the realm of the spirit. The doctors and nurses were oblivious to all this. A year later Dale was talking to the attending physician and asked him who was in the next room. It was Chuck Burns. Dale could not tell this story until writing his book, forty years after it happened. The fate of his friend, companion, mentor, and devoted friend, was more than he could bear. All the time he had flown with Chuck, he had never brought up the issue of his soul and making peace with God through Jesus and his sacrifice. He thought there would always be time. Now he is more intentional because he now knows the spirit world is far more real than this world, and nothing matters in the long term except getting right with God.

Dale spends several pages dealing with the sheer terror experienced by the victim being taken against his will to a place he didn't want to go. Chuck was a good man in the world's sense, but "No one comes to the Father except through me," Jesus said. He said his experience dealing with Chuck's death and the demons caused a sorrow too deep for words. Every day he thinks of Chuck and the bone-chilling fear he experienced and knows it is beyond what can be contained in our physical minds here on Earth. The presence of evil was that powerful that day that Chuck died in its hands. Dale felt a spiritual destruction and loss that surpassed all the combined terror he had ever experienced in life. (Black 2018, 143-152)

George Ritchie's glimpse of Hell

Jesus took George Ritchie on a trip to view three places where people go who don't reach heaven. The first was a normal city. There were lots of people, some living and some not living. The living ones could be recognized by being surrounded by a faint glow over the surface of their bodies. This luminosity moved with them like a second skin made of pale, scarcely visible light. The non-living beings did not have this sheath of light around them. (Ritchie, 59)

Two people would be walking along side by side, a living person and a non-living person. The living person was smoking a cigarette, and the non-living person would continually be trying to grab the cigarette out of his hand, which he couldn't do. At a bar, a non-living person would try to grab the drink of a living person. In an office, a young man at a desk was being given constant criticism and advice from an older non-living man behind him. In all of these instances, the dead spirit stayed on Earth but still had the effects of bad habits cultivated in life but now could not satisfy them. George was persuaded by this to avoid cultivating any bad habits.

The second visit was to a plane somewhere, an unidentified location. Here there were no living beings, and the dead ones were constantly fighting, abusing, raping, and otherwise doing all the violence they could to other non-living beings. Without physical bodies, it was all for naught, but that did not deter any of them from venting their wrath in whatever gruesome ways they could.

The third place was like a university. Here people were quietly going about studying and doing research. They were content, but it was obvious they were missing the best; they were not experiencing the love, joy, and peace of a relationship with Jesus and the Father. As much as they had achieved a measure of selflessness, they were oblivious to Jesus. It was here that George saw the nuclear submarine engine test facility.

Finally, in the far distance, George saw a lighted, beautiful city. Two beings of light were coming toward him, but at that point Jesus said he had to go back. After experiencing Jesus love, he did not want to return to his body, but that was Jesus' will.

George recognized that the beautiful lighted city was heaven, and George wasn't ready to go there. He longed to be there and walk its streets, meet the people, etc., but he needed to make some changes in his life first (Ritchie, 56-73). My opinion is that the other scenes were temporary holding places until the final judgment.

Thomas Welch and Others' Encounters with Hell

Dr. Rawlings reports a story that appeared in a booklet by Thomas Welch, *Oregon's Amazing Miracle*. Welch, a young man working at a lumber mill, went out on a conveyor belt to loosen a logjam, and fell, hitting his head on a beam. He tumbled down into the water in the pond below. It was about an hour before they found his body and took it to the house where he had been staying. His landlady had been praying fervently for him since he was not yet a believer. Then miraculously, he came back to life.

He said that after he died, he found himself beside a lake of fire, blue flames of fire and brimstone. There was no one in the fire, but many around the edge, like himself. He saw some others that he had known. Everyone was perplexed; they didn't know how they got there and what they could do about it. He describes the scene was so awesome that there aren't enough words to do it justice. The only way he can describe it is to say he was an eyewitness now to the final judgment. He saw that there is no way to escape, no way out. So you don't even look for one. This is the prison out of which no one can escape except by Divine intervention. He said to himself in an audible voice, "If I had known about this, I would have done anything that was required of me to escape coming to a place like this." But he had not known.

Then he saw Jesus passing through. Somehow he knew Jesus was his only hope, but Jesus didn't look in his direction. Just before Jesus left the scene, He turned and looked directly at Welch, and in that instant, he returned to his body. He now knows Jesus is alive; he has seen him and has forever been changed. He does not want to go back again to the hell he saw! (Rawlings, 86-89)

Dr. Rawlings describes several more very bad encounters of the afterlife. A heart attack patient saw that he was getting out of his body. Then he entered a gloomy room where he saw in one of the windows a huge giant with a grotesque face that was watching him. Little imps or elves that seemed to be with the giant were running around the windowsill. The giant beckoned him. He didn't want to go, but he had to. Outside was darkness, but he could hear people moaning all around him. He could feel things moving about his feet, although he couldn't see them. As he moved on through a tunnel or cave, things were getting worse. He remembers crying. Then for some reason the giant turned him loose and sent him back. He was being spared, but doesn't know why. (Rawlings 90)

He describes other cases that involve similar features: darkness, travel in a tunnel or cave, frightful beings, eerie sounds, foul smells of decay, and a feeling of terror. People who have these terrifying experiences come back and change their ways. Dr. Rawlings says of one of his patients, since his experience of hell, he has had a compulsion to warn others of the dangers of complacency and the need to take a definite stand in their faith. (Rawlings, 93)

Dr. Rawlings gave other stories of people being hounded by evil demons.

Richard Sigmund visits hell

At one point in Richard Sigmund's journey in heaven when he was with Jesus, Jesus told him He wanted to take him to visit the other place. He did not want to go, but Jesus took him in his arms, and he felt safe. He immediately saw that hell is the complete opposite of heaven. There were hideous grotesque beings. There were flames of punishment and cries of doom and despair. Demons torture people. There was no one too young to know about sin. Demons were screaming at the presence of Jesus. Everything he saw made him ill; it was absolute horror. Some people were skeletons with flesh hanging off. Demons would eat the rotting flesh and then it would be back to rot again. People were raped. People were in burning cages being dipped in the lake of fire. People had cancer with its pain and suffering forever. There are degrees of punishment; those who know the most and didn't do what they should have are punished the most. Jesus urged him to tell people what he saw, both what heaven is like and how much He and the Father love us, and what hell is really like. He said, "I want you to tell others of this place and warn them that *unless they are washed in my blood, unless they are born again, this is where they will spend eternity.*" (Sigmund, 116-119)

Richard Eby experienced hell for two minutes in a visit to Israel

When Richard Eby was in the suddenly darkened tomb cave of Lazarus on a visit to Israel, Jesus expunged his name from the Book of Life for two minutes so he could experience hell exactly as an unbeliever will. He described falling into the center of the Earth into a chamber about ten feet high and four feet square. It was a holding tank for sinners until the white throne of judgment takes place. He was terrified. He said voices tell the sinners why they are there and how they got there. When they die they are instantaneously there, and there is no escape. The terror he felt was indescribable, and there was the stink of demons. He was surrounded by a thousand little things like deformed dogs and cats the size of little spiders, who were chained and had fire behind their eyes. They looked up at him and in a more terrible language than anything on Earth ridiculed him for turning down the Savior. They said they would never let him out and would give him the hell they were experiencing. They crawled up the walls and over his face and continued to taunt him with very obscene words and language. They said they caused the Earthquake when Jesus was on the cross to make the nails in his hands hurt worse. The black cloud during the crucifixion was demons trying to paralyze what God was planning to do so there would be no salvation. (I have not heard this before, but how much can I trust the words of a demon since his master is the father of lies?) Richard asked them why they were in hell, and they said they had already accepted Satan as their savior and there was no other choice. They were there forever and they planned to keep him there forever also. The stench of death was terrible because Satan is the author of death. The demons enjoyed it because they knew nothing else. (Roth, 177-178)

Then Richard was suddenly in the throne room of God. There was a book there on which was written in Hebrew, "The Lamb's Book of Life." God was turning the pages at lightning speed looking for Richard's name. Jesus said, "It is not there. I expunged it to show you that there is such a book, and it will be looked at by My heavenly Father."

Suddenly Richard was back in the tomb of Lazarus and the lights came on. Jesus said, "I went there first before you were born, and I took the keys to hell and death. I had to form a new place that would be in total isolation from God." He explained, "Because that was the desire of their hearts. The only way people can get into hell is by their own volition. I've given each person a will. The desire of the hearts of those who will not accept me is that they want Us to stay out of the way. They don't want the Father, Son, or Holy Spirit. They say, 'Leave me alone, I'll make it.' They think they can make their own lives, live the way they want. That's the will of the people who deprive themselves of salvation. So I had immediately to create a place of total separation." (Roth, 179)

Experience of Three Others

John Myers' *Voices from the Edge of Eternity* records the last moments on Earth as people prepare to leave. Many of the moments are not pleasant. These are all the recordings of people who were with the one dying. Some are testimonies of victory and the anticipation of heaven. But many others are the distress of those who have rejected Christ and are in torment regarding their death and what lies ahead. It appears that many times people get a sense of the error of their ways at the very last and fear what is ahead for them.

When Jesse Duplantis was taken to heaven for six hours one day, Jesus told him when the time of the final judgment comes there will be tears in heaven. Jesus will cry tears of sadness and heartbreak when He has to tell those whom He created, loved, and died for so that they could be with Him forever, but have refused to accept Him, to be gone. It will be heart breaking to have to do this to those He loved, but they leave

Him no choice. He gave everyone freewill and He will not go against his/her choice even when it hurts Him so much. So please, do not cause the Lord who loves you to grieve on the Day of Judgment by refusing to accept His gift.

Herbert Broome had a glimpse of heaven and hell when he was on his deathbed from cancer. He said hell is a terrible, terrible place. It is so awful you have no idea how bad it is. He heard murmurings that sounded like wailings, all wailing at the same time. It was horrible and it goes on forever. He said you have to be born again. Just saying you are good and being a good fellow "doesn't cut it." You must be born again to escape hell. Doucette 2013-1)

Bill Weise Suddenly in Hell

Bill Weise went to bed Sunday, November 22, 1998, when, suddenly, at 3:00 a.m. on the twenty-third, without any notice, he was being hurled through the air, and then fell on the ground, completely out of control.

He landed in what was very much like a prison cell with stone walls and heavy bars (Weiss 2006, xv-xvi). It was very hot, too hot to survive, and had the effect of taking away his strength. He looked around and saw two enormous beasts in his cell. They were ten to thirteen feet tall and were entirely evil. They gazed at him with pure hatred. Their arms and legs were out of proportion.

He describes the first beast as having bumps and scales all over his grotesque body, a huge protruding jaw, gigantic teeth, and large sunken eyes. He said this creature was stout and powerful, with thick legs and abnormally large feet. The second beast was taller and thinner, but with very long arms and razor sharp fins that covered its body, and claws that were nearly a foot long protruded from its hands (Weiss 2006, 3-4). It too was very evil and spoke hatred for God. Then they turned on him as hungry predators, and he felt a violent, evil presence greater than he had ever felt before and greater than anything he could imagine. Their hatred far surpassed anything he could imagine. He felt totally helpless. Two more beings showed up, and together it appeared his torture would be their amusement. One creature picked him up with strength one thousand times greater than any man and hurled him against a wall. Then the second beast, with its razor sharp claws and sharp protruding fins, grabbed him from behind in a bear hug and pressed him into its chest, with its sharp fins piercing his back. Then it ripped Bill's flesh with its claws. He says the creatures seemed to derive pleasure in the pain and terror they inflicted upon him. Also there was a terrible foul stench coming from these creatures that was extremely nauseous. It was absolutely disgusting, foul, and rotten; by far the most putrid smells he had ever encountered.

He also heard the screams of an untold multitude of people crying out in torment that horrified him. It was dark, but not like darkness on Earth. This darkness, besides being totally absent of any light, was accompanied by a distinctive evil presence. He saw flames from the lake of fire in the distance. He longed for a drink, but there is no water anywhere. He knew there was no way out, no work, no goals, no wisdom, no one to talk to, advise, or comfort. It seemed like all life was over, and all that was left was a useless wasting away that permeated his being.

At one point he had gotten out of his cell, but one of the demonic creatures grabbed him and carried him back into the cell. It threw him on the floor. Another creature quickly grabbed his head and began to crush it. Then all four of the creatures were on top of him, each grabbing a leg or an arm as if he were a lifeless prey. He was so terrified that there are no words to describe it. But just before they were to pull his body apart, he was suddenly taken out of the cell and placed next to the pit of fire. (Weiss 2006, 13-14)

He looked up into that dark, eerie, tomb-like atmosphere, which seemed to be like a mouth that had swallowed death. The flames of the lake's ravenous appetite could not be satisfied with the pitiful screams of the untold multitudes. The heat was totally unbearable. He could see outlines of people through the flames, and the screams from the condemned souls were deafening and relentless. There was no safe place, no safe moment, no temporary relief of any kind. In hell, this state of fear never ceases for one second. It lasts for eternity. (Weiss 2006, 21-22)

Bill gives more details of his experience in hell, and then says that for some unknown reason, he suddenly began ascending up and came into the presence of a brilliant, pure, white light that he knew to be Jesus.

Jesus then explained to him He had taken away all of Bill's knowledge of being a Christian and all awareness of the presence of God so he could truly experience what hell is really like. He allowed Bill to experience all of this because He wants people to know that hell is very real, and it is not someplace you want to go. Jesus doesn't want anyone to go there; he wants everyone to be in his Kingdom with him and his Father. He allowed Bill to experience this so he could pass this message on to a hurting world.

Finally, Jesus told him to tell people he is coming very, very soon. Richard Sigmund (Sigmund, 77), Jesse Duplantis, and others have echoed this same warning. Bill felt a God-given urgency to warn as many people as possible, as time is running out. Jesus sternly said it again, *"Tell them I am coming very, very soon!"* Repeating Himself indicates His coming truly is getting very, very close. Time is running out. We must get the truth out so people can know there is a choice to make. Without Jesus as your Savior, you will not be going to heaven, and that is absolutely certain, and where you will be going, he can testify *you absolutely don't want to go.* (Weise, 37-38)

A Divine Revelation of Hell

Mary K. Baxter's experience of hell was the most extensive of all. It was originally a complete book, *A Divine Revelation of Hell.* In 1976 Jesus came to Mary K. Baxter every night for thirty nights and while everyone was sleeping took her in the spirit to view hell. On two occasions He left her alone there so she could completely experience what people who go there have to endure. She got to leave, but she was there long enough to experience personally the horrors of hell to such an extent it took her a very long time to recover. I have taken it from a volume that combines both *A Divine Revelation of Hell* and *A Divine Revelation of Heaven* together in one volume. Others have echoed some of what she saw. This includes the tornado-like funnels, the fire pits with occupants trying to climb out only to be pushed back into the flames by demons, and the cages.

Jesus took Mark K. Baxter out of her body and had her accompany Him to hell because He wanted her to write a book to tell people what hell is really like to get more people to repent and accept Jesus before it is too late. In the company of Jesus, her spirit left her body as if she had died and left her body behind in bed purportedly sleeping. She could see the other members of her family sleeping in the house as she left. (Baxter, 160)

Funnels to Hell

After they had traveled far enough to see Earth below, she saw many dirty spinning slinky like funnels high above the Earth. Jesus told her those are the pathways to hell. One gets to hell through one of them, so they entered one of them and encountered a deep darkness with a horrible smell. Dark gray evil forms that cried out to them as they passed by were embedded in the walls of the funnel. She also felt an invisible evil spirit moving with them in the funnel. Sometimes she could see forms moving in the darkness. Jesus told her they were evil spirits waiting to be released by Satan to go to Earth, and they called out to her with laughter. They would have touched her but the power of Jesus restrained them. She had all her senses, and they were stronger than usual. The worst odor she had ever smelled permeated the air. It was the smell of decaying flesh. She heard the cries and wails of the dead in that place. She was surrounded by fear, death, and sin. Jesus warned her that even worse was coming up next. (Baxter, 161-162)

Horrible Torments, Pain, Sorrow, and Fire Pits

There were things she could not put on paper, but the things she did are horrible beyond belief. She said hell "is a horrid place of torments, excruciating pain, and eternal sorrow." And, "There are no parties in hell. No love. No compassion. No rest." [No companionship or comfort]. (Baxter, 163)

When they left the funnel they came to an area of many fire pits four feet across and three feet deep with red-hot brimstone on the sides. There was a lost soul in the center of each one. Flames would rise up from the bottom and engulf him/her. Then the fire would die down and only to rise up and rush over him/her again. The lost soul was caged in a skeleton form with a dirty grey mist inside. She heard a feminine voice from one of the pits cry out, "Jesus, have mercy!" Decayed flesh hung by strips from her bones and her eyes were just empty sockets. She had no hair. There were worms crawling out of her bones. The worms were not harmed by the fire but the woman felt the worms. She cried again that she wanted out. Jesus had great sorrow in His face. The fire again rose up and consumed the woman. She had great cries and deep sobs. She was lost and there was no way out. (Baxter, 166-167)

There were more pits, and cries, moans, and hideous screams came from all directions. At the next pit, a man's voice said, "Lord, have mercy on me." With wailing sobs he said, "I'm so sorry Jesus. Forgive me. Take me out of here. I have been in this place of torment for years. I beg You, let me out!" "Lord Jesus," he cried, "Haven't I suffered enough for my sins? It has been forty years since my death." Jesus said it is written that the mockers and unbelievers will come here. You would not believe the truth. Many times My people were sent to you to show you the way, but you would not listen to them. You laughed at them and refused the gospel. Even though I died on a cross for you, you mocked Me and would not repent of your sins. My Father gave you many opportunities to be saved. If only you had listened." At this Jesus wept. The man cried out, "I know, Lord, I know! But I repent now." Jesus said, "It is too late. Judgment is set." The conversation with this man continued along the same lines as that of the rich man in hell while the poor man Lazarus (not the brother of Martha and Mary) was at Jesus side. (See chapter 16 in Luke) (Baxter, 169-170)

At this Mary Baxter turned to Jesus and cried, "Lord, how horrible!" Jesus replied, "Hell is real; the judgment is real. I love them so, my child." Jesus loves everyone and He died a horrible death on the cross after a cruel flogging just so we wouldn't come this place. To see someone he has loved so much in this place hurts him more than you can know. But like He said, it is too late, the judgment is real and final. Mary Baxter wondered if the people in hell feel all these things. Jesus told her, "When they come here they have the same feelings and thoughts as when they were on Earth. They remember their family and friends and all the times they had a chance to repent but refused to do so." He lamented, "If only they had believed the gospel and repented before it was too late." Jesus then told her the story of the woman's life. She had had painful cancer, but blamed God and refused to repent. He said she had known Him once but came to hate Him and said she did not need God. She turned her back on Jesus and cursed Him and resisted the Spirit's pleading with her. The woman pleaded with Jesus to let her out and she would serve Him and be good. "Haven't I suffered enough?" Jesus replied with sadness all over His face, "You had chance after chance to repent and serve Me." Mary Baxter longed for something she could do to help the poor woman, but unfortunately after the judgment nothing can be done. She says, "Sinner, please don't wait until God's Spirit quits striving with you." (Baxter, 170-172)

In the next pit Jesus and Mary Baxter came to a woman in the same state of pain and distress. She cried out and told Jesus the story of how she couldn't follow and serve him because she wanted all the fame and fortune her beauty brought her. Jesus kept seeking her for something special but she kept choosing the pleasures of this world, saying she would follow Him someday. But an auto accident took her life before she ever did choose Jesus, and so she is here forever without her beauty, fame, and fortune. As she tried to climb out of the pit, a large grizzly-bear-sized brownish-black demon pushed her back down into the pit and into the flames. Tears fell down Jesus' cheeks and Mary Baxter cried, "Dear Lord, the torment is too real. When a soul comes here, there is no hope, no life, no love. Hell is too real." She recognized there is no way out, and the poor woman must burn forever in these flames. (Baxter, 172-174)

Demons in Hell and Occupants of Fire Pits

The next night Jesus took Mary Baxter to a different part of hell where she saw many demons. A large demon was telling some smaller imps and devils, "Go, do many evil things. Break up homes and destroy families. Seduce weak Christians, and misinform and mislead as many as you can. Remember, you must be careful of those who have genuinely accepted Jesus as their Savior. They have the power to cast you out." Then the evil imps and devils flew up and out of hell to the surface of the Earth to do their evil. She describes them as being in many different grotesque forms and sizes. (Baxter, 176-177)

In the next pit of fire and brimstone, there was a large-framed man preaching the gospel. Tattered parts of his clothes hung on him and had not been burned. Burning flesh was hanging from his skeleton and his skull seemed to be in flames. A terrible odor came from him. Jesus told her he had been a preacher of the gospel and served Jesus speaking the truth. He spread his hands as if holding a book and began reading Scripture after Scripture. He said to Jesus, "Lord, now I will preach the truth to all the people. Now, Lord, I am ready to go and tell others about this place. I know that while I was on Earth I didn't believe there was a hell, nor did I believe you were coming again. It was what people wanted to hear, and I compromised the truth to the people in my church." He went on and ended with, "Let me out and I will do right. I won't take money from the church any more. I have repented already. I will love people of every race and color." Jesus reminded him of the truth of what he did knowingly, and all the ways Jesus had tried to get him back. He wanted to go his own way and was evil. He did not want to repent although Jesus waited for him. Now the judgment has been set. Mary Baxter could see that Jesus felt deep pity for this man. As they walked away many other bony hands reached out to Jesus to plead with Him. (Baxter, 177-179)

In the midst of the flames of the next pit, with worms and dead flesh in her bones, a woman cried out to Jesus, "Let me out of here. I will give you my heart now, Jesus. I will tell others about your forgiveness. I will witness for you. I beg you, please let me out!" Jesus reminded her that Scripture tells that we must repent and turn from our sins and invite Jesus into our lives if we are to avoid this place. He told her, "If you had listened to me and had repented and come to me, I would have forgiven you." He reminded her he had given her many opportunities to repent but she hardened her heart and would not repent. She had had sinful affairs with many men and had caused many homes to be broken apart, describing in detail what all she had done. Nevertheless He would have forgiven her if she had turned to Him. (Baxter, 179-180)

In one pit a woman was preaching, quoting from Scripture, proclaiming the Word of God. She had answered a call to serve Jesus and was doing good work. She studied the Word of God and prayed. She had many prayers answered, taught the way of holiness, and was faithful in her house. But her husband had an affair, which he confessed and for which he asked her for forgiveness. She refused to forgive him. She became angry and bitter. She quit reading the Word and praying. Her anger extended to others. Her heart grew bitter as she continued to harbor unforgiveness. She eventually murdered her husband and the other woman. Finally with complete yielding to Satan she killed herself. She could have been in heaven except she allowed unforgiveness in her heart to take control and destroy her. She now said she would forgive him, but it was too late. (Baxter, 185-187)

She saw many more scenes similar to these, many in fire pits with burning skeletons with burned and rotten flesh hanging in strips. The trapped souls of these skeletons never repented and followed Jesus. They wanted Jesus to save them, promising to follow Him now. But Jesus told them all of the many times He wooed them to repent and come but they wouldn't. Some told of good things they had done and being church members. But the bottom line in every case was each one never repented of his/her sins. They cursed Jesus when He could not save them now. Mary Baxter's experience of all this was very gruesome and made her all the more anxious to do what she could to keep people from coming here. She learned hell is infinitely worse than anyone can imagine.

The Belly of Hell

Jesus took Mary Baxter through a tunnel to another part of hell. The tunnel was very dark except for the light of Jesus. She saw large snakes, as large as four feet around and twenty-five feet long, large rats, and many evil imps and devils. The imps and devils were on their way to the surface of the Earth to tempt and mislead as many people as they can, and doing anything else of Satan's bidding. That dark, damp, dirty place with evil ever present caused Mary Baxter much fear, but Jesus protected her. (Baxter, 195)

Jesus called the place they came to the belly of hell. First Jesus showed her the center of the "belly of hell." Here there is great torment and it varies from soul to soul. Jesus told her, "There are many different types of torment for these souls. There is greater punishment for those who once preached the gospel and went back to sin, or those who would not obey the call of God on their lives." He wanted her to know and tell others that hell is real, Satan is real, the demon powers are real, and the powers of darkness are real. They are not figments someone's imagination or artifacts of religious ideas. (Baxter, 197-198)

She saw a man in a coffin who was being stabbed repeatedly by a dozen demons marching around the coffin. Each stabbing pierced his heart and this was going on continuously as was his agony. Mary Baxter could not stand to see this man's pain and suffering. But Jesus explained this man had preached the gospel and brought salvation to many. But having a big church with a fine automobile and a large income became more important than serving God. He began stealing from the church and preaching lies. Eventually he held seminars to teach his false doctrine. He trampled God's Holy Word under his feet. In spite of this Jesus had continued to love him and seek his repentance, but he never did repent. He lead many astray, some of whom were present in hell along with him. Jesus told her, "It is better to have never known me than to know Me and turn back from serving Me." His torture and all the others she had seen are all the work of Satan. Satan and his demons are doing all the torturing and causing all the suffering. God is not inflicting the torture, it is the work of Satan, who hates God, Jesus, and all those created in God's image (us). God provided a way for all created in His image to be with Him in His perfect kingdom, but anyone who refuses to repent and accept God's gift is left at the mercy of Satan, and he has no mercy. (Baxter, 199-201)

The "Fun Center" of Hell

There is a "fun center" in hell, but it is not for the fun of the people that go there. It is for the demons' fun. It is like a circus arena and former occult leaders are brought to the center ring. Those that they had deceived and made to follow Satan could come to the outside of the ring and could torture those in the center. In one torment the bones of the one being tormented were taken and hidden all over hell. The victim than had to go on scavenger hunt to find his/her bones. Satan ordered all kinds of torture for those being tortured, causing them to cry out that they wanted to die. But spiritual death, the only death left, was not allowed. This was Satan's fun center. (Baxter, 220-221)

When we get to heaven all illnesses and all infirmities and all injuries are immediately restored, so that the person is fully as they were designed to be. But this is not true in hell. Everyone remains as they were when they died. If blind, they stay blind. If missing a limb, the limb is still missing in hell. (Baxter, 230)

A Tower of Cells

Next she saw the tower of cells. It was seventeen miles high with three-mile circular rings of small cells all the way to the top. (Baxter, 195) It is the same thing that B.W. Melvin saw. (Melvin, 65-182) Each cell contains one soul being tortured. The torture is in keeping with how evil the person had been. At one point Mary and Jesus were halfway up the tower of cells when a hurricane force fire came up and burnt into every cell. The occupants tried to find a place to hide at the back of the cell. She saw that the fire was Satan himself, although he was not being burnt. He raised his arms and balls of fire went out. He was delighted to hear the occupants of the cells cry out in screams of pain wanting to die. Demons, too, were laughing in amusement. Jesus says that Satan feeds on evil, and gains power from the pain and suffering of those he inflicts. Jesus had longed for every soul there to turn from Satan and come to Him when they were alive so he/she could be saved, but he/she never did. Now it is too late. (Baxter, 122-123)

Many of the cells were for people who had practiced witchcraft. She observed what appeared to be a fully clothed woman in agony who changed from an old woman to a man to a young girl to a middle-aged woman and back to an old woman. Jesus explained she had been in witchcraft all her life and had taught witchcraft to others, who are with her now in hell. She enjoyed serving Satan who told her she would live forever and have a kingdom from him. She resisted all Jesus' attempts to repent and receive eternal life. When she got to hell she asked Satan for her kingdom and he laughed in her face. And gave her this cell as her kingdom. She is now a misty skeleton who goes through the Satanic transformation delusions she enjoyed in her witchcraft and is regularly dragged out of her cell by a demon and tormented. (Baxter, 210-213)

Next Mary was shown another former witch who had sold her soul to Satan and had been similarly deceived by Satan's lies. Her fate was the same as the other woman's. Jesus emphasized that He came to save all people, but that most will not repent and be born again in the Spirit. One cannot enter the kingdom of God without repentance of sin and giving your heart to God. (Baxter, 215-219)

As Colton Burpo said, "Did that man have Jesus? He *had* to! He *had* to! He can't get into heaven if he didn't have Jesus in his heart!" (Burpo, 59). And in another place, he said Jesus told him He died on the cross so we could go see his Dad. (Burpo, 111)

She describes many more experiences of lost souls locked in cells in the center of hell like these. But I will not take any more space to repeat them as they are similar to these I have shared. In each case, the person is just a skeleton with a dirty gray soul in it. The soul pleads for Jesus to take him/her out. He/she promises to repent and follow Jesus now. But Jesus goes over why that person is there and the many chances he/she had to repent and accept Him. But now "it is too late." (Baxter, 261-268)

Alone in Hell

One night Jesus took Mary Baxter into the heart of hell and left her. Demons came and bound her in chains while something was eating away her flesh. There were worms crawling out of her bones and the heat and stench were awful, the odor was more putrid than she had ever known. She was taken before Satan who ordered her be taken to the deepest part of the heart of hell and learn to call him "lord". She pleaded for Jesus to come, but she could feel no God, no love, no peace, no warmth. With the keenest of senses she felt fear, hatred, excruciating pain, and the worst sorrow she had ever known. Satan said he is her lord now and told a large evil being with a face like a bat, claws for hands, and a terrible evil odor and another hairy demon with a face like a boar to take her to the deepest part of the heart where there are constant horrors and she will learn to call Satan lord. She cried out to Jesus in desperation and then a light appeared and Jesus took her in his arms suddenly back in her bed. He told her he had to leave her there like that so she could fully experience what hell is like to be able to tell us. It took her several days to recover from that ordeal. (Baxter, 227-231)

Later Jesus again left her alone in "the jaws of hell" to know for certainty what the lost experience when they die. Her story this time was more intense and longer than the first one. I will not repeat it here, but encourage you to get her book and read yourself if you wish. It was a terrible experience from which it took her a long time to recover. But it achieved Jesus' purpose. She has been able to write and tell people what hell will actually be like if they die before repenting and having their sins forgiven. She has personally experienced hell. Fortunately for her it was just temporary, but it was far too real. It was real enough to enable her to tell others how terrible hell really is and to plead with everyone to accept Jesus and NOT TO GO THERE! (Baxter, 283-289) I hope the same message is coming through in my writing here.

This is a brief glimpse of what God showed Mary Baxter so that she might share with the world how terrible hell is to encourage people to repent and accept Jesus' gift to avoid that place. There is more in her book A Divine Revelation of Hell that I haven't covered. Hopefully this is enough along with what other witnesses have said for you to know that hell is very real and very terrible. You must do what you can to be welcomed into heaven and not left in Satan's evil hands. The real situation is much worse than what she has told. "I saw things in hell that are too terrible to tell—even more awful than the wails of torment, the odors of decaying flesh, and the dreadfulness of the fires of hell with its deep pits. I also saw things God would not let me write." (Baxter, 220)

Darkness, Cold, and Odors Accompanies Death

Dr. Reggie Anderson, in *Appointments with Heaven*, gives a detailed account of one of his patients at the point of death having terrifying visions of where he is going. This is condensed from Chapter 21, The Smell of Good and Evil, of his book. Eddie (not his real name) had a reputation as a bad man. He was a heavy smoker and had abused his wife, kids, and others, sexually and physically. He got into fights with his fists or a knife in which he caused serious injuries requiring emergency treatment. The way he treated his children, he didn't care whether they lived or died. Eddie was truly *evil*.

But Dr. Anderson also believes deathbed conversions are possible. He doesn't have the ability to look into another man's heart or soul and know where his relationship stands with God, but he believes that no matter where he is spiritually, redemption is always available. God had rescued him from a godless life he was once living, and now he believes God can and does rescue others, even up to the moment of death.

In spite of Dr. Anderson's frequent attempts to engage Eddie in discussing the issue of his soul, he would always answer, "Shut up, and just treat the cancer! I don't want to waste my time talking about something that doesn't exist."

When his last breath finally came, it wasn't the same peaceful exhale like he had experienced with his other dying patients. Eddie fought to take that last final breath, and then his heart and pulse stopped. His last breath was a grunt.

Suddenly, Dr. Anderson sensed a dark cloud present in the room. The lights seemed to grow dimmer, and the temperature fell enough that the room was freezing cold, as cold as if the temperature had dropped one hundred degrees. Dr. Anderson had previously described how he can feel the presence of heaven coming into the room of a dying believer and the holy escort coming to take the patient home. However, here the warmth he had come to expect when heaven's doors opened with his other patients seemed to have been replaced by the opening of a liquid nitrogen canister. The room appeared dark and shadowy, as if it were being swallowed by a dark abyss. Then he smelled sulfur and diesel, instead of the usual citrus and lilac he smells when heaven is present taking his patient to be with the Lord. The air felt heavy, and it was harder to breathe. Then he remembered the same smell from Donaldson, Georgia, after the murders of the Aldays. They were six cousins and coworkers who were brutally murdered one by one by three escaped convicts when they came home. Memories of those dark days flooded his mind, which it hadn't done for years. He was terrified. Though he had no rational reason to feel this way, he was afraid he would get trapped by the evil presence and be unable to leave. He said he wanted to get out as fast as he could. Evil had entered the room.

Everything about the room that day is the antithesis of heaven. There was just a stagnant coldness, no warmth, no breezes. That room reeked of death, and the sulfuric odor lingered for weeks afterward. He was aware of it every time he passed. The fear he experienced that day stuck with him as a bad memory. Although he has visited countless other patients in that room since Eddie died, he still gets a strange sensation when he walks in that door. His experience that day Eddie died was very traumatic.

He thinks that when Eddie crossed over to the other side, he didn't like what he found. He also believes he could have made a different decision at any time before he died. It made Dr. Anderson very thankful that he knows where he is going. It also made him more intentional about making sure his other patients know what heaven and hell are like, so they don't have the experience Eddie did (Anderson, 183-191). If we could accept the magnitude of this issue, perhaps we would be more intentional about reaching out to those we know and love also.

The Bad News of Denying God's Authority

This bad news is about the terrible destination of those who deny Jesus, but more it is about the bad news that is the consequence of man's denial of God's authority on Earth. This was a vision Jesus gave to Michael McCormack. After Jesus showed him the new Earth, he showed him the future old Earth from space. It was grey and dull and surrounded by a black mist, which Jesus said was sin. He felt Jesus' sadness in his heart. A closer look showed him the buildings were crumbled and destroyed and there was no life, no plants, no people, and I presume no animals. It was deserted. Jesus told him, "This is the Earth that man has destroyed. ... This is what is going to happen and you can't stop this...but you can help save more people." (Roth, 83-84)

When asked what impact it had on him to see the world destroyed by sin, he said, "I know I won't be there. I'm going to that beautiful place, so there's nothing to fear." (Roth, 85)

Suicides

Dr. Rawlings says regarding experiences with suicide, many people choose it as a way to end it all, but, according to the cases he has seen or heard about through other doctors, it may only be the beginning of it all. He doesn't know of any good out-of-the-body experiences that have resulted from suicide. However, only a few who have attempted suicide have had any experiences they will talk about.

He then gives the story of a depressed, fourteen-year-old girl who took a whole bottle of aspirin. During recovery, she experienced cardiac arrest, but recovered immediately with external heart massage. Her recollections during recovery were not good. At the time, she kept saying, "Mama, help me! Make them let go of me! They're trying to hurt me!" The doctors tried to apologize for hurting her, but she said it wasn't the doctors, but "Them, those demons in hell . . . they wouldn't let go of me . . . they wanted me . . . I couldn't get back . . . It was just awful!" But a day later she couldn't recall any of it. (Rawlings, 94-95)

John Bunyon was tempted to doubt God by an evil friend who chose to deal with his sin by deciding there is no God or heaven or hell or judgment. John didn't believe his friend but it caused enough doubt for him to wonder if his friend might be true. He decided rather than continue to live in this world of doubt he would kill himself and find out the truth. He took a knife out into a field prepared to administer his fatal attack, when a voice spoke to him and said the fatal stroke you are considering will assure your damnation, for how could you hope for mercy if you willfully destroy yourself who was made in the image of God? He didn't know where this voice came from, but it came with so much power he was sure God had intervened to prevent him. He trembled and fell face down and praised and worshiped God for His mercy. It persuaded him of the great evil of suicide and the importance of not doubting God and His power, which he had just experienced. (Doucette 2013-2)

Kat Kerr, on the other hand, says that God told her that each instance is considered separately. Although suicide is defined as intentionally killing oneself, if that person is a believer and has lost control of his/her reasoning because of physical, emotional, or mental trauma, God might consider it "ending [his/her] suffering" rather than suicide and that person would not be excluded from heaven. She then gives two stories from several she has witnessed to confirm this. In the first case, a thirteen-year-old boy had lived most his life in abusive foster homes. He did except Christ and was placed in a good home, but the damage had already been done, and he was never able to cope and ended his suffering. Kat saw him in heaven, and he was a different boy, filled with the love of God, happy, playing in a rock band, and playing junior football.

Another person was a long-time believer who at twenty years old was in a serious auto accident and was on very strong medication that took away his normal reasoning powers. Soon he ended his suffering. Kat saw him in heaven several times, and he was very sorry for the pain he caused his family, and he wanted them to know he is in heaven, because some well-meaning friends had told his parents he wouldn't be there. He was in his father's mountain home enjoying many of the things he had done with his father. She saw on the mantel a trophy with the words: "God 1—Satan 0."

She does indicate that God says He will decide, so as a child of God we must not have any part of Satan's world: witchcraft, occult games, contacting the dead, séances, palm reading, demonic cards or games, games of violence, any movies involving a spirit of death, pornography, or anything associated with evil or death. Choose Life and the things of God's Kingdom, not Evil or Death. If any of these things have been a part of your life, repent and live your life for the Kingdom of God, not Satan's world. You do have free will and this must be your choice. (Kerr 2010, 112-117)

The Antidote

So how does one avoid going to hell when he/she dies? Paul wrote, *"For all have sinned and fall short of the glory of God"* (Rom 3:23, NIV). That pretty much guarantees that this beautiful, loving place is off-limits to all of us. So why has God gone to all this creative trouble only to have the place empty? Clearly from these stories, it is not empty but filled with people. The difference is in Jesus' statement, *"I am the way and the truth and the life. No one comes to the Father except through me"* (John 14:6, NIV). He paid the debt for all our sin and rebellion when he died on the cross. We merely have to accept that gift and take his life in place of our own. Then all our sins and rebellion are blotted out. Any record of our sins and rebellion is then blotted out from the archives of heaven. There is no longer any record of them; it is as if we have partaken of Jesus' perfection. God sees us through Jesus, not what we were without him.

That means after you have accepted Jesus' gift to you, there is no record in heaven of any of your past or future sins, failures, wrongdoings, lack of faith, etc. That is why Jesus is the only way and what separates those who get to enjoy all that heaven offers from those who miss out. If it were not for his gift, even one little imperfection would prevent us from spoiling heaven by being imperfect in God's perfect world. All the people, whose testimonies about heaven to which I have referred in the preceding chapters, at some point in their lives confessed their sin and accepted that Jesus is who he claimed to be and surrendered their lives to him, receiving forgiveness for all their imperfections and receiving his perfection.

Three things we learn from Ian McCormack's experience are: first, if you, like Ian's mother, are praying for someone who is rebelling against God and living his/her own way, don't give up. Your prayers are effective. God promises to hear your prayers for the person you care about, and those prayers may be the only things that enable God to get the message to him/her before it is too late. I know that the people I care about will not listen to me and yours probably not to you either. But keep praying, so God can find a way to reach them. Don't delay just because you can't find a way to talk with that person. Be faithful in prayer until God does get through to them by whatever means He can.

Second, hell is no party; it is total darkness, total evil, total terror, total pain and suffering, total aloneness, total hopelessness, and not a place anyone would want to be. It is the complete opposite of heaven and has none of God's love, peace, companionship, wholeness, beauty, and everything else He gives us on Earth and in heaven. Those who think they will party up with their friends in hell are terribly mistaken.

Third, God will hear you and accept your plea for forgiveness even in the last minute of your life. But you may not have a last minute of consciousness before death, so like Ian said, don't wait until the last minute. Besides, waiting until the last minute deprives you of the joy and fulfillment of God's presence in your life here. Heavenly life begins now, not after you die. The heavenly life reaches its complete fulfillment when we leave the hindrances of this life behind, but we begin experiencing some of heaven as soon as we receive God's forgiveness and Spirit.

In April 1998 Kat Kerr saw Jesus take a vase of His blood and pour it out on the beautiful cloth on the altar. As He did, one by one, words on the cloth were wiped away: "fear," "hate," "disease," "grief," "murder," "homosexuality," "insanity," "adultery," "pain," and many more, ending with "death". When the blood hit each one there was a sizzling sound like water hitting something hot and the word disappeared. Finally after the last word, "death," disappeared, God stood up, raised His arms, and shouted, "YES, It is finished!" (Kerr 2007, 116-120)

All the things that are the result of sin and disobedience to God and prevent anyone from coming into God's kingdom were wiped away by Jesus blood. This emphasizes again why Jesus said, "No one comes to the Father except through me." (John 14:6b) It emphasizes, too, how important, even necessary, it is that we come before Jesus and receive Him into our lives in a second birth, a cleansing birth of the Spirit, through accepting His blood sacrifice for us.

Colton Burpo frantically said when attending the funeral of a man his father didn't know, "Did that man have Jesus? He *had* to! He *had* to! He can't get into heaven if he didn't have Jesus in his heart!" (Burpo, 59). And in another place, he said Jesus told him He died on the cross so we could go see his Dad. (Burpo, 111)

Conclusion

I hope through this book everyone will know what heaven is like and what the consequences are of not choosing to get right with God. Eddie's (Dr. Anderson's patient) problem was not being more evil than most of us are. His problem was that he refused God's grace and forgiveness that Jesus has made available to us. "*All have sinned and fall short of the glory of God*" (Romans, 3:23 NIV), and so we are all in Eddie's same predicament.

In all the stories of someone who went to hell and came back, that person was never able to change his/her destination while there. All he/she could do was pray to God to have a second chance. That second chance only came when he/she was back on Earth. There are no second chances in heaven or hell. This life is the only one where we have freewill to choose.

If you have never asked to receive God's forgiveness through Jesus, please do so soon. We each do not know how much time we have left on Earth nor whether we will leave this world suddenly or linger long enough to change our ways. Don't count on being resuscitated; most deaths are permanent. If you are on the fence, please remember the experience Jesus gave Bill Weise and the caution that *Jesus is coming very, very soon*, and accept the gift of life before it is too late. *Don't put it off and end up in the place Bill Weise described*, where Eddie went!

ANNOTATED BIBLIOGRAPHY

Alcorn, Randy. 2004. *Heaven*. Carol Stream, IL: Tyndale House Publishers. This is Randy Alcorn's seminal work on heaven that resulted from many years of study of the Bible. It is Biblically based and not based on any eyewitness testimony.

Alexander, Eben, M.D. 2012. *Proof of Heaven: A Neurosurgeon's journey into the Afterlife*. New York, NY: Simon and Schuster Paperbacks. In November, 2008, when he was 54, Dr. Alexander arose in the morning to intense pain in his spine from having contracted bacterial meningitis from a virulent strain of E. coli. It turned into a grand mal seizure and a coma that lasted a week. When the attending doctor finally determined Dr. Alexander was not going to return to life, he suddenly opened his eyes, became alert, and was back to life, miraculously healed. During his time in a coma with his brain not functioning, he visited heaven. As a neurosurgeon, he had always assumed the brain was responsible for all that happens; any NDE experiences were just brain abnormalities. With his own experience of things beyond this life, he had to come to the realization that there is a life beyond this life that goes beyond the brain's function. As a scientist he came to recognize that spirituality is as real as any science, and those members of the scientific community who are pledged to the materialistic worldview are wrong. The spiritual side of existence is greater than the physical side and must not be left out. Making this known is the primary purpose of writing his book. It was a challenge to relate his experiences to the others that have been reported because he uses terms to describe his experience that are different from those of other authors. There was a non-Earthness to his experience while others saw heaven in terms of what they experienced on Earth, which allowed him to experience a dimension of the afterlife beyond what others have seen, for which there is no Earthly comparison. As helpful as his testimony is regarding a scientific view of the spiritual realm and the many things he experienced that are far beyond what we can experience in this universe, what he does say bears little resemblance to the testimonies in Scripture, especially Revelation 21.

Anderson, Reggie, M.D. 2013. *Appointments with Heaven: The true story of a country doctor's healing encounters with the hereafter.* Carol Stream, IL: Tyndale Momentum, Tyndale House Publishers. Dr. Anderson went from being a faithful Christian to being an atheist after the gruesome murder of the whole Alday family, relatives, and coworkers. For years he knew God didn't exist because He didn't intervene for his friends. But God appeared to him in a vision in which he saw all these friends happy and full of joy and peace in their heavenly home. Dr. Anderson then knew that God was present and had taken care of his friends in a way beyond what we perceive in this life. God gave him a promise of things to come, including his marriage, four children, and role as a country doctor in Tennessee, all of which eventually became true exactly as God had foretold. God has given him a special sensitivity to the presence of the Spirit in his medical practice, and this book is the story of how God has been present in the lives of his patients and in his practice, sometimes in miraculous ways.

Baxter, Mary K. 2019. *A Divine Revelation of Heaven and Hell.* New Kensington, PA: Whitaker House. This is a consolidation of two books, *A Divine Revelation of Heaven,* July 1, 1998 and *A Divine Revelation of Hell,* September 1, 1997. Jesus first took Mary K. Baxter to show her the reality of hell so she could tell everyone the importance of avoiding it and having one's name written in the Lamb's Book of Life. Seeing hell was very hard on her and it took a long time to recover. But then Jesus took her in the spirit and showed her heaven. A lot of that book is thoughts taken from her ministry, applying what she learned from heaven. My reverences to Mary K. Baxter are taken from this two in one publication. The page numbers given only match this edition and not the page numbers of the two separate books. However, for reference, *A Divine Revelation of Heaven* starts at the beginning and *A Divine Revelation of Hell* starts on page 151. Perhaps subtracting 150 from my page references will lead you to the source of the reference in the separate edition of *A Divine Revelation of Hell.*

Besteman, Marvin. 2012. *My Journey to Heaven*. Grand Rapids, MI; Revell, a division of Baker Publishing Group. Besteman tells his story of becoming ill with insulinoma, a rare pancreatic cancer, his temporary death during surgery, seeing heaven from the gate through which he was not allowed to pass, and then his struggles afterward being able to tell people of his experience.

Black, Dale, Capt. 2010. *Flight to Heaven*. New York, NY: MJF Books, Fine Communications. This is Dale's first description of his experience in heaven. Most of my references in this book are from the second (later) description, but there have been some additions from this earlier book.

_____. 2018. *Visiting Heaven: Secrets of Life after Death*. Carlsbad, CA: Sovereign House Publishers. As a pilot in training for his commercial pilot license and ATP license, he was on a flight with his instructor and another less-experienced pilot who caused them to crash into a building at 135 miles per hour. The other two pilots died, one at the scene and the other later in the hospital. Dale died and was in a coma for three days, but came back to life. He saw many features of heaven and experienced the reality of what heaven is like. He also witnessed the demons coming to take his friend and flight instructor off to a world to which he did not want to go. This was the most terrifying event of his life, and he couldn't talk about it for forty years.

Braxton, Dean. 2010. *In Heaven! Experiencing the Throne of God*. Dean died from kidney stones, infection, and other organ failures, and was dead for one hour and forty-five minutes. His resuscitation and recovery are a miracle. His book describes his experiences while he was dead and the affect of faithful prayers of the saints on his behalf, all with many Scripture references.

Buck, Roland, Charles Hunter, and Frances Hunter. 1979. *Angels on Assignment*. New Kensington, PA: Whitaker House. Pastor Buck was pastoring a church in Idaho when angels started visiting him and giving him messages for the church. At first he ignored the messages, fearing rejection by his congregation, but on subsequent visits the angel was more persuasive, so he yielded. Most of these messages were given in his office at the church or at home. (It is interesting to note that his dog sensed when an angel was present.) However, on one occasion, the angel took him to God's throne room, so while he did not directly experience heaven, he experienced something that is in heaven: God's throne room and His archives. God gave him a set of 150 predictions of things that would happen, and as of the writing of his book, nearly all of them had happened just like God said they would. Some of them would amaze you.

Burke, John. 2015. *Imagine Heaven: Near Death Experiences, God's Promises, and the Exhilarating Future That Awaits You.* Grand Rapids, MI: Baker Books. John Burke tells many things about what heaven is like and backs those up with quotations from authors and from interviews of people who have had NDEs and experienced heaven. Sometimes he starts with the quotation and then draws summary conclusions. He includes many of the same sources I have used plus many other NDEs that don't necessarily describe heaven. It serves the same purpose as this book but from a different perspective.

Burpo, Todd. 2010. *Heaven Is for Real: A Little Boy's Astounding Story of His Trip to Heaven and Back.* Nashville: Thomas Nelson. Three-year-old Colton Burpo experienced heaven while he was in surgery for a seriously ruptured appendix. He tells of his experiences with the innocence and candor of a three- to four-year-old boy without theological or adult jargon. Many of the things he reports were things he never learned in Sunday school or from his parents.

Chennault, Willie Agnes. 2019. *The Next Time I Go to Heaven I Will Not Be Back: My Journey to Heaven.* Chennault Publishing. This story is very long, 588 pages plus 26 pages of photos! But her writing style is more like a disorganized train of thought, jumping from one thought to another as she rambles. She returns to the same subject many times throughout the book, usually not adding anything new, just repeating what she wrote before. Her description of heaven is woven into the story of her life and how she dealt with her illness. Her visit to heaven had a profound permanent effect on her life such that she is thankful for her illness that allowed her that experience. It is not an easy read, complicated by all the misspellings and other editorial errors.

Davis, Marietta. 1999. *Caught Up into Heaven.* New Kensington, PA: Whitaker House. In 1848 at the age of twenty-five, Marietta Davis went into a trance for a period of nine days. During that time she visited heaven and came back changed. She knew she would be leaving again permanently in seven months and she did just as she said, singing a hymn of praise. The vocabulary and sentence structure reflect English of the nineteenth century even with the publisher having updated the words, expressions, and sentence structure.

Ditto, Laurie A. 2019. *The Hell Conspiracy: An Eye-Witness Account of Hell, Heaven, and the Afterlife.* Shippensburg, PA: Destiny Image Publishers, Inc. Laurie Ditto was in a prayer service at Kansas City Evangelists' Fellowship when suddenly the back of the church opened up with hell in view. Hell and the prayer room were both together in plain view to her but no one else saw the image of hell. The gates of hell swung open and a fingerless arm came out and grabbed her with a strong suction and pulled her into hell with the gates closing behind her. She screamed in terror. Her story is all about what she experienced in hell and how it drastically changed the way she lives with a deeper understanding of the power of sin to destroy and the eternal necessity of obeying God and avoiding sin. Of major concern to her was her unwillingness to forgive those who had hurt her and a self-seeking pride.

Doucette, Patrick. 2013-1. *Is Heaven for Real?: Personal Stories of Visiting Heaven.* Published by Kindle. He includes Ian McCormack's testimony, an interview with Oden Hetrick, and an interview with Don Piper. (In this apparently self-published book there are no pages numbers to which I can refer.)

_____. 2013-2. *Is Heaven for Real?: Personal Stories of Visiting Heaven 2.* Published by Kindle. He includes an interview with Dale Black, an interview with Tony Davis, an interview with Gary Wood, an interview with Dan Braxton, the brief story of three-year-old Paul Eicke, the story of Marvin Besteman, the story of Allison visiting heaven in her sleep, an interview with Crystal McVea, a repeat of Ian McCormack's story, and an experience of John Bunyon. Most of these stories are in their author's own books that I have included in this bibliography.

Eadie, Betty J. 1992. *Embraced by the Light*. New York: Bantam Books. Betty Eadie died from hemorrhaging complications following an otherwise successful hysterectomy November 18, 1973. She first met Jesus, and he explained many unknown mysteries to her, especially how important it is to love. She saw some of heaven, but most of her experience was being in the presence of perfect love and acceptance and learning details of God's creation. She saw the future daughter she would adopt in heaven and then again as a vision in the hospital. When the vision came about in real life, all this came together for her.

Eby, Richard, D.O. 1978. *Caught Up into Paradise*. Grand Rapids, MI: Spire Books (Fleming H. Revell). At age 60 he tumbled off a second floor balcony when a termite-ridden railing gave way as he was throwing some boxes to the ground. He fell headfirst onto the pavement; his head split open, and all body functions ceased. The emergency responders put his body in the ambulance and leisurely drove to take it for medical examination. When his life functions suddenly returned, the ride turned into one of a red light flashing, siren blowing, and full speed emergency.

Endraske, Kim. 2019. *God Is Real: The Eyewitness Testimony of a Former Atheist*. No Publisher given. Kim does not give any actual witness to heaven itself, but rather details her life from being an atheist through college and then coming in contact with the gospel for the first time. She then details her journey learning to live for Jesus instead.

Enstad, Jeanne. 2018. *A Journey of Hope to Heaven and Back*. Maitland, FL: Xulon Press Elite. Jeanne Enstad tells the story of her life from her youth on a small farm to having open-heart surgery at age thirty-seven and numerous other medical situations. She visited heaven three times in all of that, the last being when her car was hit head on by a semi. She was also the result of a medical mistake that left her right side useless. She tells how God used all of these trials to bring her to a deep real faith in Him and walk with Him and the ability to sense the leading of the Spirit in her life..

Esther, Sister Gulshan, and Thelma Sangster. 1984. *The Torn Veil.* Hammersmith, London: Marshal Pickering an imprint of HarperCollinsReligious. Gulshan Esther had been paralyzed on her left side from a bout with typhoid fever as an infant. There was no medical remedy so the last resort was prayer. Prayers to Allah went unanswered so a Hajji to Mecca was hoped to bring healing. It didn't, and after that her father died from pneumonia and left her an orphan. But before he died he assured her that, "One day God is going to heal you, Gulshan. Pray to Him." The prayers to Allah had no effect so she started praying to Jesus also. After three years, Jesus came to her in the middle of the night and totally healed her.

Garlow, James L. and Keith Wall. 2010. *Encountering Heaven and the Afterlife: True Stories from People Who Have Glimpsed the World Beyond.* Bloomington, Minnesota: Bethany House Publishers. James gives four stories of people who have glimpsed heaven but were only there for a moment and several stories of visits by angels. He tells the impact these glimpses have had on people lives.

Habib, Samaa. 2014. *Face to Face with Jesus.* Bloomington, MN: Chosen Books. Samaa is a former Muslim from an unidentified Middle Eastern country undergoing a terrible civil war. She responded to a free Tae Kwan Do class to learn to protect herself. A Christian organization sponsored the classes, which emphasized a strong spiritual basis. She and a friend attended a service and ignored the call for becoming a Christian but did respond to a call for prayer. When they went forward for prayer, they were both slain in the spirit when prayed for. The hand of God touched both of them, and they became followers of Jesus. She secretly attended services with a local Christian group on Fridays, but one day four repeat visitors planted bombs in the church timed and located to cause the most casualties. Samaa was standing next to one when it exploded, and she died instantly. But after meeting Jesus (the title of the book) he sent her back in a miraculous healing to keep his message alive.

Kerr, Kat. 2007. *Revealing Heaven: An Eyewitness Account*, Xulon Press. God chose Kat for some special revelations of heaven. Though she didn't die, she was given visions of heaven on different occasions. While she testifies to some of the same things others have reported, she was allowed to see some things no one else has reported. Some of things answer questions people have asked about heaven. With the help of an artist, she has included sketches of scenes she observed in heaven. Some might question whether visiting heaven in the spirit while still clinically alive is legitimate. But she is not the only one like this. There is no medical record of Colton Burpo dying while under surgery, and Roland Buck's encounter with heaven (the archives in the throne room) is consistent with what others saw. Others had their experience when there was no one to confirm their deaths, so whether they actually died or not cannot be determined. This includes the apostle Paul. Some of what Kat Kerr experienced is unique and may be doubtful, but I have included it anyway. It is what she said; take it for what it is worth to you.

_____. 2010. *Revealing Heaven: An Eyewitness Account II*, Xulon Press. Volume II adds more testimony of heaven, covering things not mentioned in the first volume or expanding on the discussion there.

Kolbaba, Scott J., M.D. 2016. *Physicians' Untold Stories*. North Charleston, South Carolina: CreateSpace Independent Publishing Platform. Dr. Kolbaba reports twenty-six stories of doctors who have experienced miracles. One of these was a patient who was in heaven but didn't realize it. His story is given in Chapter 2, First Glimpses of Heaven. Another was a young girl who was suddenly totally healed of terminal muscular dystrophy by an audible command from Jesus standing behind her, "My child, get up and walk!" as a result of much prayer. The other stories are impressive, impactful, and praiseworthy, but don't bear on the subject of this book.

Komp, Diane W., M.D. 1992. *A Window to Heaven: When Children See Life in Death*. Grand Rapids, MI: Zondervan Publishing House. Dr. Komp has worked with sick children and has found sometimes they have seen things beyond this world. She reported some of what these children have told her.

Kramarik, Akiane and Foreli. 2006. *Akiane her life, her art, her poetry*. Nashville, TN: W Publishing Group, a Division of Thomas Nelson, Inc. It gives the story of Akiane's life growing up with atheistic parents but having visions of heaven beginning at age four, during which she was taught how to draw and subsequently has become famous as an artist and poet. Her painting of Jesus, Prince of Peace, is famous for reputably being what Jesus actually looks like in heaven.

LaFrance, Jacques, Ph.D. 2017. *A Composite Portrait of Heaven: What We Learn about Heaven from People Who Have Been There*. Meadville, PA: Christian Faith Publishing, Inc. This is the first edition of this book. It takes the testimony of eighteen accounts of visiting heaven and compares them feature by feature for a more complete picture of heaven than any one book gives.

_____. 2018. *Heaven Is Amazing! : A Composition of 34 Eyewitness Testimonies*, Tustin, CA: Trilogy Christian Publishers, A Wholly Owned Subsidiary of Trinity Broadcasting Network. This book is an expanded edition of the former with sixteen more testimonies and more features of heaven described.

Malick, Faisal. 2012. *10 Amazing Muslims Touched by God*. Shippensburg, PA: Ambient Press. This book tells the stories of ten Muslim who have seen God /Jesus and learned the truth of the New Testament and the Messiah. As a result they have a strong faith in their Savior and have God-given ministries to reach out to other Muslims. These Muslims include himself and Akef Tayem, Kamal Saleen, Khalida Wukawitz, Güçlü (Corey) Erman, Hamdi Erman, Cemil and Isil Akbulut, Jaafar Attaran, Mohammed Seyedzadeh, and Stephen Masood. Khalida Wukawitz saw into heaven when Jesus came to her. Jesus gave Jaafar Attaran a glimpse of the New

Jerusalem. But the others only met Jesus where they were and did not say anything about seeing heaven. Güçlü (Corey) Erman had a glimpse of hell when he was high on drugs.

Malz, Betty. 1977. *My Glimpse of Eternity.* Grand Rapids, MI: Spire Books (Fleming H. Revell). Twenty-seven-year-old Betty Upchurch (now Malz) died at Union Hospital in Terre Haute, Indiana, from an overdue ruptured appendix. Twenty-eight minutes later, she came back to life miraculously totally healed. The healing was a wonderful miracle but so was what she experienced in heaven those twenty-eight minutes and the affect on her family afterwards. Her testimony eventually allowed her husband to die peacefully.

May, Mary. 2018. *Heaven is Closer than you Think...The Dawn Cypret Story*, Forman, AR: Blue Lily Publishing. Dawn Cypert died during surgery for a significant heart attack. She went to heaven and saw many incredible things. When she came back and people learned she had been to heaven, she became quite popular in her long stay in the hospital. Her experience in heaven made her more sensitive to things of the Spirit, and she has seen angels. She also saw a clear vision of a man being electrocuted as it happened while she was lying in the bed at her daughter's house.

McVea, Crystal, with Alex Tresniowski. 2013. *Waking Up in Heaven*, New York, NY: Howard Books, a Division of Simon and Schuster, Inc. After years of sexual and other abuse, several failed marriages, an abortion, and other rebellion against God, after which she did not believe in God or heaven and was sure that if there were a God, He could never accept her. She died for nine minutes in the hospital. She describes her life that led up to that point. Then her narrative about her life afterwards is punctuated with some of what she learned in heaven. The main thing was how beautiful and full of love heaven is. She saw how much God has always loved her and came back a changed woman.

Melvin, B. W. 2005. *A Land Unknown: Hell's Dominion*, Xulon Press. The author was living a wild life, "grabbing all the gusto he could with no thought about tomorrow," when he almost died from cholera. He did die temporarily and had the most extensive experience in hell of any I have read except for that of Mary K. Baxter. It was enough to make him consider tomorrow and accept the only one who can save us from what he witnessed, Jesus Christ, "a Name and a Title." He saw many lost souls in hell and described what they were going through and why they were there. It is a very eye-opening read.

Morse, Melvin, M.D. 1990. *Closer to the Light: Learning from the Near-Death Experiences of Children*, New York, NY: Ivy Books (Ballantine Books). Dr. Morse had interviews with hundreds of children who had once been clinically dead and found a common experience and attitude over and over, including out-of-body travel, telepathic communication, and meetings with past relatives and friends.

Musick, Steven R. 2017. *Life After Heaven: How My Time in Heaven Can Transform Your Life on Earth*. New York, NY: Waterbrook, an imprint of Crown Publishing Group, a division of Penguin Random House LLC. Steven was training to be a Navy seal and go to the Naval Academy when he was inoculated with a new vaccine against the swine flu. He had an allergic reaction from which he got sick enough to die temporarily in a five-week long coma. During that time he was in heaven and walking and talking with Jesus. It had a profound effect on him after he awoke from his coma. But he had scarring in his lower lungs so that he only had 40% lung capacity until ten years later when he was slain in the Spirit at a church healing service and ended up in heaven at the same place he had been before. Jesus told him this time, "Things will be different now." When he awoke he had full lung capacity. All the scar tissue was miraculously gone, as was confirmed by his doctor. The rest of the book deals with how he was seeing more and more things of heaven happen on Earth: healings, words of knowledge, divine appointments, things he referred to as Bubbles of Heaven. It is an inspiring read as he tells how we can have an intimate relationship with God and experience these bubbles from heaven ourselves without having to die.

Myers, John. 1968. *Voices from the Edge of Eternity*. Uhrichsville, OH:

Barbour and Company. Testimonies of what people saw and said in the moments before death. Myers takes these testimonies from three other books: *Dying Hours* by D. P. Kidder, *Dying Words* by A. H. Gottschall, and *Dying Testimonies* by S. B. Shaw.

Neal, Mary C., Dr. 2011-2012. *To Heaven and Back*. Colorado Springs, CO: WaterBrook Press. Dr. Mary Neal was on a white water kayak adventure in Chile when an inexperienced kayaker ahead of her got stuck between rocks in a falls. Mary could not get around but went under the other boat and was trapped under water. The force of the current prevented her from getting out of her kayak. Her breathing stopped, and she had her adventure into heaven. Fortunately, her friends were able to revive her, so we could hear her testimony.

_____. 2017. *7 Lessons from Heaven: How Dying Taught Me to Live a Joy-Filled Life*. New York, NY: Convergent Books. Dr. Neal reviews some from her previous book and adds insights she has gained over the intervening five years. Mostly the book is about lessons learned from her temporary death experience in heaven and applying those lessons to life. It is a good follow-on to such an experience and is worth reading. She also adds research she has done on NDEs, Angel visitation, and miracles. It is the hope of this author that you can gain similar lessons from the composition of all these testimonies of life in heaven recorded in this book and how that impacts our life here.

Olsen, Jeff. 2012. *I knew their hearts*. Springville, UT: Plain Sight Publishing, an imprint of Cedar Fort, Inc. Jeff was in a terrible roll-over auto accident at 75 mph. His dear wife and youngest son died in the crash. He met his wife in heaven and she insisted he had to go back for their eldest son. He did and saw that in the spirit he could tell everything about the people he saw in the hospital before he returned to his body, hence the title of the book. He had a long painful recovery. His book details his struggles, both physical and emotional, and how he recovered and gained hope, eventually with a new wife and family.

Panagore, Peter Baldwin. 2015. *Heaven Is Beautiful*. Charlottesville, VA: Hampton Roads Publishing Company. Peter was ice climbing with a friend in Alberta when his rope got stuck and he couldn't move. He died of falling and hitting his head on the rock wall under exhaustion and hypothermia. While he was gone from this life, he talked with God and gained understanding of this fallen world compared to the perfection of God's kingdom. God allowed him to come back. He and his climbing companion finally got off the mountain, and he eventually recovered.

Payne, Matthew Robert. 2017. *My Visits to Heaven: Lessons Learned*. Linchfield, IL: Revival Waves of Glory Books and Publishing. Matthew has visited heaven many times in the spirit. What he has seen in these visits confirms other reports of those who visited heaven under more adverse circumstances (temporary death). Their reports confirm his visits as genuine, not fabrications.

Piper, Don. 2004. *90 Minutes in Heaven*. Grand Rapids, MI: Revell. Don was in a terrible auto accident on a bridge in Texas. He was pronounced dead at the scene, but a Christian friend came along, crawled in the back, and prayed for him. While he was singing, Don started singing also, so the friend ran to the paramedics who initially wouldn't believe he was back to life. He eventually recovered, and his doctor had never seen anyone with those injuries ever recover.

_____. 2018. *People I Met at the Gates of Heaven: Who Is Going To Be There Because of You?* New York: FaithWords. Don identifies eight people who met him at the gates of heaven, and then tells how each one played a significant role in helping him become the follower of Jesus he is today. He then deals with questions he is frequently asked at speaking engagements. He concludes the book by helping his readers see how they might be significant in someone's life like all these eight people were in his life.

Rawlings, Maurice, M.D. 1978. *Beyond Death's Door*. New York: Bantam Books. Dr. Rawlings was prompted to collect these stories and write this book after a cardiac patient died in his presence and, during repeated recoveries, fearfully said he did not want to go back to hell! Ultimately, he didn't because the experience frightened him so much he accepted Jesus.

_____. 1993. *To Hell and Back*. Nashville, TN: Thomas Nelson, Inc., Publishers. In this book Dr. Rawlings focuses on eyewitness testimonies of hell from his and other clinical cases. I don't comment directly from this book but do refer to the examples he mentions that Bill Weiss considers.

Reppert, Dale. 2017. *Detour to Heaven: One Man's True Journey*. Kurztown, PA: Odenheim Press. Dale was a hard-working and successful financial advisor bent on providing financially for his family, even if it meant time away from them. But at age forty-five, he was diagnosed with Type I Chiari malformation, a congenital condition in which the bottom of the brain herniates down into the spinal canal. As he was being treated, he got sicker with more intense pain. As the pain became unbearable, it was learned he had contracted bacterial meningitis. He finally succumbed to the pain and spent forty-five hours in a coma, during which time he had a brief detour to heaven, after which he awakened back in the hospital. He was out of his body and in heaven even while his body continued to function. There was no medical indication of death. Through surgical procedures, the meningitis was eliminated, and a cranial patch corrected the Chiari malformation. However, part of the arterial blood supply to his brain had been cut off, disabling him from continuing to pursue his financial career and requiring him to accept retirement. The book is about this whole experience with one chapter devoted to his brief encounter in heaven.

Ritchie, George. 1978. *Return from Tomorrow*. Waco, TX: Chosen Books. Dr. Richie died of double pneumonia at an Army training facility in West Texas in 1943. Nine minutes later, he was miraculously resuscitated. During those Earthly minutes, he experienced being a bodiless spirit, meeting Jesus, falling in love with Jesus, and being shown what happens to those who die without being redeemed. He never actually made it to heaven but experienced some spirit domains prior to God's eternal punishment. His life was transformed by being in the presence of Jesus' love that whole time.

Robinson, Mickey. 2014. *Falling into Heaven: A Skydiver's Gripping Account of Heaven, Healings, and Miracles*. New York, NY: Broadstreet Publishing Group, LLC. This book is basically the story of Mickey Robinson's life. It describes his childhood and his love of sports and then extreme sports. He became extremely fond of skydiving. Along with this is the development of his relationship with Julie. But on a skydiving trip, the pilot mishandled his new plane and crashed it shortly after takeoff. Mickey was trapped inside when it burst into flames. The others had escaped and one came to his rescue and got him out. But his burns were excessive and he spent more than a year in a recovery that included several medical miracles. At one point he had a glimpse of Heaven, mostly meeting Jesus and God face to face. The rest of his story is about how his life was transformed into one of following Jesus rather than the following the dreams of this world he had always pursued. Seeing how he responded to God's love and slowly learned how to live with an eternal purpose is worth the read.

Roth, Sid. 2012. *Heaven Is Beyond Your Wildest Expectations*. Shippensburg, PA: Destiny Image Publishers. Sid Roth tells ten stories of people's experiences with heaven: Dean Braxton, whose own book is included here and who died in a hospital three times before he was allowed to stay in heaven; Rhoda "Jubilee" Mitchell, who reached the end of her rope and pleaded with Jesus, who came and took her to visit heaven; Ian McCormack, who died from a jellyfish sting and had a deathbed conversion but initially visited hell anyway before he was taken to heaven; Michael McCormack, Ian's son, who had an encounter with Jesus and heaven when he was ten years old while he was sitting in church and praying to Jesus; Khalida Wukawitz, a former Palestinian Muslim who encountered Jesus and heaven after years of abuse but eventually landed in America and became friends with a Christian woman; Dr. Gary Wood, who visited heaven after dying in an auto accident; Robert Misst, who was taken up to heaven during a prayer retreat in Christchurch, New Zealand;

Richard Sigmund, whose own book is included here and who died in a single vehicle accident and came back to life after eight hours; William Smith, who was adopted as an infant but had a deep longing to know God and one day was taken to heaven as he lay on his bed; and Richard Eby, MD, whose own book is included here and who was conceived by a mother who was told she had no reproductive organs, died of a miscarriage at six months, but suddenly started breathing, and at age 60 died from a two-story fall head first onto concrete.

Sharkey, Jenny. 2013. *Clinically Dead, I Have Seen Heaven and Hell.* No publisher given. This is Ian McCormack's story. He had lived a wild life as an atheist, even though his mother had tried to share God with him and prayed for him every day. Then he was stung by several box jellyfish while surfing off the coast of Mauritius. He made it to the hospital but died anyway and was dead for fifteen minutes or so. Fortunately in the ambulance he remembered his mother's prayers and prayed what he could remember of the Lord's Prayer. He began his death experience in hell but soon was transported out of hell into the presence of Jesus, who allowed him to come back to life here.

Sigmund, Richard. 2010. *My Time in Heaven: A True Story of Dying and Coming Back.* New Kensington, PA: Whitaker House. Richard Sigmund was driving along and suddenly was in a single car accident for which there is no explanation, and he immediately went to heaven. He was dead for eight hours. His is the most extensive heaven experience I know of since he was dead for eight hours Earth time.

Springer, Rebecca. 1984. *Within Heaven's Gates* (originally *Intra Muros*). New Kensington, PA: Whitaker House. She took a journey to heaven during a lengthy illness, whether she actually died or just had an out of body experience, she didn't say. There was no medical record of her death, since she was alone at the time. (There is no medical record of Colton Burpo being medically dead when he went to heaven either.) There she met her brother-in-law who showed her around heaven, including his house he had built and the place he was building for her and her husband. She saw many other houses and experienced the eternally living plants, water that does not drown or wet, and other things common to other people's experience.

Storm, Howard. 2005. *My descent into Death: A Second Chance at Life.* New York: Doubleday. Howard Storm, an avowed atheist, died in a Paris hospital from lack of medical attention for a punctured duodenum. He was confused because he felt more alive and his senses sharper than he had ever experienced before. Then some voices called to him to come with them. But they were anonymous deceivers, which he eventually figured out. But by then, they were far from the hospital. He was in hell being tortured by demons. But he called out to God and that made them all go away. Then Jesus came, and he had many conversations with Him that changed his life.

Taylor, David E. 2011. *My Trip to Heaven: Face to Face with Jesus.* Shippensburg, PA: Destiny Image Publishers. The book begins with a teaching Biblical study guide about the many facets of our relationship with Jesus. Then the other chapters are about times he was taken in the spirit to have a meeting with Jesus. The one chapter I focus on in this book is Chapter 6: The Special Trip to Heaven.

Weise, Bill. 2006. *23 Minutes in Hell.* Lake Mary, FL: Charisma House. At 3:00 am November 23, 1998, Bill was suddenly awakened and thrown into a cell in hell. For twenty-three minutes, he was allowed to experience hell, first with Jesus' light present and then in total darkness. Without God's presence, evil was horribly present. It was an awful experience. But Jesus came and took him out of there and explained to him that he had chosen Bill to take the message back to Earth that hell is very real and *you do not want to end up there.* Too many people today, especially in the Western world, don't think hell is real and don't see any need for religion. Jesus wanted to use Bill to help wake up the world to his soon return and the pending judgment.

_____. 2013. *What Happens When I Die?* Lake Mary, FL: Charisma House Book Group. In this book Bill Weiss tells many stories from other books, such as several of the ones listed here, to illustrate what is on the other side of life. These include both experiences of heaven and of hell. He also draws from Scripture. These stories echo what the others have said, namely how experience of either heaven or hell changes everyone's perspective on what is important in this life.

Wood, Gary L., Ph.D. 2008, 2014. *A Place Called Heaven*. Kingwood, TX: RevMedia Publishing. Dr. Wood died in an automobile accident at age eighteen. He went to heaven for twenty minutes before his sister prayed for him in the name of Jesus and he had to return. As a result of his time in heaven he has had a ministry in which he has seen people healed of various illnesses and even raised from the dead. God promised him that wherever he told his story of heaven, people would be saved, healed, and delivered.

Woodford, Jim, with Thom Gardner 2017. *Heaven an Unexpected Journey: One Man's Experience with Heaven, Angels, and the Afterlife*. Shippensburg, PA: Destiny Image Publishers, Inc. Jim Woodford is a former airline pilot who contracted the rare Guillain-Barré disease. The disease was very painful, casing him to become dependent on narcotics to subdue the constant pain. One day he took too many of the opiod pills and died. He did not know he had died and initially thought the medicine had miraculously taken away all the pain. But when he saw his body sitting in his truck, he perceived he had died. At that point he was taken up into heaven, saw the pit of hell with demons after him, but his plea for God to help caused three angels to come and banish the demons. They then took him on a tour of heaven. He came back from his experience a changed man, and subsequently has traveled across the continent telling people about his experience and the reality of hell, heaven, and God's love.

ABOUT THE AUTHOR

Dr. Jacques LaFrance became a follower of Jesus as a freshman at Harvard University. Throughout the rest of his undergraduate and graduate work he was active in InterVarsity Christian Fellowship. After completing his Ph. D. in computer science, he taught at Wheaton College, Wheaton, Illinois, and then at Oral Roberts University in Tulsa, Oklahoma. His final teaching assignment was as Adjunct Associate Professor in the master's program at Oklahoma State University, Tulsa campus. After retiring in 2000, he has done various things, mostly tutoring in mathematics and science. In the 1970's he was introduced to George Ritchie's *Return from Tomorrow* and Maurice Rawlings' *Beyond Death's Door*. He was so fascinated with what he read that he has ultimately read the books in the bibliography. By noting the consistency and differences in each of these accounts, he conceived the idea of this book to create a thorough overview of what heaven is like in all of its features by putting together different authors' descriptions of each feature. He currently lives in Sand Springs, Oklahoma, and is a member of First Presbyterian Church of Tulsa. He enjoys nature lore, hiking, bicycling, and N scale model railroading. He would love to hear from you after reading this book by writing to him at Dr.JELaFrance@gmail.com.

Made in the USA
Las Vegas, NV
30 September 2022

56131556R00184